RESEARCH IN PARAPSYCHOLOGY 1977

Abstracts and Papers from the
Twentieth Annual Convention of the
Parapsychological Association, 1977

WILLIAM G. ROLL

Editor

The Scarecrow Press, Inc.
Metuchen, N.J. & London
1978

This volume is the sixth in a Scarecrow Press annual continuation of the former series, Proceedings of the Parapsychological Association, of which numbers 2 through 8 (the end) are available from the Psychical Research Foundation, Duke Station, Durham, N. C. 27706.

ISBN 0-8108-1131-6
Manufactured in the United States of America
Library of Congress Catalog Card No. 66-28580
Copyright © 1978 by the Parapsychological Association

CONTENTS

PREFACE

The year 1977 is the 20th anniversary of the Parapsychological Association. The PA was formed on June 19, 1957, during a workshop at the Parapsychology Laboratory at Duke University, Durham, N. C. The initiative for creating a professional society came from J. B. Rhine, director of the Duke Laboratory. Rhine saw the PA as a means to extend leadership in the field beyond the Duke group and at the same time to solidify adherence to rigid scientific standards, which had come to characterize the work at Duke, to the research of anyone who wished to join the professional community. To insure the PA's independence, Rhine declined nomination to either the Council or the Presidency and has consistently done so these 20 years.

The roots of parapsychology and of the PA obviously go deeper and extend further than North Carolina and the United States. Parapsychology as a science began with the formation of the Society for Psychical Research in Great Britain in 1882 and important research accomplishments were made there, at the American Society for Psychical Research, and in Holland, France and elsewhere. The PA was created as an international organization which would cooperate with existing societies for psychical research.

There are several changes in this year's PA program and in this volume from previous years. Instead of having the reading of research briefs, the Program Committee arranged a series of roundtable discussions where presentations could be made on selected topics. In the evenings, times were set aside for workshops where the convention participants themselves could choose areas for discussion. The workshops are not reported here, but the roundtable presentations appear as abstracts prepared by the participants and the chairpersons.

Research in Parapsychology has suffered a loss this year: Joanna and Robert Morris have had to withdraw as

vii

editors for family reasons (the arrival of twins!). Fortunately, the Program Committee did a careful job of scrutinizing the papers and clarifying unclear points, making the task of editing a relatively painless one.

W. G. R.

THE TWENTIETH ANNUAL CONVENTION

The Twentieth Annual Convention of the Parapsychological Association was held at American University, Washington, D.C., August 10-13, 1977. A total of 250 persons attended. William Braud was chairperson of the Program Committee, which also included Helmut Schmidt and Rex Stanford. Irvin Child was consultant to the Program Committee for field studies and theoretical papers. Howard Zimmerman was chairperson of the Arrangements Committee.

The volume has three parts. Part 1 contains abstracts of the roundtable discussions, Part 2 has the full papers, and Part 3 consists of the Presidential Address by Charles Tart.

Part 1:   Roundtable Discussions

TWENTIETH ANNIVERSARY*

CHARLES T. TART (University of California, Davis)

The Parapsychological Association was created 20 years ago by a small, but dedicated group of parapsychologists following a workshop at the Duke University Parapsychology Laboratory in Durham.   Since its founding the PA has played an important and central role in the development of the field.   This roundtable was organized both to honor those founding members who are still active in the PA, and to gain some perspective on where we have been in the past twenty years and where we may be going.

Founding members Robert A. McConnell, Carroll Nash, Karlis Osis, Gertrude R. Schmeidler, J. Gaither Pratt and William G. Roll participated in the roundtable. Margaret Anderson, J. B. Rhine and Rhea White were unable to attend the convention, but Rhine sent his prepared remarks which were read.

J. B. RHINE (Institute for Parapsychology, FRNM, Durham, N.C.)

The founding of the Parapsychological Association in 1957, at the Parapsychology Laboratory of Duke University, was in many respects a development of the times.   Much had happened in the nine years since the attempt at a meeting in Washington in 1948 to found the Society for Parapsychology--a hopeful step which proved to be premature.

This time the Duke Laboratory had completed on June 19th of that year a quite successful workshop, with 16 registrants and four "imported" instructors to supplement the research staff.   All these, together with a few visitors, repre-

---

*Chairperson: Charles T. Tart.

sented a relatively good geographic distribution and a har-
monious range of interests. The reaction to the proposal of
a professional society was very well received by the group,
and a founding committee was promptly appointed, consisting
of J. G. Pratt, Dorothy H. Pope and Wadih Saleh (an attor-
ney).

The Committee then proceeded to nominate the following slate of officers: R. A. McConnell for president; Gertrude R. Schmeidler, vice president; Rhea White, secretary;
Remi Cadoret, treasurer; and three additional members of
the Council: Karlis Osis, Margaret Anderson, and W. G.
Roll. The Committee and the Council were responsible also
for the preparation of a constitution, to be submitted for ap-
proval by the charter membership. In due course the Council was authorized to hold a regular election of officers for
the succeeding year.

But there were other factors too that favored this development in 1957. It was the 20th anniversary of the founding of the Journal of Parapsychology, and in the preceding
(March) issue the editorial had sounded a strong note of confidence in the professional progress of the research field.
The textbook which Dr. Pratt and I had been asked to write
was appearing that year. There was a clearly observable
unity felt among us following the extravagant attack by George
Price in Science only two years before; even some of the
critics expressed their condolences to us about that. We
were consequently more conscious of our status as a group
than we had ever been.

It seems to me we had developed among ourselves a
natural fraternity that proved to be of binding value to the
new organization. The officers who were selected for the
launching of the Association are the people to salute for the
growth and accomplishments of the PA in its formative period, and perhaps the very trials they had to meet, and the
dangers they knew only too well, contributed something to
the achievement.

But I do think that the generation following, perhaps
with enough major challenges facing them still, can well produce the greater accomplishment we now have good reason
to expect from them.

It is, for me at least, a pleasure to look back. But
if I were proposing such a beginning again from today's ex-

perience I would want to make a study of what works well
and what does not in the functioning of conventions such as
these of the PA. I would want more continuity of personnel
and objectives through the years, so that gains could be better sustained, mistakes more certainly averted. Instead of
the democratic selection of all members, I would want to see
a more permanent use of the skills, methods and experience
of some, in order to increase the effectiveness of the meetings, designing them more directly to suit their aims to the
best advantage. Yet I am truly proud to have had even a
small part in this fine organization. I think it has enormous
potential for the future.

R. A. McCONNELL (University of Pittsburgh)

While it might be interesting to reminisce with you
about the beginnings of our Association, I decided, instead,
to concentrate on a specific question that concerns both the
past and the future, namely: How far has parapsychology
progressed in the last 20 years towards acceptance by those
members of the intellectual elite who have been designated
by society as the guardians of relevant, accepted scientific
belief? I am referring, of course, to the recognized lead-
ers of physics and psychology.

To the best of my knowledge--and I would like to be
corrected if I am wrong--the first treatment of parapsychology in a college textbook of psychology appeared in 1961,
some four years after the founding of our Association. It
was 30 pages in The Personal World, an eclectic and discriminating synthesis written a generation too soon by Professor Harold McCurdy of the University of North Carolina.

The subject did not catch on, however, until after
1967, when Ernest Hilgard and Richard Atkinson served as
bellwethers by giving four pages to an open-minded discussion of parapsychology in their best-selling Introduction to
Psychology. Today, nearly all of the dozens of general textbooks of psychology give ESP some kind of recognition.

I need not remind you that it was in 1969, 12 years
after its formation, that the Parapsychological Association
was admitted to affiliation with the American Association for
the Advancement of Science. Are there any other indications
of acceptance of this field by orthodoxy? I know of none of
importance. Moreover, admission to textbooks and to the

AAAS do not constitute any degree of acceptance by the mandarins of psychology and physics who decide what scientific truths are true enough to deserve further elaboration by research. This failure to carry conviction I regard as primarily our own fault rather than the fault of the scientific establishment. We have failed to think of ourselves as revolutionaries. I do not mean that we have failed to proclaim our revolutionary intentions, but rather that we have neglected to study the sociology of science so that we might understand why skeptics do, and must, reject psi phenomena.

GERTRUDE R. SCHMEIDLER (City College of the City University of New York)

What have been the changes in the PA since it began twenty years ago? The most conspicuous of them is that now, happily, there are more of us. During one of those earliest meetings in Durham, I remember that while Dr. Rhine was ferrying a carload of us around, he said that if we had a fatal wreck there would be no parapsychology left. He was joking, of course; but anyone who tried to make the same joke nowadays would have to update and reword it to a busload of parapsychologists, or even a medium-size airplane-full.

And we have changed qualitatively, too. I think we do better research for a number of reasons: better apparatus available, a wider variety of useful techniques, and more sophisticated statistical methods. Even more important is that we are tying our thinking more closely to that of other disciplines, and asking how changes in psi relate to changes in psychological or physical parameters. (We have not been asking many incisive biological questions yet; let's hope they'll be coming along.) And I think I can add another reason that our research is better now: the last twenty years have taught us something about psi. We can build on our own prior findings when we plan a new experiment.

All this comes back, in a kind of spiral, to an amplification of the first thing I said. We not only have more people, we also have more good people. Among the ones with theoretical interests we can be especially glad about the influx of theoretical physicists, who suggest to us experimentalists how to tie psi research in with quantum theory. And most noteworthy and good is the astonishing number of high scoring subjects, who often give us such good procedural advice that they really are also consultants or co-experimenters, and who produce the massive ESP and PK results that we all feel excited about and that stimulate us to livelier theorizing.

J. G. PRATT (Division of Parapsychology, University of Virginia)

The chairman has called us together before you because we were there when it all began at Duke University 20 years ago. His instructions were that each one should reminisce, evaluate past accomplishments, or offer words of wisdom--anything that seemed appropriate to the occasion.

It has become evident that some of our listeners are not satisfied with only backward glances, but they insist upon also knowing our views about what lies ahead for parapsychology over the next twenty years. I will therefore try to play both roles, historian and prophet.

What contribution has the PA made to the development of parapsychology over the past two decades? I see the organization as primarily providing a stimulus to individual workers in the field to maximize their research efforts. Undoubtedly, the thought of having some new work completed in time to present it at the annual convention--the necessity of meeting deadlines--has quickened the pace of research. At the same time the emphasis upon the completion and reporting of new research as the primary requirement for membership in the PA has preserved the character of the Association as a professional scientific society. Finally, I point to the growing collection of annual volumes summarizing the work presented at the conventions as the most readily available public record of the developments in the field over the years.

The PA has become the leading force for fostering relations between parapsychology and the larger community of science. This can be seen most clearly in the growing number of papers and symposiums offered at scientific gatherings outside our own field. I think that the PA is also to be credited to some degree with the trend toward spreading more of our scientific papers among nonparapsychological periodicals.

What about the future? On this topic I think we cannot expect to be detailed and precise in our predictions, nor

do I regard this limitation as being a bad thing in a pioneer-
ing enterprise such as ours. In 1948 the Journal of Parapsychology ran a symposium on the topic of a research program for the next ten years of the field, with most of the
field's active workers participating. Ten years later I compared what had been done with what had been projected, and
there was virtually no correlation. I feel that while wise
researchers take advantage of consultations with their colleagues, the current state of our field does not allow it to
be organized like research in an industrial laboratory. If
I had to choose one thing as the most important for the future of parapsychology, it would be the necessity of somehow gaining the acceptance by our colleagues in science that
would bring the professional status and provide the financial
security needed to insure the survival of the field. I agree
with what Bob McConnell has said on this topic.

CARROLL NASH (Saint Joseph's College, Philadelphia)

        It may be of interest for you to know that this con-
vention of the Parapsychological Association at American
University is not the first connection between this science
and this University. In 1944-45 a PK experiment which was
performed here under my supervision was published in the
Journal of Parapsychology. It indicated that the scoring rate
was no less at a distance of 30 feet between the subject and
the dice than at a distance of three feet.

        At the present time there are no specific credentials
for being a parapsychologist, and numerous individuals claim
to belong to this profession who have little education and no
record of research in this field. The fact that a parapsychologist may be psychic does not warrant that an individual
call himself a parapsychologist on that basis alone. A parapsychologist is an individual who is qualified by training to
conduct research and/or education in this field. He studies
psychics, but is not necessarily one himself. In my opinion
the Parapsychological Association should take upon itself the
obligation of certifying individuals who are properly qualified
for this profession.

KARLIS OSIS (American Society for Psychical Research, New
        York)

        At the time of the PA's birth, parapsychology was like

an archipelago of rather disconnected and often hostile islands. Integration was therefore the first natural task of the PA. Indeed annual conventions provided the necessary forum for both personal encounters and the exchange of information. The PA helped us learn to live in a pluralistic society where no one has the only Right Truth and all are striving for new relative knowledge. (Of course, the islands themselves are not necessarily pluralistic.) While the experimentalists and the methodological puritans at times gained clear dominance of our program committees, thinkers, clinicians, case workers, survivalists and even the creative avant-garde still were heard. In my opinion, the integrative function of the PA has contributed enormously to the growth of parapsychology and should not ever be abandoned for the sake of dominance of one group over another.

Another obvious task for our conventions was to attract and recruit new workers and supporters in the worlds of science and finances. If research output is an indicator of these lines, our success has been dismal; that is, there are disproportionately small gains as compared to the tremendous expansion of public interest and the avalanche of college courses in parapsychology. Our conventions simply did not inspire. Obsession with selecting papers low on relevancy but high on technicalities and boring presentations might be part of the cause. Not we, but such pseudo-research problems as pyramid power, plant communications, bioplasma, psychotronic generators, and endlessly expanded consciousness, inspired and carried away our youth to nowhere. It is high time indeed for reprogramming PA programs, leaving the nitty gritty for the journals.

WILLIAM G. ROLL (Psychical Research Foundation, Durham, N. C.)

The first report on parapsychology this week did not appear at the 20th PA convention, but in The Washington Post on August 7. Since this article is concerned with what the world might hold in store for us during the next few decades--or rather what parapsychology might hold in store for the world--it deserves the attention of the PA as much as the convention presentations. According to the Post, classified psi research is now supported by government agencies here and in the communist world. A psychic arms race is in progress where espionage is beginning to live up to its name and where PK is looked on as a trigger device for nuclear bombs. John Wilhelm, author of the article suggests, "If there is reason to believe that psychic functioning performs according to the 'mind war' scenarios described in the few classified studies that have leaked out, public debate can help shape safeguards to insure benign application. If there is the slightest shred of evidence that psychotronic weaponry is at all possible, it should be considered biological warfare and banned in accordance with existing agreements."

Certainly, it seems to me, debate is called for by members of the professional and, significantly, international society in the field. It may be objected that the issue has no urgency: if we look at the level of results achieved in most psi tests, the possibility of practical application, benign or malign, is remote. However, there are reports of high-accuracy ESP and of striking displays of PK which suggest we are not dealing with trifling forces.

We can approach the issue in two ways. As an organization, we should explore the possibility of outlawing military applications of psi and, as individual researchers, we should increase research into areas which may lead to improvements in life in general.

Psi research is one of many sciences which explores connections among people, and between people and their physical environments. It is the only science, however, which is concerned with the possibility that connections which span space and time may also be channels of consciousness. In psi conducive states there often is a sense of identification with persons and things which usually are experienced as outside the borders of the self. If psi research should point to an empirical and experiental extension of the human self, then "mind war scenarios" and other confrontations which plague human society may lose their appeal. If it should also turn out, as suggested by studies of psychic healing, that physical and psychological health may be aided by such states, psi research should lead to overall improvements of the human condition.

RESEARCH ON OUT-OF-BODY EXPERIENCES*

ROBERT L. MORRIS (University of California, Santa Barbara)

OBEs are of general interest in parapsychology because they appear in anecdotes as psi-conducive and because
they suggest a discrete aspect of self that may be able to
exist apart from the physiological body. To help understand
psi during OBEs we need to explore procedures in which information seems to flow from the environment to the OBEer
(e.g., OBEer is asked to "visit" and describe remote events)
as well as procedures in which information seems to flow
from the OBEer to the environment (e.g., OBEer is asked
to "visit" and influence remote events).

If we are to assess specific theoretical concepts about
OBEs, such as the notion that they may represent an actual
extension of the experiencing self beyond the boundaries of
the physiological body, we must construct specific, testable
(e.g., falsifiable) models which are amenable to controlled
investigation. In constructing such models we may find ourselves developing rather weak, tentative versions at first,
ones which must rely upon subsequent research to allow
sharpening to the point of useful accuracy. An example is
the detection model we have used at the Psychical Research
Foundation. We hypothesized that during OBEs an aspect of
self extended tangibly to the location experienced, such that
it could be detected by physical, animal and human detectors
at that location in much the same way as a magnetic field is
detected by a magnetometer. We tested this model by asking an OBEer to "visit" detectors at an assigned target location. Our detectors' responses had to be consistent from
time to time, although perhaps varying in strength with variations in qualitative aspects of the reported OBE such as vividness, lack of fantasy components, etc. Response strength
should also vary with distance from the detector to the OBEer's
perceived location as well as with the onset and termination

---

*Chairperson: Robert L. Morris.

of the OBEer's visit to the target location.   By researching
a variety of detectors under a variety of circumstances, we
can explore the generality of the above model.   Any detection responses from any detectors can be assessed for consistency as well as systematic variations in strength with
variations in their characteristics of the environment and/or
the characteristics of the OBE as reported by the experi-
encer.   Sporadic "detection" responses would be likely to
represent either standard ESP-PK responses or true detection responses that correlate with some yet-unmeasured variable.   Continued data collection at both a descriptive and experimental level would allow a gradual shaping of what kinds
of detectors work and under what conditions.   As potential
detectors successively fail, the range of viable detection
models for OBEs gradually diminishes, thus increasing the
specificity of those for which one does not get positive evidence.   Our Psychical Research Foundation work, as noted
in earlier RIP volumes, has yet to find a perfect detector
although we have been encouraged by some results with a
kitten.   One possibility is that our model may have to incorporate the possibility that living detectors may habituate.
It would also be hoped that as our models undergo gradual
evolution there be room to incorporate some of the OBEs'
experiential richness.

KARLIS OSIS (American Society for Psychical Research)

      The interesting aspect about the OBE is that it might
be real, i.e., a projection of the psyche beyond the body.
Needless to say, research on the externalization aspect of
the OBE is extremely relevant because of its obvious implications for the psychology of personality and for the problem
of postmortem survival.   In spite of Tart's effort clearly to
conceptualize the definitive characteristics of the "classical
discrete" OBE, confusion prevails.   Nowadays it is fashionable to label "out-of-body" even those experiences which are
fundamentally either altered states or "remote viewing,"
i.e., undifferentiated ESP.   I agree with Palmer and Vasar
that the OBE appears to be illusory when experimentally "induced" in subjects during only one short session.   Four
years of research led me to believe that Hornell Hart's "full-
fledged" OBE or Tart's "classical OBE" actually exist but
are rarely voluntarily controlled.

      We tried to identify characteristics which, when taken
together, might discriminate the OBE from other phenomena

it often gets confused with. The following promising leads
have emerged: (1) decrease in amplitude of occipital EEG
and absence of REMs during reported OBEs; (2) perception
from a perspective of the area in which the OB consciousness is, according to subjects, experienced to be; (3) visi-
bility of the OB projection reported on rare occasions in
laboratory and in spontaneous, real-life situations; (4) reported effects of "classical OBEs" on the personality of the
experient, such as a change of one's whole outlook on life,
and/or reduction or extinction of fear of death; and (5) the
modus of the experience is reported, in "classical" cases,
to be uniquely OBE and dissimilar to dreaming, daydream-
ing, other altered states and other ESP experiences.

Research on the OBE is, of course, still very scarce
and in the formative stages. Although final answers should
not be expected so early in a new field of inquiry, the results are, so far, very encouraging.

JOHN PALMER (University of California, Davis)

The out-of-body experience (OBE) is a subjective
state during which a person experiences his consciousness
as localized in space outside his body. As such, it is no
more a psychic phenomenon than is an ordinary dream.
However, as with dreams, psychic phenomena (i.e., interactions with the environment not currently explainable by
known physical laws) sometimes occur in conjunction with
OBEs. It is this association between OBEs and psi (e.g.,
ESP) that has prompted some researchers to suggest a theory
of psi (which we might call the "OB theory") which assumes
that a "non-physical" aspect of self (i.e., Roll's theta agency) is capable of leaving the body during the course of psychic interaction with the environment.

However, mere documentation of psi sometimes occurring in conjunction with OBEs is not sufficient to establish such an association. It must be shown that psi occurs
more frequently or at least differently in OBEs than in other
states before the OB theory can begin to claim any support.
I found such an association in my own research on OBEs induced in the laboratory, but I then confronted the additional
problem of a confounding between OBE reports and reports
of a hypnagogic state, an internally deployed attention state
that has been shown to be ESP-conducive independent of
OBEs. Insofar as OBEs outside the laboratory arise from

hypnagogic states (and there is evidence that many do), this problem exists for these cases as well. One approach to a solution is to determine whether OBEs associated and not associated with verifiable psi differ phenomenologically, and if so, whether the differences are attributable to the psi-conducive nature of the state of consciousness underlying them.

CHARLES T. TART (University of California, Davis)

I want to reinforce John Palmer's remarks about the importance of getting clearer conceptualizations of just what we mean by out-of-the-body experiences (OBEs). In what we might think of as the classical OBE, there is a distinct quality of "location." Location is used in the ordinary sense of the word, just as I would say now that I perceive myself as located in this meeting room. In the classical OBE, the experience has this element of direct realization that you are located elsewhere than where your physical body is.

This clearly distinguishes classical OBEs from phenomena like remote viewing, where, if asked about your location, you know that you are "in" your body but absorbed in imagery you hope is about a distant location. Although some people have casually lumped OBEs and remote viewing together, we should not do so.

Further, the quality of consciousness during many or most classical OBEs is "ordinary," i.e., one's mental processes seem to function in about the same way as they do in ordinary, "in-the-body" experience. I used to define OBEs by the joint qualities of knowing you were elsewhere than your physical body and experiencing your consciousness as ordinary, but now I would make the latter characteristic common, but not essential. An altered state of consciousness can occur in conjunction with an OBE. Further clarification here will depend on increasing our understanding of altered states of consciousness.

ARE THERE ESPECIALLY PSI-CONDUCIVE
INTERNAL STATES?*

CHARLES HONORTON (Maimonides Medical Center, New York)

Our psi state methodologies appear to be producing strong and moderately replicable psi effects. The "psi resolution" capability of state methodology is evident in the small number of trials typically required for significant psi detection. Replicability is indicated by the number of studies, experimenters and laboratories achieving significant detection rates.

To what do we owe this success and how may we improve upon it? We can identify at least five components of state methodology which are psi-conducive: (1) Psychophysical noise reduction. Psi input may normally be masked by the noise generated by ongoing somatic and perceptual activity. If so, the probability of psi detection should increase as the noise level is reduced. Noise reduction is usually induced via relaxation and perceptual isolation techniques. (2) Spontaneity and neural indeterminancy. Psi state methodology usually involves free-response techniques which may increase response spontaneity and minimize guessing habits. Stanford's model-of-function model suggests that Ganzfeld and similar techniques may increase neural indeterminacy, thereby enabling psi input to be encoded and/or triggered. (3) Motivation. Receiver motivation is probably enhanced through "stimulus hunger" induced through perceptual isolation, and by (4) relaxed interpersonal contact with "significant others" in the experimental setting. Relaxation techniques, if used successfully, promote relaxed interpersonal contact between receiver, experimenter, and/or target person. (5) Permission to function psychically. As Braud notes, psi state methods are somewhat ritualistic and may serve as "permission giving" or "placebo" influences on psi performance.

---

*Chairperson: Charles Honorton.

Our task now is to refine and optimize existing methodologies, to develop better ones, and to confirm, revise or refute the various theoretical models we have tentatively erected. Refinement and optimization will require more systematic assessment of the individual and interactive contribution of the above components on psi performance. There are many methodological and measurement problems to be resolved along the way. But if, as seems likely, the level of concentrated effort in this area continues to accelerate, we should soon see further substantial increases in the magnitude and reliability of laboratory psi performance. We clearly have our work cut out for us.

WILLIAM BRAUD (Mind Science Foundation, San Antonio, Texas)

Although good psi results are being obtained in experimental studies of "psi conducive states," the crucial psi-influencing aspects of these experiments are not known. Seven "mechanisms" are outlined which, either alone or in combination, might account for the "psi-conduciveness" of these procedures. If the various psi-conducive procedures (relaxation, ganzfeld stimulation, hypnosis, meditation, etc.) are effective to the extent that they reduce psi-interfering "noise," three possibilities suggest themselves: (1) reduced noise may allow improved access to "psi signals" themselves; (2) reduced noise may allow improved access to psi-mediating vehicles (images, memories, etc.); (3) reduced noise may reduce externally- and internally-generated constraints which structure the percipient's brain, allowing it to become more labile and more readily restructured in ways that match the structure of the target (in Stanford's terminology, increasing the likelihood of "conformance behavior").

Four additional "mechanisms of action" of psi-conducive procedures do not necessitate "noise-reduction" at all: (4) "psychological" changes associated with the procedures (e.g., a shift from LeShan's "sensory reality" to the "clairvoyant reality" or Ehrenwald's "existential shift") may allow psi to manifest more readily; (5) the ritualistic aspect of well-specified procedures may itself be psi-conducive, reducing such psi-interfering factors as anxiety, personal responsibility, egocentric effort, lack of confidence or belief, "ownership resistence," etc.; (6) conventional experimenter effects may play a role; and (7) psi-mediated experimenter effects may play a role.

Following a more detailed discussion of these seven interpretations, we need a serious and intensive research effort which might test their validity, relative contributions and interactions in producing instances of dramatic laboratory psi.

JAMES KENNEDY (Institute for Parapsychology)

The question under discussion is not whether psi can occur in supposed "psi conducive" states but rather whether psi effects are stronger in these states than in other states of consciousness. In evaluating this question, several methodological points must be considered. First, the term "psi conducive" is an over-generalization of the existing data. The vast majority of the states of consciousness studies in parapsychology have used ESP tests and recently most experiments have involved the specific case of ESP information mediated by imagery--only one of many possible psi manifestations.

Operationally, the investigation of internal states reduces to administering a psi test after a formal induction procedure (e.g., hypnosis, Ganzfeld). Before conclusions can be drawn about the relative efficacy of psi conducive states, three questions about these induction procedures must be answered. (A) Are psi results stronger with the induction procedures than without them? (B) Do the induction procedures produce the desired psychological effects in the subjects--i.e., is there construct validity? (C) Do the induction procedures introduce other confounding psychological effects that influence psi scores?

My impression is that question C has been essentially unaddressed; B has been answered affirmatively in the few pertinent investigations, and most discussions have been limited to question A.

The methodological problems for question A center around the use of control groups. Most psi-conducive state experiments have not employed control groups and the few that have are open to criticisms of experimenter effects. The best control procedure may be to have other experimenters, without biases towards the hypothesis, carry out control studies. For example, as a control for Ganzfeld studies, free response tests with one trial per session and with no internal state induction procedure should be carried

out by experimenters having a high expectation for success--
conditions which seem to be met by the remote viewing experiments.   It is doubtful that the Ganzfeld results could be
shown to be superior to those of remote viewing.

The loose handling of statistics in internal states research also hinders an overall evaluation.   Again, using the
Ganzfeld research as an example, the majority of reports
present two or more analyses without specifying which ones
or how many were planned in advance.   This raises the difficult problem of multiple analyses which must be considered
when evaluating the overall significance of a line of research.

REX G. STANFORD (Center for Parapsychological Research;
    Austin, Texas)

One possible explanation for the apparent facilitation
of ESP performance by certain "altered internal states" (e.g.,
hypnosis, deep relaxation, dreaming, effects of Ganzfeld
stimulation) is that these states reduce external and internal
distractions and confusion which interfere with the detection
and recognition by the subject of the internal ESP signal.
This is termed the noise-reduction model.

An alternative explanation is the mode-of-function
model.   It proposes that psi can influence neural activity
only under certain circumstances.   The brain is presumed
susceptible to psi influence to the degree that the neural
activity needed to encode the "target information" (or to make
a goal-relevant response) is not constrained.   Such constraints
include circumstantial, sequential and rational ones.   In an
ESP-favorable internal state, possibilities exist for mentation which would not otherwise emerge under this set of
physical circumstances; the mentation of a given moment is
less dependent upon the preceding mentation; and both the
content and sequence of mentation need not "make sense."
All of the psi-favorable conditions discovered thus far seem
to facilitate such constraint reduction.   In short, brain function conducive to ESP is proposed to be function which is
ready for and capable of change but in which the activity is
not constrained in the sense described above.   During such
function brain activity might best be compared with the operation of a random event generator (such as the "Schmidt machine" used in PK testing) rather than with the function of
a computer or other deterministic system.

The noise-reduction and mode-of-function models yield different predictions under certain circumstances. Without experimental investigation of these divergent predictions, we cannot say whether there exist truly psi-favorable internal states or whether "altered states" manipulations influence only judgmental factors which occur later than the psi process itself.

SPECIAL PROBLEM AREAS
IN RESEARCH METHODOLOGY*

REX G. STANFORD (Center for Parapsychological Research)

Same-subjects designs are often used in parapsychology, and they have the advantage of economy and, sometimes, of increased statistical power. These advantages do not warrant such a design whenever we cannot clearly justify the assumption of symmetry of transfer (relative to sequence effects) which is required for effective counterbalancing. Use of such a design in violation of this assumption results in a confounded experiment. Also, such a design cannot be justified unless the experimenter is specifically interested in the effects of juxtaposing two (or more) tasks for the same subject rather than, as is usual, a concern with the effects per se of the conditions studied. This is because same-subjects designs do not allow differentiation of the effects of the experimental conditions per se from the effects of their juxtaposition. Moreover, if task juxtaposition results in a negative correlation of performance under the two conditions, as has been observed in several psi studies, the statistical power of the design is reduced, often drastically, due to an increased error term and the loss of degrees of freedom found in any such design. Unless one is interested in task juxtaposition per se or wishes directly to compare the results with independent-groups and same-subjects designs, use of the latter design is generally questionable.

It is also desirable to introduce ESP trials for which there is no target but for which subjects make calls, anyway, without knowing that. Such trials allow assessment of sensitivity to particular types of target materials.

In studies involving free-response methodology, the use of the subjects themselves as the judges (raters or rankers) confounds the effects upon ESP performance of the ex-

---

*Chairperson: Rex G. Stanford

perimental manipulation or individual differences with the effects of these same factors upon judging performance.

ROBERT L. MORRIS (University of California, Santa Barbara)

Researchers pay much attention to what goes on during ESP and PK trials, e.g. specific attempts by the subject to use psi, but they largely ignore what happens between trials. Yet the participants are processing a lot of information between trials. Within a run, subjects may be processing whatever feedback they got about the specifics of a target, whether or not they "got a hit" and how they feel about that, and their feelings about any other experiences that took place during the preceding trial. Should they form any hypotheses, e.g. that body sensations are informative, they may then become overly attentive to body sensations, thus greatly reducing the usefulness of body sensations as being informative about the target. If they make a string of hits in a row, they may stop to reflect on this, perhaps with great changes in anxiety level, deployment of attention and so on. We need to give subjects tools to help them stabilize across trials such that they can make effective use of feedback. Possibilities include the use of highly specific attention deployment procedures that will keep the person busy; teaching concentration techniques that allow the person to register information accurately without immediate cognitive elaboration; verbal instructions to notice but set aside; and so on.

Processing of feedback goes on between runs and sessions also, including feedback from the experimental environment and the environment outside the laboratory. Ideally we should allow the environment to exert a reasonably stable yet positive influence. Since participants change from time to time, the participant-environment interaction may best be stabilized by allowing the environment to change with participant changes (e.g., personally administered progressive relaxation rather than relaxation tapes). It may also be important to deal at the start with any concerns or fears the participants (or experimenters) may have about success at psi studies, so that stable, positive attitudes can be more easily maintained.

A final between trials factor is that of alternative paths of psi information flow, e.g. the participant or experimenter may be making decisions or influencing events psy-

chically in between trials that will facilitate success at the
psi task.   The opportunities to do so should be reduced as
much as possible.

The above factors are rarely taken into account as
we design and report our studies; yet if we hope to do conceptual replications and extensions of each other's work we
must acknowledge them, measure them, stabilize them and
use them.

JOHN PALMER (University of California, Davis)

Let us consider the evaluation of free-response material in parapsychology when a judge is asked to compare
a target with one or more controls randomly selected from
a pool.   Although simple rankings have proven adequate in
some experiments, ratings provide a more continuous and
sensitive measure of psi.   This added sensitivity is especially important when the effects are relatively weak and/or one
desires to look at the ESP scores in relation to other variables.   It was stressed that while ratings can always be con-
verted to ranks, the reverse is not possible.   Ratings have
customarily been transformed to standard $(\overline{Z})$ scores, which
in my experience in this context tend to be distributed rec-
tangularly and thus are most suitably analyzed by non-para-
metric statistical tests.

We also need to consider the advantages of having
free-response ratings made by independent judges rather than
by the percipients themselves.   Percipient judging has obvious economic advantages, and the percipient has access to
aspects of his imagery not available to an outside judge.
However, the outside judge's handicap can be mitigated by
careful interviewing of the percipient.

Independent judging has the important advantage of not
requiring the percipient to see the control pictures, thereby
substantially reducing the possibility of displacement effects.
Naive percipients bring highly variable criteria to the judging task, thereby introducing much error variance that can
be eliminated by independent judging.   When more than one
judge is employed, measures of reliability can be computed.
This is not possible with percipient judging.   There are other statistical advantages of Z scores computed from independent judges' ratings.   In most group experiments, independent judging is the method of choice.

WHAT NEXT IN SURVIVAL RESEARCH?*

IAN STEVENSON (Division of Parapsychology, University of Virginia)

Since 1962 a group of parapsychologists particularly
concerned with the evidence of survival after death has met
every few years. The membership of this group has varied,
although some of its latest members were also among participants in the 1962 meeting. The group has met most often
at the time of the annual convention of the Parapsychological
Association. At the convention held at the University of
Edinburgh in 1972 the deliberations of the group were included in the official program of the convention. And the
topic of survival research was again included in the program
of the 1977 convention held at the American University in
Washington, D. C. The presentation of the topic of survival
research within the program of the Parapsychological Association's conventions reflects some increased interest in it
on the part of parapsychologists in recent years.

Every parapsychologist who believes that present
evidence justifies a belief in paranormal events is also committed to considering at least the possibility that such events
are caused by aspects of human personality that may survive
death. Thus evidence of extrasensory perception is, in
principle, a type of evidence of survival after death. (Not
all parapsychologists necessarily concur with this statement.)
Evidence of paranormal communication between living persons provides, however, only an indirect kind of evidence of
survival after death. Many parapsychologists have believed
for years that the search for more direct evidence of survival after death is at best premature and at worst futile.
This, however, was not the view of the founders of psychical
research, parapsychology's precursor. And it is not the
view of the participants in the roundtable held at the Washington convention. Several members of the roundtable have

---

*Chairperson: Ian Stevenson

actively sought improved types of direct evidence of survival
after death for many years; all are committed to the value
and the feasibility of such research, although not to a single
line of investigation in it.   They met in Washington to present in public their latest views and plans for further research in this important part of parapsychology.

WILLIAM G. ROLL (Psychical Research Foundation)

I have been asked to review some of the concepts in
survival (theta) research.   There are two important ones,
personality and consciousness.   Most of our work has focused
on the continuation of personality, such as the memories and
traits of the deceased.   From these we infer the existence
of that person as a conscious being.   However, a living person may express his memories, traits and so on without
conscious attention, in normal as well as in paranormal activities; personalities may continue after death in states of
unconsciousness.

It is generally assumed that the only way to determine
whether someone else is conscious is inferential: I infer
that you are conscious if you behave in the manner that I do
when I know myself to be conscious (by acting the same way,
showing the same type of brain wave, etc.).   It is assumed
that a person cannot be directly aware of the consciousness
of another person because there is a separation between
them.   Explorations into "expanded" states of consciousness,
particularly psi conducive states, call this assumption into
question and raise new possibilities for survival research.
If consciousness is continuous, then a person may become
aware of the existence and state of another person's consciousness by introspection of his "own" consciousness.   A theta
researcher-experient might in this way observe or become
aware of the presence of the theta consciousness of a deceased person.   Since the resulting change of consciousness
in the researcher might be associated with brain wave
changes characteristic of the theta consciousness, EEG
measures could be used as a test for the presence of this
consciousness.   This would provide a means of relating direct awareness with inferential knowledge accessible to con-
sensual validation by researchers in whom the ability of direct awareness of theta consciousness has not been developed.

There is another way to test the hypothesis that consciousness is continuous.   If there is direct interaction be-

tween the consciousnesses of people, then the consciousness of one person to whom a second person's attention is directed would be expected to become similar to the state of consciousness of the second person (as determined by state reports and EEG recordings). LeShan claims that psychic healing may occur when the healer enters an altered state where he experiences himself as merging with the patient. Research into psychic healing may be a way to explore whether consciousness can function as a means of interaction and observation and, thereby, as a tool in survival research.

IAN STEVENSON

In 1972 at the convention of the Parapsychological Association held at the University of Edinburgh, I described a fantasy of the "perfect case" of the reincarnation type. Such a case would have a number of features that are sometimes or often found in different cases, but not yet altogether in any single case. It is perhaps unlikely that they ever will be found altogether in a single case. We may, however, find less than perfect cases and we should intensify the search for these.

For cases of the reincarnation type we have numerous hypotheses alternative to reincarnation, such as fraud, cryptomnesia, paramnesia and extrasensory perception on the part of the subject. Of these, the one most difficult to exclude, and therefore the most important, is that of paramnesia. This refers to the possibility that the informants for a case have, usually quite unconsciously, mingled and confused their memories before the case's investigation, so that the subject has been credited with more knowledge about the previous life he claimed to have lived than he really had. From this arises the need to find and investigate more cases in which an investigator can make a written record of what the subject says before any attempt at verifying his statements is made; this means also before the subject's family meets the family of the presumed previous personality and thus gains normal knowledge about his life.

Fifteen cases of this rare type--in which the families concerned have not met before the investigation began--have been found and investigated. It is encouraging to note that these cases have, in general, the features found in the more numerous cases in which the concerned families have met before the investigation began. It is planned to give top priority to the search for additional cases of this type as funds and personnel become available.

India appears to be an excellent country for the discovery of such cases. The subjects of Indian cases often give numerous details about the previous lives they claim to remember. The two families often reside in towns and villages separated by some distance so that verifications of what a subject says requires some effort, and attempts at it may be postponed by his parents. It seems feasible to arrange for investigators to be notified earlier than they now are of the occurrence of cases; and when this can be arranged, so can the prompt investigation of the cases notified. In this way we can hope to accumulate a substantial series of cases in which we can at least exclude errors of memory on the part of the informants as an appropriate explanation of the case.

DAVID READ BARKER (Division of Parapsychology, University of Virginia)

Intensive research by Ian Stevenson has located more than 1600 cases of the reincarnation type. Although the primary evidence for reincarnation originates in individual cases, important features of these cases recur with sufficient frequency to become both intra-cultural and trans-cultural patterns. My research is aimed at identifying and interpreting these cultural patterns.

We are now able to make objective descriptions of cultural patterns in these cases through the use of a detailed coding sheet containing 215 variables. Key data from individual case files are being transfered to these coding sheets and then to computer cards for statistical analysis. The preliminary results are very encouraging.

The broad conformity of individual cases to cultural modalities poses several problems of interpretation. If a distinct model of reincarnation exists in a particular culture, it is possible that cases may develop in conformity with it. However, preliminary data from the computerized cases suggest that the patterns in the cases are not the result of cultural conditioning but are, at least in India, unknown to the subjects and their families before the start of a case.

Belief in reincarnation is to be found in every culture

area in the world, in societies which range from hunting
bands to great civilizations. In every society with a belief
in reincarnation, cases have thus far been identified when
fieldwork has been undertaken to locate them. The great
diversity of beliefs and social organization among these societies provides a control for the hypothesis that cases are
simply behavioral manifestations of beliefs. Several of the
most important features of cases of the reincarnation type
appear to be almost trans-cultural. Our continued anthro-
pological study of large numbers of cases in many societies
will extend an understanding of and, possibly, evidence for
cases of the reincarnation type.

BRUCE GREYSON (Medical Center, University of Virginia)

        Persons who come close to death often report appar-
ently paranormal experiences that convince them that man
survives physical death. Data derived from such experiences have been proposed as one type of evidence suggestive
of survival after death. Only through rigorous investigation
of such cases can the significance of these experiences for
the question of survival or for the dying process itself be
ascertained. Most "near-death" experiences must be studied
retrospectively and under uncontrolled conditions. We are
planning a prospective analysis of such experiences in dying
or critically ill persons, after first reviewing and completing
the investigation and pattern analysis of our existing cases,
with particular attention to characteristic features of the reported experiences, recurrent aspects of the subjects' physical and psychological or social situations at the time of the
experience, recurrent factors leading to the reporting of the
experiences, and consideration of alternative hypotheses to
survival and ways of discriminating more valuable from less
valuable experiences with regard to evidence for survival.

        The prospective study will be part of a clinical coun-
seling service provided in a hospital setting to a suitable
and cooperative group of persons expecting to die. By systematically recording the experiences of all the patients in
a particular group, we shall eliminate the self-selection of
subjects that weakens most studies of near-death experiences.
We shall be particularly vigilant for possible paranormal
features in the experiences of these persons and, in the case
of apparent extrasensory perceptions, will attempt to cor-
roborate or verify their statements. We will also offer to
willing persons within this group the opportunity to engage

in controlled experiments of extrasensory perception or "out-of-body" experiences.

KARLIS OSIS (American Society for Psychical Research)

Our study of deathbed visions comprises three surveys over an 18-year period and includes more than 1000 cases. The most rewarding data came from 600 terminal patients who saw apparitions. The phenomena of near-death and resuscitated patients were less consistent.

We developed multivariate methods of fitting the data to a bipolar model. The model hypothesized how the visions would be in case they contain ESP glimpses of a postmortem existence and also how they would be if the other world does not exist and death is the ultimate destruction of the personality. The survival pole of the model fitted the data of our two transcultural surveys surprisingly well while the destruction hypothesis made a rather poor fit. Visions of the dying do seem to have their basis in ESP, that is, awareness of postmortem existence. Medical and psychological factors which are known to enhance hallucinations did not increase the frequency of visions suggestive of postmortem survival. Cultural factors did not sway the core phenomena.

Our model might provide a basis for subsequent studies, but it needs extension and incorporation of all that has been learned since. The range of observations also needs expansion and should include at least the following four variables, which we did not cover: Prognosis prior to visions, because numerous patients seem to die against their own expectations and the medical prognosis, but following the ostensible wishes of the apparition. Diminution of discomfort and pain, which might indicate changes in the mind-body relationship. EEG recording during comatose states which may contain OBE. Lucidity of patients before death who have been out of touch with reality for a long time.

Methods of observation have to be congenial to the patients to permit them free expression of highly unusual experiences. The methods should also provide sufficient data for critical evaluations of response biases, observer biases, "doctrinal compliance" with observers' views and, most important, the possible influence of cultural factors, such as religion and other belief systems related to the after-life hypothesis.

GERTRUDE R. SCHMEIDLER (City College, City University
   of New York)

   Research on survival gives provocative findings, but
it might have more conclusive ones if it utilized modern
methodology.   Up to now it has been almost exclusively retrospective rather than predictive (investigations beginning only
after a person's death); it has been largely qualitative rather
than statistical; and it has seldom or never been double
blind.   These are weaknesses.

   I propose (and if it is funded, will perform) a project
with falsifiable predictions and double-blind data to examine
the hypothesis that an identifiable personality survives death,
i. e. , that individual differences so noticeable in life can predict post-mortem messages.   The idea was suggested by
Ashby's findings on attitudinal differences toward survival
messages.   The project has five steps, as follows.

   (1)   Subjects will be same-sexed volunteers who are
terminally ill but not sedated or extremely weak (N = 30?).
Trained clinicians will use semi-structured interviews and
personality tests to find the volunteers' attitudes, needs,
values, styles, memories, etc.   (2) Psychologists (taking
survival as a working hypothesis) will predict differences in
post-death communication.   Some possible examples are:
(a) will attempt to communicate or not; (b) will emphasize
physical appearance or not; (c) will attempt identification by
specific memories or will be vague; (d) will refer to unfin-
ished business or not.   (3) After the volunteers die, blind
note-takers will ask blind mediums for messages.   (4) Blind
coders will put each set of messages into one of the pre-
stated categories for each prediction.   (5) Each prediction
will be evaluated statistically.

   The hypothesis as stated will be falsified if few or
none of the predictions are confirmed.   But what if a substantial number are supported?   This will be irrelevant to
a super-psi hypothesis, which is unfalsifiable.   However, it
would support the survival possibility; and if an increasing
number of refined predictions are confirmed in subsequent
research, then convergent validity would make the survival
hypothesis increasingly strong.

A TAKE-HOME TEST IN PK WITH PRE-RECORDED TARGETS

Helmut Schmidt (Mind Science Foundation, San Antonio, Texas)

A typical PK experiment with pre-recorded targets proceeds in three steps.   First, a binary random number generator is automatically activated to produce a string of random numbers, "heads" or "tails."   Two identical records of these events are made, one for the experimenter to evaluate, and one to activate the later feedback to the subject. At this stage, nobody looks at the data.   Second, the recorded sequence of heads and tails is played back to the subject in some psychologically stimulating arrangement while the subject tries to enforce the appearance of, say, more heads than tails.   Third, the experimenter evaluates his copy of the data and checks whether, indeed, it contains more heads than tails.

In one previously reported experiment, for example, the heads and tails were represented by weak and strong clicks recorded on cassette tape, and the subject listened to the tape at home, trying to obtain more weak than strong clicks.   At the end of the experiment, the two records, the tape given to the subject and the record in the experimenter's files still agreed, but they showed an excess of heads.

Such an arrangement where the subject can work at home at his leisure might be psychologically advantageous for obtaining PK results.   Furthermore, the experiment is safe in so far as we do not have to trust the subject's honesty, because the data evaluation is based on the record which never left the laboratory.   It appears that this arrangement enables us to channel the subject's PK effort through time and space from the time when the subject makes his effort at home to the earlier time when the random number generator produces the random events in the laboratory.

The two experiments to be reported follow the described procedure with minor modifications. In both experiments, the feedback to the subject was given by up- and
down-moving tones rather than by weak and strong clicks.
At the beginning of a run, the feedback tone started at the
middle of the available tone range, and then each recorded
head or tail (played back at the rate of five per second)
shifted the tone frequency by one step upward or downward
respectively. Whenever, in this manner, the tone happened
to reach the upper or lower limit of the 16-step tone scale,
the tone was reset to the center frequency and after a one-
second intermission, the randomly up- and down-moving tone
sequence was continued. The reaching of the upper or lower limit was clearly indicated by an additional very high beep
or a very low tone respectively. With this feedback, the
goal of obtaining many heads was equivalent to pushing the
sound predominantly upward so that the upper tone limit was
reached more often than the lower limit.

The purpose of the first experiment was to test the
usefulness of the new display which the subjects particularly
liked. In this experiment, the ten participating subjects
were already used to PK experiments from previous visits
to the laboratory. Furthermore, the subjects could play in
the laboratory with the new feedback before they took the
tapes for the home test. This first experiment showed a
significant PK effect.

The second experiment was done on a less personal
basis. The subjects, respondents to newspaper advertisements, were called by a secretary and received, through the
mail, the tape together with a form letter describing the
task and the philosophy of PK testing with pre-recorded targets. This experiment was intended to study two more factors besides the existence of the PK effect under the given
conditions. In all previous experiments with pre-recorded
targets, the outcome of the data had not been inspected by
anyone in the laboratory before the subject made his PK effort on these data. In half of the tests for this experiment,
however, an assistant did look at these data. He was required to do some simple calculations with the scores in
order to make sure that, indeed, he had noticed them, but
he did not know the meaning of the recorded numbers so that
he did not get emotionally involved, wanting to find high
scoring. The other factor to be studied was a possible addition effect resulting when several subjects worked on the
same recorded data. Therefore, part of the recorded runs

were sent on identical tape copies to four subjects simultaneously.   These interesting factors could however, not be
analyzed because the second experiment did not show a sufficiently large PK effect.

First Experiment

Ten subjects participated in this experiment.   Before
the PK test with pre-recorded targets, these subjects had
the opportunity to play with the test machine under the following conditions: A binary random generator was automatically activated to generate a run of 512 events, heads
or tails, at a rate of five per second.   This generator was
connected to the mentioned tone display.   The subject listened through headphones, to the tones, trying to push the
stepwise varying frequency up or down respectively.   After
each run, or sometimes after a longer sequence of runs,
the scores were printed out by a mini-computer.   The scores
of these informal runs will not be reported.

For the formal part of the experiment, each subject
received two cassette tapes marked H and L respectively.
East side of a tape contained six test runs, separated by
ten-second intermissions.   Each of these pre-recorded test
runs was obtained by activating the random generator 512
times in the described manner and by recording the resulting
up- and down-moving sounds and the special sounds which indicated the reaching of the upper or lower tone range (and
which thus gave an objective indication of the subject's success) on the tape.   Thus, in this experiment, the subject had
the same task and received the same kind of feedback as in
the preliminary tests in the laboratory.

The subject's goal was to make the sound step upward or downward for the tapes marked H (high) and L (low)
respectively.   When the tapes were recorded, the experimenter did not yet know which tapes would be marked H or
L, but this was already decided by a specific entry point in
a random number table.   After a tape was prepared, the
computer printed for each of the 12 runs the numbers of
heads and tails.   This printout was, however, not inspected
at this time but only sealed in an envelope.   Only after the
subject had worked on the tape did the experimenter open
the envelope and inspect the data.

The expected main effect (PK hitting) was an increase
in the frequency of heads (corresponding to upward steps of

the sound pitch) for the H tapes and a corresponding increase
of the tails for the L tapes.

Considering the H tapes, let us call a step upward
(head) or downward (tail) a hit or miss respectively. The
subject could hear these events directly, but at the speed of
five steps per second the subject had not much time to concentrate on each event. Whenever the tone reached the upper or lower limit of the tone scale an additional sound was
displayed, a very high beep or a very low sound. These
events, which we call "grand hits" and "grand misses" respectively, occurred only a few times per run and served as
major milestones in the subject's progress. By counting
mentally the grand hits and grand misses, the subject could
easily keep track of his scores. After a grand hit or miss,
whenever the difference hits minus misses reached the value
of +8 or -8, the next grand hit or grand miss was scored.
This implies the relationship

integral part of $\left\{ \dfrac{\text{(hits) - (misses)}}{8} \right\}$ = (grand hits)-(grand misses)

This same relationship holds for the L tapes. The subjects
were, on the average, successful in both tasks of pushing
the sound up or down respectively. The total score was significant (CR = 3.34) at the 0.001 level, confirming the existence of a PK effect with pre-recorded targets.

Similarly a t-test applied to the ten total scores of
the ten subjects gives t = 3.87 (9 df). The differences in
the scores of the ten subjects on the H and L tapes are not
significant (t = 0.86, 9 df).

Second Experiment

This experiment was similar to the preceeding one,
the main differences being the following:

(1) The 64 participating volunteer subjects were
phoned by a secretary and then received the tapes with instructions through the mail. Thus, the subjects could not
get used to the experiment in the laboratory and they could
not discuss the many questions which are usually raised in
connection with PK tests using pre-recorded targets.

(2) Half of the runs (one side of each tape) were
"group runs" rather than "individual runs." For the group
runs, four identical copies of sound recordings were sent to
four different subjects. In these runs therefore, we have

four subjects making their PK effort on the same random
sequence of tones.

(3)   For half of the subjects in the individual and
group tests, the data printed out by the computer were seen
by an assistant before the subjects made their PK effort.
The assistant had to notice the printed numbers in order to
do some simple manipulations with the data, but he did not
know the meaning of the numbers so that he would not get
emotionally involved and would not wish for a particular result.

Thus each subject contributed 12 individual runs
(called his individual contribution) and each set of four subjects
also contributed 12 group runs (called a group contribution).
Each contribution contained two types of runs, where the subjects
tried to increase or decrease the sound frequency respectively, but since the previous experiment indicated no scoring
difference between these two cases, the scores of both cases
are combined for the following discussion.   We do distinguish,
however, between the sessions for which the data were inspected and those for which they were not inspected by an
assistant, previous to the PK test with the subject.

Data Evaluation

Four hypotheses or questions were to be studied:
Hypothesis 1: On the total of all not-inspected runs a significant positive score is expected.   We can evaluate the existence of this PK effect either in terms of the total CR
value or through a t-test, taking sessions as units.   The resulting values, CR = -1.13 and t = 1.16 (39 df), do not
confirm this hypothesis.   Hypothesis 2: The group runs are,
according to one earlier study, expected to show higher
scores.   The group sessions gave slightly, but not significantly stronger negative scoring, with t = -1.16 (38 df).
Question 1: Do the inspected runs (all combined) show evidence for a PK effect?   The answer is negative, CR = 0.4,
t = 0.36 (39 df).   Question 2: Are the scores of all inspected runs different from all scores of the not inspected
runs?   They are not significantly different, t = 0.72 (78 df).

Thus, the data do not suggest the existence of any PK
effect in the present experiment.   Only the CR^2-values in
the second experiment, which are all above their chance expectancy $=1$, might indicate that we had a mixture of PK
hitters and missers.   Combining all CR^2 contributions, the

resulting $\overline{CR^2}$ = 1.31 (80 contributions) is only suggestively high (p = 0.03).

Conclusion

The first experiment confirmed the existence of PK effects under a test arrangement with pre-recorded targets. Such an arrangement appears useful in reaching conveniently a large number of subject who can do a PK test at their leisure at home. The failure of the second experiment to produce PK effects, however, suggests that the rather impersonal manner of sending out test tapes with form letters was not psychologically favorable for obtaining PK results. Further experiment might show whether, for a successful PK test, the personal interaction between experimenter and subject is necessary or whether some better formulated instruction letter combined with verbal contact through a cassette tape might provide a sufficient psychological bridge between experimenter and subject.

CONSCIOUS AND SUBCONSCIOUS PK TESTS WITH PRE-RECORDED TARGETS

James Terry† and Helmut Schmidt (Mind Science Foundation)

A previously reported experiment suggested that subjects might subconsciously affect the spacing of clicks which were presented at random time intervals. The clicks were barely audible and the subject's conscious task was to recognize each of the clicks which arrived at an average rate of about ten per minute. A significant increase in the rate of the generated clicks was observed much as if the subject's eager concentration on the next click had subconsciously activated a PK mechanism to make this click come earlier than expected by chance.

In the three experiments to be reported, the arrangement for testing the subconscious PK effect was slightly different and furthermore, test runs with a subconscious PK task were alternated with runs in which the subject tried consciously to exert a PK effect. These experiments were

---

†Presented by Terry; dagger will indicate speaker.

set up in a two-experimenter design where both experimenters could independently watch all relevant steps of the tests, so that any improper procedure applied by one experimenter in the tests or evaluations could have been detected by the other experimenter.

The Subjects and Their Task

The three experiments (I, II, and III) took up 20, 20 and 30 sessions respectively. Each subject participated in only one of these 70 sessions. The first two experiments were done with one subject per session, but in the third experiment we had two sessions with one subject, 12 sessions with two subjects, and 16 sessions with three persons simultaneously linked to the same PK task. The subjects were volunteers, ranging in age from 15 to 81 years.

Each session consisted of six runs, three "subconscious PK runs" alternating with three "conscious PK runs" so that the first run in each session was of the subconscious type. Each run lasted approximately four and a half minutes and short breaks were taken between runs. During the run, the subject sat in a comfortable armchair and listened through headphones to tones.

For the conscious PK runs, high tones were offered at random time intervals so that the average number of sound expected per run was 128. The subject's (conscious) PK task was to increase this number of sounds, i.e., to shorten the random intervals between successive sounds.

For the subconscious PK test, high and low pitched tones were presented statistically independent of each other, at random time intervals so that the expected number of high as well as low sounds per run was 128. The subject's conscious task was to listen to the sounds attentively and to react, by the pressing of a hand-held switch, to each presented high sound as fast as possible, but not to react to the low sounds. The subjects' reaction time however, was not measured. It was rather expected that the subject's intense concentration on the sounds might activate a subconscious PK mechanism such as to shorten the waiting intervals between successive sounds.

The Two-Experimenter Design
with Pre-Recorded Targets

Previous experiments had indicated that for PK effects

to occur, it is not necessary that the subject make his PK
effort (and receive feedback) at the same time a random generator produces the random events to be effected by the PK.
In these experiments, the random generator was repeatedly
activated and its output recorded in the absence of a subject,
and only later did the subject make a PK effort while the
pre-recorded output of the random generator was played back.

Such a test arrangement is certainly interesting for
theoretical and practical reasons. Furthermore, this arrangement is particularly suitable for a tight two-experimenter design. The specific procedure used in our experiment was as follows:

Previous to a session with the subject, the following
steps had been made. J. T. makes a binary decision to
specify which of two tapes, A or B, will serve as test tape
in the experiment. J. T. does not communicate the decision
to anyone at this stage. The decision is made with the
help of the random number program of a pocket calculator.
This program transforms an arbitrarily entered eight-digit
number through a complex mathematical deterministic calculation into a quasi-random number. If the last digit is even
or odd, the decision is for A or B respectively.

Next, H. S. prepares a pair of digital cassette tapes,
labelled A and B respectively. Each of these tapes contains
six sequences (corresponding to the six runs) of 2048 random numbers each, in the following arrangement. The numbers 0, 1, 2 are, with the help of an indeterministic random number generator, an IMSAI mini-computer, and a
Memodyne digital cassette recorder, recorded so that the
number 0 occurs with the relative frequency 15/16 and the
numbers 1 and 2 occur with the relative frequency of 1/32
each. At this stage, the generated sequence is not known
to anyone.

Finally, H. S. and J. T. meet, H. S. turns over the
cassette tapes to J. T. and J. T. tells H. S. which of the
tapes, A or B, is the "test tape." The other tape serves
as "control tape."

In the following session with the subject, J. T. used
the "test tape" only and left the "control tape" untouched.
Only at the end of the experiment were the control tapes, as
well as the test tapes, read automatically by a computer
which printed out the relevant results.

During the test runs, the test tape (which contained the numbers 0, 1, and 2 randomly distributed with relative frequencies of 15/16, 1/32 and 1/32 respectively) was read automatically at the rate of ten numbers per second.

In the subconscious PK runs, each recorded 1 or 2 was displayed to the subject as a high or low tone respectively, whereas in the conscious PK runs, only the recorded 1's produced a (high) tone. The numbers of 0's, 1's and 2's in a run were given to the experimenter by display counters and were manually recorded. These numbers could be verified by the mentioned later computer printout.

Results

The main goal of the experiment was to test for the existence of a PK effect on prerecorded targets in the two-experimenter arrangement. The most relevant question was, Are the test tapes on which the subjects made a PK effort different from the control tape on which no such effort was made? Note that the test and control tapes were prepared by H.S. under identical conditions while H.S. was not yet aware which tape would serve as test or control tape respectively. At the time when these tapes were prepared J.T. had already made the decision, but this decision became known to H.S. only later when he gave the tapes to J.T.

As primary measures for testing the existence of PK on the test tapes, we had chosen the following: In the conscious PK tests, there was only one primary measure: the frequency of sound signals, i.e., the number of 1's in the test runs. In the unconscious runs we consider two measures: the frequency of high tones and the difference in the frequency of high and low tones.

From past experience, we would not commit ourselves to predicting whether conscious PK would work in the hitting or missing direction because this might depend on subtle unrecognized factors.

For the unconscious tests we expected an increase in the number of high tones on which the subject concentrated (corresponding to an increase in the click rate in the previous experiment) but we could not predict whether the high and low tones would be affected in the same manner or not.

Considering the combined results of the three experiments, there were only two significant values. The test runs for conscious PK displayed PK missing (CR = -3.07, P < 0.005, two-tailed). And the same runs showed a high variance. Considering the individual CR values for the 70 sessions, we get $\overline{CR^2}$ = 1.50 which is significantly high, with (one-tailed) p < 0.005. The corresponding control tapes show no such significant effect.

The results suggest that, indeed, the scores on the test tapes are different from the scores on the control tapes. On the other hand, a t-test comparing the 70 conscious PK sessions with the 70 corresponding control sessions gives only t = 1.65 (138df) p < 0.1, two-tailed.

This reduction in significance is not surprising because of the significantly high variance of the test sessions and because the control sessions happen also to be biased toward a smaller number of high tones.

This non-significant bias, which also appears in the subconscious runs and the corresponding control runs, raises the question whether perhaps the random generator was biased. An extensive randomness test at the completion of the experiments, however, indicated no such bias. In this test, with a theoretically expected number of high tones of $\overline{H}$ = 204,800, the observed deviation was +236, slightly in the opposite direction (CR = 0.53).

Special Features of the Third Experiment

The third experiment was different from the first and second experiments in two respects. First, during the PK sessions we had (except for two sessions) two or three subjects simultaneously listen through individual headphones to the same sounds, with the same tasks. Second, before and after the PK tests, J. T. administered clairvoyance tests to each subject with pictures, using Honorton's binary coding method for the evaluation. Before the PK part of the experiment, the subjects met in the library with J. T., read instruction on the binary coding, and then worked on a slide (different for each subject) inside a heavy brown envelope. Directly after the PK test, they worked on a second slide and then they could check their guesses by looking at the two pictures. The obtained scoring rates of 52.4 per cent and 53.6 per cent before and after the PK test, respectively, are (combined) significant at the 1 per cent level (one-tailed, CR = 2.34).

Conclusion

The reported experiments confirm the existence of a PK effect in tests with prerecorded targets in so far as the part in which the subjects made a conscious PK effort led to significant PK missing (p < .005). The test was not sensitive enough however to establish a significant difference between test and control tapes. The test tapes showed, furthermore, a significantly high variance (p < .005). The search for a subconscious PK effect in half of the test runs did not show clear indications of any PK effect under these conditions. A clairvoyance test was added to the third experiment and this test, using Honorton's binary evaluation method, gave positive scores (p < 0.01) even though the conscious PK runs in the third experiment produced rather high PK missing.

A PK INVESTIGATION OF THE EXPERIMENTER EFFECT AND ITS PSI-BASED COMPONENT

Richard Broughton, Brian Millar, John Beloff and Kathleen Wilson† (Department of Psychology, University of Edinburgh)

At the 1976 PA Convention in Utrecht, R. B. presented a paper entitled "An Exploratory Study on Psi-Based Experimenter and Subject Expectancy Effects" [RIP 1976, pp. 173-7]. This suggested that the experimenter effect may be largely psi-based. The present investigation, which pursues this indication in a large-scale project, was designed and carried out by four members of the Parapsychology Unit of the Department of Psychology at the University of Edinburgh.

The project outlined herein is an investigation of what happens when various parapsychologists and interested researchers are given an identical PK experiment to conduct. Any differences which may appear would generally be attributed to normal psychological mechanisms. However, insofar as detailed attention is paid here to the distribution of feedback to the participants, certain inferences may be drawn regarding the psi-component of experimenter effect.

Both Schmidt's mathematical model of psi and Walker's quantum mechanical model focus upon feedback of the event

as the key factor in paranormal occurrences. Three implications of this aspect of the models are of special relevance
to the present study. They are (1) that a psi-source is
activated only when feedback has been received, (2) that the
experimenter no less than the ostensible subject may represent the critical psi-source, and (3), which follows directly
from (1) and (2), that psi effects are retroactive. This follows because if a psi-source is activated only at the moment
of feedback it can only operate retroactively in determining
the prior ESP response or PK effect as the case may be.
Schmidt has in fact provided some evidence for (3) from a
PK experiment using pre-recorded digits.

    What still remains problematic in these models is how
far one must assume a retroactive influence stemming from
later psi-sources. This is what Schmidt himself calls the
"divergence problem." In other words, on these new models,
when does an experiment end? If the experimenter can retroactively influence the subject's response or if the principal
experimenter can retroactively influence the findings of the
sub-experimenters, does the reader who studies the principal
experimenter's report likewise have an influence on its content? Only further research can determine how rapidly these
subsequent retroactive influences tail off and become negligible and how far we can regard the later vicissitudes of the
data as no longer relevant. The experiment described below
is predicated on the assumption that, if the sub-experimenter
is the first to inspect the cumulative data, he will exercise
a decisive influence upon the way they have turned out so
that if he happens to be a psi-positive experimenter his positive influence will not be nullified by the principal experimenter or anyone else who subsequently inspects these results. Considerable, though largely informal, evidence does
in fact suggest that the experimenter powerfully affects the
outcome of his experiment even when he has no sensory contact with the subjects.

    The basic technique used in this experiment is one in-
volving pre-recorded PK trials which was successfully pioneered by Schmidt. In this procedure the outcomes of a
random number generator (RNG) are recorded without human
observation and the record subsequently used to activate a
feedback device in the same way as for a contemporaneous
PK task. In our experiment the trials were recorded on
cassette tapes which were distributed by post. For the first
time this technique allowed us to conduct a large-scale study
in which many investigators, using a broadly-based subject

population, had access to a single system with which psi effects could be monitored.

Method

As understood by the subject, the task consisted of trying to increase by PK the frequency of "bleeps" (high-pitched tones) as heard through an earpiece in an otherwise random sequence of high and low tones which was supposedly being generated then and there by an RNG. This illusion was sustained by having the earpiece visibly connected to a dummy box labelled "Edinburgh Parapsychology Laboratory Portable PK Unit." Actually, the sequence which the subject heard was pre-recorded onto a tape-cassette at Edinburgh using a computerized RNG with a tone generator which performed the task automatically (i.e., with no exposure of any trials to the Edinburgh personnel). Thus so far as the subject was concerned, the task was one of contemporaneous PK although, in reality, any PK effect he would be able to exert would, in the nature of the case, have to be retroactive in its operation (we were here assuming that no gross PK effect would occur which would alter the tape once the recording had been made).

Two categories of participants were involved besides the four principal experimenters who are the authors of this paper. These are the sub-experimenters (SEs) and the subjects (Ss). The SEs were drawn from among those known to be active in parapsychology who had access to a cassette tape recorder and to subjects who had expressed willingness to collaborate in this experiment. There were 16 SEs in all and each SE was responsible for finding 16 willing Ss. Each SE was issued with a complete experimental kit together with a full set of instructions as to its use. No stipulation was made as to what kind of person should act as subject but Ss, unlike SEs, were kept in the dark as to the non-contemporaneous nature of the experiment, at any rate during the course of their experimental session. The SEs, on the contrary, understood this but were allowed to conceive of their own role in the experiment as essentially that of collaborators rather than, as we conceived of it, as affording evidence for the psi experimenter effect.

After an SE received his experimental kit but before he introduced his first subject, he was instructed to try a demonstration run on himself as recorded on the cassette in his kit. The object of this was to acquaint him with the

task which his Ss would have to do. The S was briefed by
the SE who explained the task to him, presenting it as a
straightforward PK task.   The S was provided with the earpiece and the dummy box to which it was attached.   The cassette machine remained in the SE's room where, when ready,
he pressed the playback button (having positioned the tape
prior to S's arrival).   At the end of five and a half minutes
the session was over and SE switched off the machine.   A
monitoring earpiece was provided for SE to check when the
end had come if he was uncertain about his timing.   This
was designed to serve a second function in that it made available to the SE, at least in the background, the trial-by-trial
feedback to which S is attending.   In addition to making the
experiment more closely approximate a "typical" experiment,
the procedure increased SE's feedback exposure.   The S com-
menced with a practice run of 25 trials so as to get the
"feel" of the thing but the formal, or scored, trials consisted of the 30 short runs of 25 trials with pauses between
each, giving 750 trials in all.   A run lasted five seconds;
the reason for cutting up the session in this way is that there
is evidence from Schmidt and others that PK tends to undergo a rapid decline so that the best means of tapping it is in
such short bursts.   When S had completed his session, the
SE opened the appropriate score envelope (one for each session was included in the kit) and transcribed the results onto
his master record (again simulating the likely procedure in
a "typical" experiment).   He then went to S's room, inquired
how well he thought he had done and proceeded to give him
his results (including his score, CR, and associated probability), explaining what they mean.   The score represented
the total number of bleeps or high-pitched tones which he had
heard in the course of the session.   Since there was an equal
probability of a high or low tone, the score he could expect
on the basis of chance alone in 750 trials is 375 (=MCE).
Finally, before sending him on his way, SE debriefed S by
revealing to him that the task was not contemporaneous.

When SE had completed running all 16 Ss, he then
opened an envelope containing a summary of the results and
a t-test evaluation of the entire experiment.

It should be noted that failure to comply with any part
of the instructions, e.g. opening the envelope containing the
scores before instead of after the sessions, could not falsify
the results; at worst they could negate any potential effects
that may have been present.   The design of the experiment
precluded absolutely any fraud, conscious or unconscious, on

the part of either the Ss or the SEs although not, of course,
on the part of any of the principal experimenters.

The tape generating system consisted of a computerized noise-driven RNG controlling an audio-oscillator and
cassette recorder. For S the target was always the high
tone but to avoid any possibility of bias the program established a "target" for each run of 25 by sampling the RNG
and assigning target status to the outcome (0 or 1) opposite
to that just obtained (e.g., if the program samples the RNG
for the target and gets a 1 then 0 becomes the target and
all 0's in the following run produce bleeps). Apart from
starting the program and cassette recorder no operator was
present.

The experimenter's kit sent to each SE consisted of
(1) a cassette-tape on which have been recorded the trials
for each of the 16 Ss plus the initial demonstration run;
note that no two cassette-tapes contain the same information,
i.e. each run is unique; (2) dummy RNG with earpieces and
long lead (to cassette machine); (3) SE's operating instructions
and an instruction sheet to be given to S; (4) 18 sealed envelopes containing print-out scores never previously seen by
any person (these were made up as follows: one containing
SE's score on the demonstration run; sixteen containing subject scores, one for each; and one containing the overall results of the experiment as evaluated by a single-mean t-test);
and (5) a paid return mailer, provided for the return of
everything except for the print-outs and any records, all
necessary data for analysis having been retained on magnetic
computer tape at Edinburgh.

Method of Analysis

Basic to the analysis is our "predictor/confirmation"
design used in previous work. The rationale is the same
as underlies the standard pilot/confirmation procedure, in
which examination of data from a pilot study suggests a hypothesis to be tested formally in a confirmation experiment.
The only difference in our design is that the data comprising
predictor (pilot) and confirmation are collected in a single
combined experiment. This largely eliminates any real difference between pilot and confirmation due to change in experimental conditions.

It is customary when using the pilot/confirmation
method to set out statistical tests to be done prior to per-

forming the confirmation study. In the present experiment
the confirmation data are already in existence when the statistical tests are framed. However, because of the automated nature of the set-up, the experimenters can have no
knowledge of the confirmation results at this time, thus no
post-hoc "statistical scrounging" is possible here. Since
the pilot data can be used only for making predictions and
are otherwise discarded, this method is less efficient than if
appropriate tests could be canvassed at the outset. However,
the flexibility, combined with rigor, of this "statistical
sharpening" procedure are particularly valuable when only
the general nature of the expected effect is known, while the
details cannot be deduced on a priori grounds.

In this experiment each S completes 750 trials; each
SE thus contributes 16 x 750 = 12,000 trials. At the time
of target generation, the trials were split by the computer
on an ABB ABB ... basis and the total number of hits for
each of the 250 pilot (A) trials and the 500 confirmation (B)
trials for each S were automatically recorded on computer
magnetic tape for later analysis. The one-third/two-thirds
split represents a compromise between securing a representative prediction while retaining the maximum of data for the
formal confirmation analysis.

The question at issue in this experiment is whether
there are differences between the data collected by the various SEs. The literature suggests that differences between
experimenters may manifest as positive or negative scoring,
variance effects, declines etc. With so many possibilities,
it is impossible to decide in advance how to analyze the data.
As a first step the pilot data only will be printed out by the
computer. On the basis of these one or more specific statistical tests will be formulated. In addition the overall
scoring rate and associated probability will be calculated for
the experiment as a whole.

Results

In the one-third predictor instalment, none of the 16
sub-experimenters was found to have departed significantly
from chance expectation. Two sub-experimenters, however,
produced scoring rates, which, if sustained in the confirmation instalment would attain significance, of 51.23 and 51.40
per cent. The chronological trend of the data for each of
the sub-experimenters was examined in terms of the difference between the totals of the first and last eight subjects.

The largest differences occurred in the data from the same
two sub-experimenters already mentioned. Both represented
an incline, which was statistically significant when the two
sets of data were pooled. The variances for subject scores
did not depart from chance for either of these sub-experimenters, although two others yielded notably small variances.
Of the 256 subjects only nine produced individually significant
departures from chance expectation in the predictor instalment, which is insignificantly less than would be expected by
chance. In the event only two hypotheses could be formulated
on the basis of the predictor data: (1) that two particular
sub-experimenters would show a significant above-chance
deviation at the 2.5 per cent level using a one-tail test, and
(2) that these same two experimenters would show a significant increase in score as between their first eight and second eight subjects using the differential CR again at the 2.5
per cent level of significance. At this stage it was hoped
that the experiment had been successful in "capturing" two
psi-positive experimenters whose results would not be nullified by the principal experimenters.

Neither of the hypotheses were confirmed by the confirmation data. Both sub-experimenters had CR's of around
zero and in neither case was there a significant incline effect.

Conclusion

In spite of the fact that 16 keen parapsychologists
were involved here as sub-experimenters, some of whom
claim to have obtained positive psi-effects in their published
reports, not one of them here managed to elicit psi in his
sub-experiment. Furthermore, a population of 256 subjects,
contributing a total of 192,000 PK trials failed to show any
evidence of psi in their distribution of scores. The discrepancy between these results and those of other workers
is massive and cries out for explanation. If the ability to
conduct a successful psi experiment is a matter of a "knack"
for coaxing psi from subjects, as it has often been portrayed,
why did none of the 16 parapsychologists involved in this study
manage to demonstrate it here? That the task was not impossible seems to be indicated by the fact that a number of
previous experiments have used retroactive PK successfully.

The first thought is that maybe the sub-experimenters
were not sufficiently motivated to produce psi, perhaps because the experiment was not their "own baby" or possibly

they did not feel comfortable with the rather indigestible idea
of retroactive PK.   This possibility is being followed up.

It is conceivable, too, that our manipulations were
successful in eliminating psi on the part of the experimenters
and that these data reflect the real rarity of psi ability in
the general population in the absence of experimenter psi.
The most plausible alternative we feel, however, is that our
design did not eliminate the nullifying psi contributions of the
principal investigators.   The consistently null results of
some of the members of the Edinburgh team are well known
and the obvious implication is that the best intentions of the
experimental design failed to avoid incurring the Edinburgh
fingerprint (or is it footprint?) on the data.

With or without the contemporary models of psi,
which naturally are yet to be validated, it appears that there
is a large and growing body of evidence indicating that little
progress can be made until parapsychologists can find a
more satisfactory means of locating the source of psi influences than the arbitrary division between experimenter and
subject which has been used up to now.

A PRECOGNITION TEST USING GUIDED IMAGERY

Judith Kesner and Robert L. Morris† (University of Cali-
    fornia, Santa Barbara)

The question whether or not true precognition exists
has been puzzling for many centuries.   Both laboratory and
spontaneous case studies have shown the phenomenon to exist,
but never totally without the possibility of deliberate fraud
or, unintentionally, using normal means of prediction or an
alternative form of psychic functioning.   Such alternatives
depend on the mode of target randomization employed after
the subject's guesses have been recorded.   If the randomizing process involves future physical events, such as those
produced by a random number generator, then subject or experimenter PK becomes a possible alternative to precognition.
If the randomizing process involves future mental events,
such as reaching into a hat and picking a number, then clairvoyance on the part of those performing the mental event becomes a possible alternative.   The present experiment attempted to bypass the problem by specifically picking an

event determined by the choices of many unconcerned people:
a column of numbers representing hundreds of shares sold
in the New York Stock Exchange. By having subjects attempt to receive an impression of the future that is determined by a particular number in the stock market, which
acts as a random number generator in that there is no systematic influence on the particular numerals, the procedure
should avoid any conflict in causality.

A state of relaxed alertness has been shown to be
conducive to a free response psychic experience in general.
The present experiment used a progressive relaxation technique followed by a guided imagery fantasy trip into the future in the attempt to induce a precognitive experience in
subjects. They were asked to try to imagine both a particular piece of music from an album and its accompanying record jacket, to which stimuli they would be exposed the following week. Both the auditory and visual modes were
utilized in an effort to increase the chances of success by
appealing to those good at auditory imaging and those good
at visual imaging.

Method

The subjects were 20 males and two females between
the ages of 18 and 30, all volunteers. The design originally
called for 20 subjects; two extra were run to allow for the
possibility of no-shows for the second session.

The apparatus consisted of a cassette tape deck and
tape with a progressive relaxation and guided imagery talk
on one side; ten selections from a variety of different albums
were recorded on the reverse side. Also used were stereo
headphones, 22 construction paper signs with individual names
of subjects written in magic marker, Stock Exchange results,
and a preliminary questionnaire dealing with subjects' attitudes towards precognition tests and their imagery ability.

The signs with subjects' names were posted individually on the wall of the subject's room prior to each subject's
arrival at the research rooms at UCSB. Subjects were
verbally given the questionnaire consisting of 11 questions,
whose responses the experimenter then recorded. They were
then instructed to lie down on a comfortable bed and listen
through headphones to the prepared tape that went as follows:

"Lie down on your back with your legs uncrossed, arms

at your side; let yourself get very comfortable. During the process of my talking you will become relaxed
and receptive to any images in your mind. Tense or
stretch any part of your body that needs it, and then
settle back and relax. Take several deep breaths in
and out. With each breath you will become more and
more relaxed. Imagine all the thoughts and cares in
your mind as tiny grains of sand ... now some warm
and soothing water washes the grains of sand down
your body and far away. Breathe deep and relax, let
your mind clear; you are very relaxed and comfortable.
Your eyes feel round and soft; feel them inside your
head. Your ears relax and sounds soften. Your
breathing has a relaxed rhythm, in ... and out. Now
imagine your head rocking back and forth. As you in-
hale, imagine your head tilting forward so that your
chin moves closer to your chest. As you exhale your
head rocks back, relaxed. Feel the rocking motion
with your breathing, and relax.... Now imagine your
body as a suit of clothes, laid flat on the bed. You
have no thickness, but are very flat. The wrinkles in
the clothes flatten themselves out to the edges; feel the
wrinkles moving toward the edges and disappearing.
You are relaxed, breathing rhythmically in and out.
This state of consciousness you are in allows energy
to flow freely into your mind. It is a quiet and relaxed flow of energy which you now feel moving to your
mind. Now imagine yourself beginning to drift ahead
in time. Your skin tingles a little and your body feels
light. You're moving slowly ahead in time to tonight,
lying in bed just about to fall asleep. Now feel yourself drifting forward to tomorrow when you wake up.
Now go in time through the day until it's nighttime and
you are in bed, about to fall asleep. Breathe deep....
Now it is morning and you're drifting in time through
the day ... and into the next day. Follow the days,
one by one ... until the time when you are to come
back into this room. You walk in and lie down just as
you are now. You will see the sign with your name
on it, just as it is now. Everything is exactly the
same as it is now. You will hear my voice and the
waves. The music is entering your head through both
ears now and you listen very carefully and fully; your
attention is focused on the music in your head. Hear
the music. When the music ends I will show you the
record jacket, which you will look at and see everything on the jacket. The record jacket will form an

image in your mind.   The image will be very clear to
you and you will remember the music you are hearing.
Just relax, listen to the music, enjoy it, look at the
record jacket.   It's very pleasant, very attractive,
very pleasing to you. [Five minutes of silence.]
Okay, good.   Now take three deep breaths, very slowly,
feel the energy moving to all parts of your body, feel
free to move your body, stretch, and slowly open your
eyes, remembering the music and the record jacket.
You're all done."

Synthesized ocean waves were played in the background, including the five-minute imagery period.   After the tape's
completion, subjects verbally related any visual or auditory
images that came to mind and the experimenter wrote down
their responses and asked them to sketch any images they
received.   Subjects then set a date to return the following
week and listen to one of ten recorded music selections (they
were unaware of the particular pieces in the target pool).
Which of the selections was heard was determined by that
later date's New York Stock Exchange results in the "Sales
per Hundreds" column.   Only those numbers with three digits
were used; the farthest right digit (0, 1 ... 9) indicating
the order number of the ten pieces of music.   A large
sample of the digits thus generated has been found by us to
be quite random, on the basis of a chi-square analysis.
Each subject was assigned their own stock number, which
was determined by the order in which they had previously
arranged to appear on that date.   On subjects' return a
week later, they were instructed to lie down on the bed
again and listen to their designated piece of music through
headphones.   During the listening session they were shown
the record jacket of their piece for inspection.

Subjects' descriptions were examined by a blind judge
who assessed to what extent, on a scale of 1 to 100, the
descriptions approximated each of the ten record selections.
The judge individually rated subjects' visual and auditory
imagery descriptions.   Next these scores were ranked from
one to ten, one being the highest score, so that each subject's actual target received three rating scores: visual,
auditory, and total (combined ratings).   A score of 1 was
counted as a direct hit and scores between 1 and 5 were
seen as suggestive of precognition.

Results

Using the binomial expansion, two-tailed p values were

derived of the outcomes.   Twenty people gave visual imagery
reports.   Of these, two scored direct hits (p = n.s.) and
13 had the correct target ranked in the top five (p = n.s.).
All 22 people gave auditory imagery reports.   Of these,
three scored direct hits (p = n.s.) and 13 had the correct
target ranked in the top five (p = n.s.).   For combined
rankings, four scored direct hits (p = n.s.) and 17 had the
correct target ranked in the top five (p < .02).

None of the questionnaire data was significantly related to the precognition scores.   Of some interest is that
of 16 people who stated their imagery was better in one
modality than another, 11 scored better in their preferred
modality.

Discussion

The significant p value for the combined visual and
auditory ratings suggests that this procedure warrants further
attention.   One other plausible explanation (besides chance)
might be that of blind judge's ESP.   The present experiment
failed to employ multiple judging to reduce the likelihood of
this factor.   This method is suggested for future replication.
Although insignificant, p values for the separate visual and
auditory ratings tended toward positive outcomes.   Perhaps
by employing the more gifted subjects (those whose responses ranked highest), and by emphasizing imagery in
modes preferred by the subjects, the present procedure
could be made to work more effectively.

EXTRASENSORY EFFECTS UPON ASSOCIATIVE PROCESSES
IN A DIRECTED FREE-RESPONSE TASK:
AN ATTEMPTED REPLICATION AND EXTENSION

Rex G. Stanford† and Winona Schroeter (Center for Para-
    psychological Research)

Stanford tested several hypotheses in the context of
a word-association ESP task.   In a major part of his study,
subjects free-associated to a word list.   They knew that a
response had been randomly chosen as a target which it was
hoped they would give, but they were asked to approach the
ESP task just as they would a normal word-association test
with the intention simply of "doing well" but without concern
about trying to give a "correct response."

The results of the 1973 study confirmed deductions from three hypotheses: (1) Extrasensory response as activation of memory traces. This hypothesis assumes that the expression of ESP consists of psi activation of memory traces--i.e., mediation into consciousness of (ESP) target-relevant information stored in an individual's memory--and that frequently-reinforced memories, or engrams, should easily become the vehicles of ESP (i.e., the associative-mediation hypothesis). (2) Response bias. In an ESP task, all else being equal, responses favored by a non-ESP bias tend to be less accurate than responses not favored by such a bias--to the degree that such a bias exists. This is conceived to occur because of the increased false-alarm rate which can be expected when responding in a way that is favored by a bias (i.e., the response-bias hypothesis). (3) Inhibition. Impulsivity (as contrasted with inhibition) facilitates extrasensory response. This dimension is conceived as measurable in terms of individual differences (i.e., the inhibition hypothesis).

The present study was intended to replicate and extend the other study and to examine some additional hypotheses. These additional hypotheses were (4) Defensiveness. Defensiveness as a characteristic of individuals works contrary to the production of positive (above-chance) ESP results since it would seem to militate in favor of constraints on the kind of spontaneity often believed to be associated with success. In other words, persons relatively free of defensiveness should more readily give expression to the impulses which mediate extrasensory responses. Considerable earlier personality-ESP work using several operational definitions of defensiveness supports this hypothesis in its general form (i.e., the defensiveness hypothesis). (5) Suggestibility. Stanford reported that high-suggestible as contrasted with low-suggestible subjects did better at a symbol-calling ESP task. Honorton had reported a similar result, though his outcome fell slightly short of statistical significance. This evidence suggests a weak, positive relationship between suggestibility and ESP performance on forced-choice tasks. We expected a positive relationship between suggestibility and ESP performance, for we expected the earlier forced-choice ESP results to generalize to the free-association ESP tasks (i.e., the suggestibility hypothesis).

Subjects

Subjects were unpaid volunteers of both sexes who

ranged in age from 14 to the 60's, though the vast majority
were of roughly college age. Most were, however, not college students but had at one time attended college. They
were recruited by word-of-mouth and by an ad placed in the
student newspaper at the University of Texas at Austin. The
majority were members of the Association for the Understanding of Man, the organization which funds the Center for
Parapsychological Research, and many of those had attended
or were attending a 16-week course, taught by R. G. S. on
parapsychology.

The Instruments of Testing

The Word-Association ESP Task: This consisted of
20 words administered at 15-second intervals via tape recording. The voice on the tape recording was that of W. S.,
who also acted as telepathic agent in the manner described
below. (See Procedure.) Subjects were to free-associate to
each word, giving a single-word response. Six seconds
after each stimulus there was a "beep" sound on the tape
which acted as a signal to the subject to relax and await the
next stimulus and to end all concern with the previous stimulus or the response to it, regardless of whether a response
had been made prior to the "beep." The six-second interval
had been carefully chosen, however, such that persons rarely
failed to respond within the limit. This task was preceded
by tape-recorded, detailed instructions also in the voice of
W. S. The stimuli on the tape had been carefully chosen on
the basis of word-association norms, primarily those of
Palermo and Jenkins, such that each stimulus word could be
expected to have a reasonably high-commonality primary response and a moderately low-commonality, but definite, secondary response. The norms used were rather old, so careful consideration was given to eliminating any words for
which one could easily infer a possible change in norms over
the years. The target domain for a given word consisted of
the primary and secondary responses to that word as given
in the Palermo-Jenkins (or other book) norms. An assistant
(Birgit Stanford) used the RAND table of random digits to
select and list, for each stimulus, for each subject, either
the primary or secondary book-norms response as the target on an equal (p = 1/2) probability basis. The test was
not scorable whenever subjects made a response which was
neither a book-norm primary or secondary response. The
ESP targets prepared by the assistant were enclosed in
aluminum foil and were sealed in an envelope which was not
opened until W. S. began her role as telepathic agent in a
separate room from the subject.

Three ESP scores were derived from this test. (1)
An overall ESP score was derived, consisting of the proportion of responses in the target domain which were correct,
to be used in assessing the inhibition, defensiveness, and
suggestibility hypotheses. (2) The proportion of hits whenever subjects produced book-norm primary responses on
stimuli which in our data yielded a minimum of 25 per cent
commonality for the book-norm primary (as per the criterion
of the previous study which this was replicating), was to be
used in assessing both the response-bias hypothesis and the
associative-mediation hypothesis; responses to 18 of the 20
words were scorable in this regard. Henceforth, this type
of score is termed primary-response success. Unfortunately,
it was not possible in the present study to derive a comparable measure for secondary responses (secondary-response
success) because the frequency of appropriate secondary responses was so low that such a measure would not have been
meaningful. An appropriate secondary response is a book-
norm secondary of less than 25 per cent commonality (in
these data) made to a stimulus with a clear (25 per cent-
plus in our data) book-norm primary. (Nineteen subjects
produced no such secondaries; 42 produced only one; ten,
only two; and one, only three.) (3) A measure of sensitivity
to primary targets was derived consisting of the difference
of the proportions of time a subject made a scorable primary
response when a primary was actually the target and when it
was not the target. This analysis, unlike the others, considers the target circumstances in which subjects made non-
scorable responses--i.e., responses falling outside the target domain. (This score had not been derived in the earlier
study but since it seemed highly appropriate in relation to
the associative-mediation hypothesis, scores of this kind
were derived on the data of the earlier study prior to gathering any data for the present study.) Although this type of
score (sensitivity) could be derived for the data of the earlier
study for both primary and secondary targets, this was not
feasible in the current study, except in the case of primary
targets, because of the extremely small frequency of scorable secondary responses produced by our subjects.

The Chair Test: Whereas in the earlier study all
subjects during word association were required to recline
completely in the padded recliner chair provided, this was
not the case in the present study. We decided, first of all,
that positive scoring might be favored, or at least score
variability decreased, if we allowed subjects to choose whether they wished their chair back to be in the upright, middle,

or fully-reclining position. After two subjects had been
tested it occurred to us that since all chair positions were
being demonstrated for each subject in advance of their using
it for word association, and since they were being encouraged
to try all positions and assume the most comfortable one,
the position chosen for the test might be an indicator of sali-
ent individual differences. In particular, it was felt that
persons relatively free of strong, maladaptive defenses might
readily assume the positions farther back, and especially the
far-back one. That position was very far back--farther than
in the usual recliner chair--and the person would have to lie
there in a passive, ventral-side exposed position to take the
test. We felt this would be more inviting or less threatening to persons sufficiently free of defenses that they were
willing to become greatly relaxed and very passive in the
test situation. Evidence possibly relevant to our interpretation of chair position was obtained by Nakamura and Wright.
They found that neurotic over-controlled subjects produced
more uncommon responses when they had to lie down to free-
associate than when they had to sit up for word association.
This did not hold for neurotic under-controlled subjects. For
over-controlled subjects the lying position may have been
stressful or threatening. Some studies suggest that persons
give fewer primaries and generally decrease response commonality when they are under psychological stress. If this
reasoning is correct, highly defensive persons or over-con-
trollers may be able to anticipate that association in a declining position will be more stressful or threatening and
may tend to avoid it.

We therefore attempted to note for all subsequent persons whether the chair was fully back when we reentered the
room at the end of the word-association task. If it was not,
they were unobtrusively asked which position in the chair
they had assumed for the largest part of the task. We neglected to ask two persons about chair position. One subject
could not be scored in this regard because she preferred to
sit in the lotus posture, a yogic meditation pose. This gave
us 67 persons scored in this regard. Forty of those chose
the fully-reclining position; 25, the middle position; and two,
the upright position. We therefore collapsed the two latter
categories and examined performance for and the difference
between performance of persons who reclined fully and those
who did not.

The Physical World Attitudes Questionnaire: This test
was administered during our experimental session, but scores

derived from it will not be discussed here because no analyses of its data in relation to ESP performance were planned or done. It was given to examine specific correlations with suggestibility and consisted of 17 items concerning ways of experiencing the physical world with which subjects expressed their amount of agreement or disagreement.

Suggestibility: The test of suggestibility was a modification of the Barber Suggestibility Scale (BSS). Like the original scale, it contained eight items, many of them taken directly from the BSS, in the following order: arm lowering, arm levitation; arm catalepsy; hands moving together; itch hallucination (right cheek); body immobility; post-hypnotic-like response (for coughing on cue); and selective suggested amnesia (for the arm levitation test). The test was administered under instructions which stated that it was a measure of responsiveness to suggestions and would serve as an indicator of how readily one would respond if one were subjected to an actual hypnotic induction procedure. The test was scored behaviorally in a manner precisely analogous to the BSS. Additionally, two phenomenological scores were developed. One consisted of counting the test items for which the subject afterward reported feeling a real effect of the suggestion, regardless of whether or not he/she had responded behaviorally to that test item, i.e., regardless of whether that item had been scored 0, .5, or 1. (This score is henceforth termed noncontingent subjective score.) The other measure consisted of counting the items on which the subject had a behavioral score (.5 or 1) other than zero and on which he/she had reported feeling an effect (termed, henceforth, contingent subjective score). The contingent subjective score was used to try and extend to the present, different, ESP task an earlier finding on ESP and this measure of suggestibility. The two other scores were used to explore any possible relationship of suggestibility and ESP performance.

Procedure

Each subject was first greeted by W.S. and was shown around the laboratory and was offered something to drink (coffee or tea). This tour included the experimental room where most of the subject's time would be spent. The subject was told, "This will be your own room." The subject was then introduced to R.G.S. who spent 20 to 45 minutes briefing him or her regarding what would be experienced and why it was being done this way. The time variation de-

pended upon how much subjects already knew about psi research and on their curiosity and the number of questions
asked.   R. G. S. attempted to insure that all subjects came
to a common understanding of the study.   At the end of the
briefing each was asked to read and sign a consent and release form.

The briefing began with questions from R. G. S. about
participants' past experiences vis-à-vis psi--whether they had
had anything which might be a psi experience or had tried
any ESP or psi tasks previously.   This was to gain information which might aid in orienting them toward the experiment
and to make them feel more like a participant than like a
subject.

They were told that word-association was being used
because it seemed to be a good circumstance for the occurrence of psi, one which invites relaxation and spontaneity
rather than self-conscious effortfulness or logical approaches.
They were told the stimulus words were very familiar, common words which would be easy to respond to and were
chosen only to study ESP, not to try to probe their depth
psychology.   Exactly how a word-association task can be an
ESP task was explained.   They were urged to approach the
task as they would regular free association, not by trying to
"guess a correct answer."   They were told that their intention to do well would be all that was needed to activate psi.
Psi, working unconsciously, would then tend to select the
correct response from the several competing available responses and would increase its probability.   They were told
that the target domain consisted of "fairly common" responses (based on norms) to each of the words, but they
were not told how many such responses were involved in the
target domain for the words.

They were told that their own ESP (clairvoyance)
could allow them to favor the correct response in this setting,
but that we were providing an additional source of possible
ESP information by means of their telepathic agent, who
would be W. S.   She would, they were told,[4] use a special
method to try to make her role as agent more effective.
The special method was that of looking over all the correct
responses just before the subject began the word-association
task, then letting go of all thoughts of this information when
she returned to her normal duties while they were actually
word-associating.   It was explained that this method might
have special advantages.   The method would be explained

further on the introductory lead-in on the tape which would be heard just prior to the word-association.

Prior to beginning the word-association ESP task, it was also explained to subjects that no data would be evaluated during the course of the experiment, but that when all 72 persons had been tested, the ESP task would be evaluated. When that was done, they would receive a letter, at a time which was specified approximately, telling them of their own performance and the general results of the study.

Subjects 1-37 in this study then were given a brief description of the physical world attitudes questionnaire. They were then briefed on the suggestibility test. They were told that this test would help to understand the finding that hypnosis can boost ESP performance, that the test would help us to learn whether or not some of that effect is due merely to the fact of a person being hypnotizable. We could learn whether suggestibility or hypnotizability is related to ESP performance. They were also told that hypnotizability or suggestibility is not related to such factors as gullibility, weak-mindedness, mental illness, or even, in any intrinsic way, to intelligence. The appropriate approach to the suggestibility task, they were told, was just to listen to the suggestions, try to enjoy the procedure and to watch what would happen. We, they were told, had no concern about how "well" they did, and they were discouraged from deliberately "going along" with a suggestion in order to "look good." If they did respond, that was fine; if they did not, also fine. They then went into the experimental room, listened to the detailed instruction for the word-association ESP task and did the word association. Subjects sat alone in the experimental room to hear the instructions on tape and the stimulus words. W. S. retired to a remote experimental room, closed the door, looked over the target list and then put it down. She went about her other activities while the subjects did word association.

Subjects 38-72 were briefed only regarding the initial phase of the study, the word-association ESP task, before retiring to the experimental room for that task. R. G. S. briefed them about each of the other tasks, the physical world attitudes questionnaire and the suggestibility test, immediately before they were to begin each. The change in procedure with these latter subjects was occasioned by concern that complete briefing prior to the ESP task might be so long that subjects would become bored. Also, they might feel less

like they were being manipulated if the briefing were given
for each task just before it began--a more natural-appearing
arrangement. (An analysis at the end of the study showed
that this change in procedure produced no difference in ESP
scoring, and all the data from the study could therefore be
pooled, as had been hoped from the start.)

     Subjects filled out the physical world attitudes ques-
tionnaire sitting alone in their experimental room. After
they came out with the questionnaire at the end, W. S. returned with them to their experimental room. The suggestibility scale was administered by tape recording and W. S.
scored subjects' responses. The queries regarding what
was actually experienced, the basis of phenomenological
scores, were also on tape. R. G. S.'s voice appeared on the
tape giving the suggestions and making the post-test queries.
Just before subjects left they were reminded that they would
receive a letter about the experiment's results and their own
ESP score. Finally, they were thanked for participating.

Results

     Associative-Mediation Hypothesis: Because of the
paucity of scorable secondary responses, there was no meaningful way of comparing primary- and secondary-response
success. We were able to evaluate this hypothesis in terms
of an attempt to see whether the earlier finding of significant,
positive primary-response success was confirmed in the present study. The mean primary-response success across subjects was .52, where chance expectation is .50 ($t = +.92$;
$df = 71$; n. s.). Performance, although quite positive, failed
to reach statistical significance. There were far too few
secondary responses, and especially too few per subject
(mode = 1 per subject), to compute comparable figures and
do a statistical (inferential) analysis upon them. It may be
of interest, however, to note that the pooled 53 scorable
secondary-response trials had a success rate of .434; on an
average subject basis (for those who had scorable primaries)
the analogous figure was .463.

     As was mentioned earlier, a measure of sensitivity
to primary targets, although it was not originally done (prior
to publication) on the data of the previous study, is a very
appropriate--perhaps even a more appropriate--measure for
assessing the associative-mediation hypothesis. This is because that hypothesis has the clear implication that one should
be more psychically sensitive relative to targets which are

related to well-established associations. Further, this test
of the hypothesis is, as can be seen from reviewing the nature of this measure given above, less subject to effects due
to response biases (e.g., a tendency to give relatively few
or many primary responses), unlike the measure (reported
above) of primary-response success. Prior to beginning the
current study we evaluated the sensitivity to primary targets
in the earlier work, and it was strongly positive but fell a
bit short of statistical significance. The mean sensitivity to
primary targets in the earlier study was $+.0343$ ($t = +1.62$;
$df = 59$; $p = .11$, two-tailed). In the earlier study sensi-
tivity to secondary targets was significantly negative ($\bar{x} = -.0238$; $t = -2.05$; $df = 59$; $p < .05$, two-tailed). In the
present study, mean sensitivity to primary targets was
$+.0349$ ($t = +1.27$; $df = 71$; $p \cong .10$, one-tailed). This
means that in both studies subjects on the average produced
a primary response approximately 3.4 per cent more often
when a primary response was the target than when it was
not; the effect, however, fell short of significance in both
studies. In the present study we could not evaluate the sensitivity to secondary targets because of the small number of
scorable secondary responses.

Response-Bias Hypothesis: The current study provided two opportunities to test this hypothesis, both attempted
replications of findings from the earlier study. One such
opportunity is in examining the product-moment correlation
between the number of primary responses produced and the
primary response success across subjects. In the previous
study this had produced a correlation of $r = -.294$ ($df = 58$;
$p < .025$, two-tailed). In the current study the same statistical evaluation yields $r = +.213$ ($df = 70$; $p \cong .07$, two-
tailed). Another analysis from the previous study which is
related to this hypothesis was product-moment correlation
between mean $\log_{10} RT$ and accuracy of primary responses
across subjects ($r = +.400$; $df = 58$; $p < .01$, two-tailed).
The rationale for this analysis is that mean log RT (mean
log reaction time) is to a large extent a measure not merely
of how often persons sample off the top of the response hierarchy but, also, of how strongly they tend to do so. It
should very well express a person's bias toward sampling
off the top of the response hierarchy and thus should relate
positively to the level of primary response success. (Note
that a small mean log RT represents a fast average reaction time and thus a tendency to sample from the top of the
hierarchy; such persons should produce a smaller proportion
of primary response success because of the relatively high

false alarm rate.) In the present study the comparable correlation is not significant (r = +.054; df = 70; n.s.).

Inhibition Hypothesis: In the previous study this hypothesis was assessed with subjects tested under either a
six- or an eight-second word-association time limit and by
a product-moment correlation between their overall ESP
scores and mean log RT's. The expectation was for a negative correlation since earlier studies had shown that person-
ality-test measures of inhibition related negatively to ESP
performance and that inhibition related negatively to average
response speed of subjects not tested under time pressure;
uninhibited subjects tend to respond rapidly. In the earlier
study the correlation between overall ESP score and mean
log RT was in the expected direction and was significant
(r = -.368; df = 38; p < .015, one-tailed). In the current
study the same correlation is of opposite sign (r = +.106;
df = 70; n.s.).

Defensiveness Hypothesis: According to our performance measure of "defensiveness," the 40 persons who
placed the chair in the far-back position were the least defensive. They were expected to do well on the test. Their
mean overall ESP score was .545 where .500 is chance expectation (t = +2.10; df = 39; p = .04, two-tailed). Also
according to our interpretation, the 27 persons who placed
the chair in the middle or upright positions were more defensive and were expected to do less well. Their mean
overall ESP score was .498 (nonsignificant). The difference
of performance of these two groups, although substantial and
in the anticipated direction, failed to reach significance (t =
+1.30; df = 65; p = .20, two-tailed. This hypothesis was
not tested in the previous study; all persons in that study
were required to have the recliner in the far-back position.

Suggestibility Hypothesis: The results of the current
study failed to support this hypothesis of a positive correlation between suggestibility and ESP performance. Since a
study by Stanford successfully used the contingent subjective
score of a suggestibility scale as the predictor of ESP performance (in a quite different setting), we sought to replicate
the general outcome by correlating that score with overall
ESP performance. The result failed to support the hypothesis (r = -.012; df = 70; n.s.). To further explore any possible relationship of suggestibility and ESP performance, the
behavioral and the noncontingent subjective scores were also
correlated with ESP performance. They yielded correlations
of +.02 and -.03, respectively, both insignificant.

Discussion

Associative-Mediation Hypothesis: The results of the
current study, although they are disappointing in not reaching statistical significance, should not, in our opinion, be
regarded as discouraging about this hypothesis. In the first
place, the results involving sensitivity to primary targets
are fairly strong in both studies, albeit not quite significant
and are essentially identical in magnitude. It should be
borne in mind that in this study--and in the former, too, to
a lesser degree--the actual number of primary-target ESP
trials per subject is very small. This results in greater
error of measurement. What the current and earlier results
suggest is the need for further testing of this hypothesis--
especially using a measure of sensitivity to high-association
targets--when there are more trials per subject. In the second place, the associative mediation hypothesis has earlier
received support from another study by Stanford involving different methodology and from another, also with different
methodology, by Kanthamani and Rao. None of these studies,
except the current one and the reanalysis reported here of
Stanford's earlier data, has reported analyses which directly
measure sensitivity to targets of a given association value.
This general approach should constitute a major effort in future work on this hypothesis, for it is the most direct, con-
ceptually straightforward test of the hypothesis. Any conclusion about whether we have uncovered a new finding in the
observation (in the earlier study) of significant negative sensitivity to secondary targets must await work which successfully provides an opportunity to replicate that finding.

Future work studying sensitivity to targets of a particular association value should include trials with no target
at all; in this way entirely independent sensitivity scores
could be derived for primary and secondary targets. This
was not the case with the present design, and this is the
reason we cannot statistically contrast sensitivity for primary
and secondary targets.

Response-Bias Hypothesis: The results of the current
study clearly fail to replicate the earlier results with respect
to this hypothesis. Nor can we think of any mitigating circumstances which would help to explain why this should be
the case. We may be confronted with a situation in which,
if the response-bias phenomenon is valid elsewhere, it does
not, for whatever reason, hold here.

Inhibition Hypothesis: Results of this study clearly fail to replicate the earlier word-association results with respect to this hypothesis. However, we can think of one possible mitigating circumstance in the current study. Unlike the previous one, subjects were in this study reminded on every trial of the six-second time limit. Previously, there was not a signal of the end of the time limit on every trial. Instead, the experimenter said "stop" if the subject had not given a response by the end of the time-limit period. Otherwise, subjects had no reason to think of the time limit. In this study subjects heard a "beep" at the end of six seconds on every trial. It is conceivable that this made them more sensitive about time and made them feel a sense of time pressure not present in the earlier study when persons were tested under the six- or eight-second time-limit conditions. As was reported in the earlier study, when subjects were tested under a four-second time limit, they did experience time pressure as evidenced by their increase in response speed (as contrasted with the six- and eight-second conditions), and they showed a reversal of the negative relationship between log RT and ESP success found in the six- and eight-second groups. Thus it is possible that our current six-second study was experienced by the subjects, in terms of a sense of time pressure, more like the four-second condition was in the earlier study. If so, it might be understandable that the earlier finding could not be replicated. Uninhibited subjects respond faster than inhibited subjects only in circumstances where there is no pressure to respond.

Defensiveness Hypothesis: This hypothesis received some support. Those persons who did recline the chair maximally showed overall positive, significant performance in the study. Performance of the others was essentially at chance level. We do not know, of course, how well this performance measure of "defensiveness" would correlate with pencil-and-paper or perhaps projective tests supposed to measure defensiveness, but we felt that its face validity made it worth the test, given the considerable evidence which shows that defensiveness is negatively related to ESP performance.

Suggestibility Hypothesis: The results of the current study clearly suggest to us that in the type of conditions and testing studied here, there is no relationship between suggestibility and ESP performance. The suggestion of a low positive relationship of suggestibility and ESP performance in the two studies cited earlier does not appear to generalize to the present, very different ESP task.

PAIRED-ASSOCIATES RECALL AND E S P:
A STUDY OF MEMORY AND PSI-MISSING

K. Ramakrishna Rao,† Melissa Morrison, and James W.
    Davis (Institute of Parapsychology, FRNM, Durham,
    N. C.)

Memory, like ESP, involves representations of objects and events with which the organism is not directly in
sensory contact. While we know something about the way
memory representations are stored and retrieved, as well
as their biochemical and physiological basis, our knowledge
of ESP does not provide any evidence that psi representations
have a cortical base. Further, much of our memory material is accessible for introspection, whereas most ESP
phenomena, being unconscious, are unavailable for any in-
trospective analysis. These important differences notwith-
standing, memory and ESP seem to have a good deal in common as psychological processes, and the understanding of
one day may aid the understanding of the other. Therefore
it is not surprising that from the time of F. W. H. Myers
to that of J. B. Rhine, a role for memory in ESP was anticipated. For example, J. B. Rhine wrote in his Extrasensory Perception (1934/1973): "It [ESP] is simple cognition ... but it uses memory, visual or other imagination
... in its functioning" (p. 191).

Hermann Ebbinghaus, who pioneered quantitative
studies of memory, wondered, as most experimental parapsychologists have since, how to control "the bewildering
mass of causal conditions which, insofar as they are of
mental nature, almost completely elude our control, and
which, moreover, are subject to endless and incessant
change." The challenge for him was how to "measure numerically the mental processes which flit by so quickly and
which on introspection are so hard to analyze." He solved
the problem by inventing nonsense syllables which the subject
learned and recalled under controlled conditions, a tradition
which is strikingly similar to the one heralded by early ESP
testers who used card-guessing methods.

There is also considerable similarity in the topics for
research chosen by memory researchers and parapsychologists. As memory researchers were concerned with the effect on recall of differences in the material to be remembered,
so were parapsychologists concerned with the effect of target

differences on subjects' ESP scores. Individual differences
are extensively investigated in memory studies as they are
in parapsychology. The search for states favorable to improved ESP scoring bears similarity to the research into the
conditions for optimal memory. While the classical card-
guessing tests are like the methods employed by Ebbinghaus
and those following him, the open-ended, free-response
studies of psi remind us of the Bartlett tradition in memory
research. Again, the position effects, the differential effect, and psi-missing seem to have their analogs in memory; e.g., U curves in serial learning, retroactive inhibition,
and parapraxes. If both memory and ESP involve informa-
tion-processing mechanisms, as some hold, memory psychologists and parapsychologists may find common points of
theoretical interest. For example, the "retrieve-edit" model
of William James or its later development in Underwood's
notion of retrieval and discrimination attributes may be applied to understand the ESP process. Also, some of the
concepts found in memory literature such as short-term and
long-term memory, episodic memory and semantic memory,
productive memory and reproductive memory may be relevant
not only in suggesting new lines of ESP research, but also in
clarifying some of the questions already raised. The memory psychologist also has much to gain by reflecting on such
concepts as psi-missing and the methodological advances
parapsychology has made in recent years.

There are two views which give opposing predictions
about the nature of the possible relationship between memory
and ESP. If, as Bergson contended, the cerebral processes
controlling memory are essentially selective in that we are
all potentially capable of recalling everything that has ever
happened to us, but are prevented from doing so by the pro-
tective functioning of our brains, then one would expect a
negative relationship between memory and ESP. Such a
theory would imply that the more efficient our memory processing is, the less likely we are to have ESP, for the ESP
representations would have to escape cortical surveillance in
order to manifest in our response. The other theory assumes a more positive relationship between memory and ESP.
As W. G. Roll put it: "It appears not only that a person's
memory traces influence his ESP responses, but, more
fundamentally, that his ESP responses consist of revived
memory traces.... In a way, memory images are the
'sense data' of ESP." These two points of view are not ir-
reconcilable at some level. But what is important is that
we must first acquire empirical data suggestive of a relation-

ship between one's ESP ability and his ability to remember
or of memory factors that seem to influence psi.

Expecting a positive relationship between memory and
ESP, Roll carried out a series of tests in which the subject
took a memory test and then carried out three ESP runs.
Roll reported: "There was a sharp initial decline in the
memory curve, with the typical upswing toward the end.   The
ESP scoring was also highest in the beginning of the run,
but there was no final salience."

Sara Feather was one of the first to report a positive
relationship between ESP and memory test scores. In two
series of preliminary tests in which the subject was first
shown a list of ESP symbols or digits for 15 or 20 seconds,
then tested on a regular ESP card-calling test, and finally
asked to recall the symbols or digits seen initially, she
found that the subjects whose recall was better obtained more
ESP hits then the subjects whose recall was poorer. In a
confirmatory series of three experiments, she again found
positive correlations (Series I: $r = .433$; Series II: $r = .277$; and Series III: $r = .656$) between memory and ESP
scores, which when pooled, were significant at $p = .012$.
While these results suggest a relationship between memory
and ESP, we cannot rule out the possibility that ESP oper-
ated in the memory test as well.   The memory test itself
was a forced-choice test and the subject guessed the memory
targets more often than he recalled them.

Stanford reported that his high-memory subjects
scored significantly better than the low-memory subjects on
"counter-story" responses, where the subject's responses
went counter to the information given in the story they were
asked to recall.   However, the ESP scores of the high- and
low-memory groups did not differ significantly on items which
did not have answers stated or implied in the original story.
Stanford therefore concluded that "memory per se is not related to ESP performance; its effect is an indirect one in
terms of its relation to response bias."

C. J. Peterson also attempted to study the relationship between memory and ESP, but did not find one.

Roll predicted on the basis of his memory theory of
ESP that frequently reinforced memory traces would serve
better as ESP vehicles than less frequently reinforced ones.
Interpreting this to imply that a subject would do better if

his ESP response were a primary response to an associated
stimulus than if it were a secondary response, Stanford reported evidence which accorded with this prediction (p < .03).

Significant experimental studies to explore memory-
ESP relationships were initiated by H. Kanthamani and H. H.
Rao.   Their subjects in one experiment memorized 20 pairs
of words and were asked to recall them after an interval of
two or three minutes.   An ESP test was embedded in the recall task by having the subjects guess which one of the pair
of words was the correct ESP target.   (In the two confirmatory series the ESP task was changed by having the subjects
write the recalled word in the correct one of two blank
spaces on the response sheet.)   Kanthamani and Rao found
that ESP seemed to operate best on correctly recalled trials
(p < .005 in the confirmatory series).   In another experimental study, they used a different set of 20 word-pairs,
half of which contained high-association words and half, low-
association words.   Again, the ESP test was built into the
task of recalling the appropriate missing word in the pair.
The subject wrote his response in one of the two blank spaces
to match the position of the concealed target in an envelope
attached to the record sheet.   The results supported the
previous finding that the subjects were more successful in
their ESP task on words they recalled correctly than on incorrectly recalled words (p < .05).   Further, this effect
seemed to be confined only to the low-association word-pairs.
The difference between the rate of ESP scoring between recall-correct and recall-wrong trials was highly significant
for low-association pairs and insignificant for high-association pairs.   The subjects scored significantly more hits than
mean chance expectation on correctly recalled low-association
words (p < .01) and significantly more misses on incorrectly
recalled low-association words (p < .01).

Kanthamani and Rao interpreted these results as providing some support to Roll's hypothesis, since it indicated
that "low-associated material might facilitate ESP scoring
more than high-associated material...."   This deduction appears to be at variance with the prediction that Stanford made
on the basis of the same theory, viz., that primary responses
would provide a better vehicle for ESP than secondary responses.   If, instead of being primary words, high-association words are regarded as words for which the subjects had
a favorable bias, then of course there would be no direct
conflict between these interpretations.   Kanthamani and Rao
also conceded the possibility of a psychological explanation

for the effect. The low-associated material, they noted, may provide a psychologically more favorable state than the high-associated material; "relatively difficult material tends to increase the attention and motivation of the subjects, and to that extent may facilitate the ESP function."

S. B. Harary attempted a replication of the Kanthamani and Rao finding and reported nonsignificant results. Harary's experiment, however, differed from the Kanthamani and Rao studies in two important respects. First, Kanthamani and Rao tested their subjects individually; Harary's subjects were tested in a group situation. Second, in the experiments by Kanthamani and Rao each subject performed with high-association as well as low-association word-pairs, whereas Harary's subjects worked with either high-association or low-association words, depending on the group they were assigned to. Therefore, it seems reasonable to assume that either Harary's experiment simply did not obtain the necessary ESP to test the ESP-memory hypothesis, or that the Kanthamani and Rao results do not imply any intrinsic memory-ESP relationship and are simply an outcome of differential scoring under contrasting psychological conditions.

Ronald Lieberman also attempted a replication of the Kanthamani and Rao results without success. However, he reported an unexpected interaction effect ($p < .01$). High-association words yielded higher ESP scores than low-association words when the subjects were tested in a group situation, whereas in the individual condition low-association words gave higher ESP scores than high-association words. Also, the number of ESP hits obtained in the individual tests with high-association words was significantly smaller than chance expectancy ($p < .01$).

Kathryn Parker, using a variant of the Kanthamani and Rao model, sought to relate memory-span scores with ESP scores. She utilized a standard digit-recall test. In one series she obtained a significant negative correlation ($r = -.347$) between memory-span scores and ESP hits $p < .05$). This result was not confirmed in the second series, but she found that the ESP scores elicited in conjunction with correct recall were significantly greater than ESP scores obtained on incorrectly recalled trials ($p < .01$). The ESP scores on incorrectly recalled trials gave evidence of significant psi-missing ($p < .01$).

Gambale, Margolis, and Cruci attempted a replication

of the 1974 study of Kanthamani and Rao and found no significant difference between the ESP success on the recall-
correct and recall-wrong trials. They reported, however,
that the ESP scores on recall-correct trials were negative
to a marginally significant degree (p < .05). In another
memory-ESP study, Gambale found no evidence of "any interactions regarding the variables of association strength,
word frequency-of-use or correct vs. incorrect recall...."

     David Emmerich carried out three series of tests to
study the role of memory as a psi mediator. In a free-
association task, the subjects recorded a primary response
(the first thing that came to mind) and a secondary response
(the next thing that came to mind) for each of 40 stimulus
words. The ESP task consisted of subjects writing their
responses in one of the two spaces provided for each of the
primary and each of the secondary responses. The results
indicated significant success (p < .01) on correct memory
words in the secondary association category. Scoring on the
counterpart primary-association words was at chance.

     Dennis O'Brien explored frequency and recognition
variables in addition to recall-correct and recall-wrong responses. He found in a pilot series that ESP scores with
correctly recalled, low-frequency word-pairs were marginally significant (p < .05, two-tailed). This result was not
supported by the two confirmatory series.

     The memory-ESP studies reviewed so far employed
different techniques and made diverse assumptions about possible memory-ESP relationships. One approach typically is
that of Feather who assumed a straightforward relation between memory and ESP. Her results did indicate that the
better one's memory, the better one's ESP. This finding
was in a sense confirmed by the first study of Kanthamani
and Rao in which a post-hoc analysis gave a significant positive correlation of .284 (p < .01) between subjects' ESP
scores and their memory scores. However, in Parker's
first series there was a significant negative correlation between memory and ESP scores. Other studies either did not
look for such a correlation or did not find any such significant relationship. We have noted that Feather's results can
be interpreted as ESP operating in both the memory and ESP
tests, because her memory test was so difficult that several
subjects obtained below-chance memory scores. In the Kanthamani and Rao test also, the significant correlation between
memory scores and ESP scores may not necessarily be con-

strued to indicate any intrinsic relationship between memory
and ESP inasmuch as the feeling of success on the memory
task may have created a psychological state conducive to psi-
hitting, while the inability to recall correctly may have had
the opposite effect. Therefore, it is reasonable to conclude
that the assumption that the better one's memory, the better
one's ESP, is something that has not yet been established.

A second approach may be illustrated with reference
to the studies of Kanthamani and Rao. Here the recall situation was ingeniously employed to create two opposing psychological sets that may have differentially affected the subjects'
ESP performance. The recall-correct set and the recall-
wrong set do appear to produce differential effects. If this
interpretation is correct, memory in this case becomes a
variable to manipulate a psi-conducive psychological state.
This interpretation can be extended speculatively to explain
why low-association words were more sensitive to psi effects
than high-association words in individual tests. It should
give one a more satisfying feeling to recall correctly a low-
associated word than a high-associated word. Also, the fact
that a number of studies did not confirm the Kanthamani and
Rao results and that group and individual tests appear to
have different effects is more in line with our interpretation
than with the suggestion of any intrinsic memory-ESP relationship.

A third approach, that of Stanford, appears to be
more relevant to testing the memory-ESP relation than others. The approach differs from the previous two in both
method and assumptions. Stanford's method involved no recall of a previously learned association between two words
in a pair. Therefore, in his data there were no correct
recalls or wrong recalls. The subjects' responses were
classified into primary and secondary categories on the basis
of known norms. Either "primary response" or "secondary
response" was randomly chosen as the target call for each
trial. If the subject complied and gave the correct type of
response, it would be considered an ESP hit. Stanford compared the ESP success when the targets were primary associates of the stimulus word with the scores when the targets were secondary associates. The assumption here is
that ESP is mediated by memory traces and therefore that
the stronger the associations a target word invokes, the
greater the probability that it is mediated into an ESP response. If memory traces are carriers of psi, it follows
that those which are more readily accessible to recall will

be better carriers of psi signals.   Stanford's results support
this assumption.   The fact that primary responses are more
likely to be biased responses than secondary ones makes it
all the more interesting that the subjects in this experiment
scored significantly better when they made such responses.

      An interesting aspect of Stanford's results is the fact
that when the subjects made secondary responses, they did
not score at chance, but tended to psi-miss.   It does not
follow from the "memory-trace" theory of ESP that subjects
will psi-miss when they make secondary responses.   Any
attempt to postulate a relationship between memory and ESP
should take into account the negative, missing aspect of psi.
In fact, the association aspects of memory may indeed provide some clues for understanding the role of psi in the
missing trials.   A fourth approach, which has guided the research reported in this paper, is directed toward this problem.

      Both memory and ESP are cognitive processes.
Memory has a physiological basis and is affected by psychological factors.   It is not known whether ESP has any such
somatic base.   It is, however, affected by psychological factors which may be influenced to a degree by physiological
processes.   Its extrasensorimotor function does not seem to
imply a cortical base.   It is at the psychological level that
memory and ESP seem to share common ground.   Therefore,
similar psychodynamic factors may underlie both remembering and psi-hitting on the one hand and forgetting and psi-
missing on the other.   It does not, however, follow from the
above assumption that persons with good memories will also
be good ESP subjects because these two abilities stem from
two different sources; rather, insofar as they may be subjected to similar influences at the psychological level, they
may covary significantly.

      The present study involves two sets of tests.   The
first set, the exploratory study, had two main objectives:
to discover (1) whether some significant relation exists between subjects' ESP scores and their memory scores; and
(2) whether memory processing and ESP processing at the
psychological level have certain similarities.   This set of
seven series which make up the exploratory study involves
the data of 150 subjects.   The basic test procedure is similar in all the series, but the memory materials used in the
first two series differ from the rest, as will be explained
later.   The second set of tests, involving seven more classes,

was conducted in the attempt to replicate the findings of the first.

Method

The subjects in all series except the fifth were high-school students in psychology or biology classes. In the fifth series, college students from an experimental psychology class were tested.

A total of 162 individuals participated in this study. The number of subjects to be tested was not specified in advance, but the experiment was terminated before the results of the last two series were analyzed.

Paired-Associates Learning Sheet: In the first two series, the subjects received a list of 50 trigrams (three-letter nonsense syllables) with low-association values. In the other five series, they received lists of 25 trigrams with relatively higher association values. In both cases the trigrams were paired with 10 meaningful words, namely, "ball, dad, eat, fish, game, love, moon, pine, sun, tree." These words were selected by K. R. R. for their close association with at least one of the others; for instance, ball is closely associated with game. According to the instructions at the top of the learning sheet, the subjects were asked to study the list of trigrams and their associated words for five minutes, after which they would be given a list containing only trigrams, their task being to recall and write down the associated meaningful words.

Recall-ESP Response Sheet: To record the recalled material and the ESP responses, each subject was provided with a response sheet. On it were two columns of trigrams, containing 25 of the previously seen trigrams randomly inter-mixed with 25 new ones which had similar association values. To the right of each trigram, a short blank line indicated the place for the subject's response, i. e. , one of the 10 meaningful words.

For the memory task, the subject attempted to recall the appropriate meaningful word associated with the stimulus trigram he had seen before. The ESP part of the test was linked to the 25 new trigrams which the subject had not seen before. One of the 10 meaningful words was chosen at random as the ESP target for each of these new trigrams. In the first two series, the whole test was presented as a mem-

ory task and the subjects were not told about the ESP aspect
until they completed the test. Thus, for these series, it
was an unintentional psi test. In Series 3 through 7, the
subjects received opaque manila envelopes which contained
all the correct responses to the memory part of the test plus
the ESP targets. They were told that they could use their
ESP to "see through" the envelope and obtain information
about associated words they were unable to recall from memory. Thus, the last five series, unlike the first two, involved intentional psi.

For all series the instructions at the top of the response sheet directed the subjects to fill in the blank spaces
with the associated meaningful words. The directions continued: "Even if your memory does not help, guess it anyway. You may still be right."

Association Ranking Sheet: This sheet was designed
to measure the way subjects associated each of the 10 meaningful words relative to the other 9. On this sheet, the 10
meaningful words were written in a column in alphabetical
order. Facing each word were the 9 other words, with blank
spaces beneath them. At the top of the sheet were the following instructions: "For each of the following key words,
order by appropriateness the nine matching words by writing
the numbers 1 through 9 in the spaces provided (1 for most
appropriate, 9 for least appropriate). Each matching word
on a line should have a different number."

Target Envelopes: In the last five series in which the
subjects received manila envelopes containing the target
sheets, the target sheet was sandwiched between two pieces
of dark blue construction paper and then enclosed in the
manila envelope. The envelope was sealed with paper seal
and stapled on both sides. This was done by J.W.D., who
was responsible also for generating the targets and preparing the test materials as described below. The test materials were prepared separately for each subject in all series
except in Series 4. In this series the targets from Series
3 were used. Here again, serial numbers 1 through 10 were
inadvertently repeated.

The paired-associates learning sheets and the recall-
ESP sheets were individually printed under computer control.
The three-letter nonsense syllables (trigrams) were taken
from Glaze. Randomization for ESP trials was accomplished
through the Rand table. Syllable selection and random order-

ing were based on the intrinsic FORTRAN random-number
function. For the first two series a pool of one hundred
nonsense syllables were extracted from the low-association
value categories (13. 33, 6. 67, and 0 per cent) with the re-
striction that syllables were selected for maximum differences in first and second letters. For the paired-associates
learning sheet, 50 "memory" syllables were selected from
this pool, randomly ordered, and then randomly associated
in pairs with one of the 10 key words. These pairs were
then listed in two volumns of 25 pairs each.

Twenty-five of the 50 "memory" syllables were randomly selected along with 25 of the 50 "nonmemory" syllables for the recall-ESP sheets. This total of 50 syllables
(half of which the subject had seen before and half of which
were new) were then randomized and printed in two columns
of 25, with blank lines next to them for the subjects' responses. Both the paired-associates learning sheets and the
recall-ESP sheets had serial numbers to identify them (and
to preclude mix-ups). A record of which syllables were
used as "memory" syllables, their associates, their positions
on the paired-associates learning sheet and their positions
on the ESP-recall sheet was stored in a computer key file
for later use by the scoring program. The association ranking sheets were identical for all subjects and were simply
photocopied from a master and numbered to correspond to
the serial numbers on the recall-ESP sheets. The targets
were selected from the Rand table, using a random entry-
point printed in digit form and stored in a locked drawer
by J. W. D.

The third and subsequent series employed some substantial modifications. First, a pool of 50 high-association
syllables (100% and 93. 33%) were selected from Glaze, using
the criterion of differentiability previously mentioned. From
these 50, 25 were selected as "memory" syllables, were
randomized as to order, and were randomly associated with
the 10 key words. These 25 pairs were then printed in a
single column on the paired-associates learning sheet. For
the recall-ESP sheet, the 25 "memory" syllables were randomly mixed with the remaining 25, and blank lines were put
beside each one for the subjects' responses. The association
ranking sheets were like those in the previous studies. A
separate program prepared target sheets for these series.
The sheets were individually placed in sealed envelopes and
were given to the subject. The key file and the target file
were used to print sheets identical to the recall-ESP sheets

except that the blank lines were replaced with the correct
memory or ESP target for each syllable. This work was
all done by J. W. D. , who had no contact with the subjects.

Procedure

The experimenters went to each school on a day arranged for the experiment. Except in the first two series,
they gave a brief talk about ESP, explaining the basic concepts before administering the tests. In the first two series,
however, M. M. introduced K. R. R. as a professor who came
from India and was interested in giving them a psychology
test. After they had taken the tests, M. M. gave a talk on
parapsychology and briefly explained the psi aspect of the
test they had just completed.

In all series, the testing began with the presentation
of the paired-associates learning sheet. Subjects were told
that they had five minutes to memorize as many of the word-
pairs as possible. For the first two series, this meant trying to associate each of 50 low-association trigrams with one
of the 10 meaningful words. For Series 3-7, subjects tried
to memorize 25 word-pairs consisting of high association trigrams and 10 meaningful words. The change in the number
and nature of the trigrams was deemed necessary because
there was no evidence of memory in the results of the first
two series.

After the five-minute learning period, subjects were
given the recall-ESP sheet with 25 familiar and 25 new trigrams listed in random order. They were asked to complete
each word-pair. No mention was made in the first two
classes of the fact that 25 of these trigrams were new and
could only be correctly paired with one of the meaningful
words through ESP. For the remaining series, students
knew that half of the trigrams were unfamiliar and impossible to recall through memory. In these series, subjects
were encouraged to try to use their ESP to guess the correct
target response, or meaningful word. In front of each student was the envelope containing the target sheet with all the
correctly completed word-pairs.

After all the subjects in a group had finished this
part of the experiment, they were given the association ranking sheet. At this point the instructions printed at the top
of the sheet were rephrased verbally. Each student then did
10 sets of rankings. The entire experiment lasted about 35

minutes.   Each group was thanked for participating and told that they would be sent the results of their performance. These were mailed to the schools.

When the recall-ESP sheets and the association ranking sheets were returned to the laboratory, they were photocopied and the two sets were independently entered as response files.   These two files were compared by the computer and discrepancies were rectified by the enterers with reference to the data sheets.   They were then processed in conjunction with the appropriate key files and target files to produce memory scores, ESP scores, and association scores for each subject.   In cases where subjects left blanks or made inappropriate responses not exceeding five in a total of 50, random digits were inserted.   In cases of two or less errors on the association ranking sheets (ties, etc.), random numbers were used to correct them.   Sheets with more errors were classed as such by the computer and dropped from the evaluation.

Hypotheses and Planned Statistical Analyses

The following two null hypotheses were stated in advance: (1) That there would be no significant relationship between the subjects' memory scores and their ESP scores. The memory scores are operationally defined as the total number of correct recalls of the missing words in the memory pairs.   ESP scores are the total number of correct matches of the subjects' responses to the ESP targets.   It was planned to test this hypothesis by means of the Pearson product moment correlation.   (2) That there would be no significant relationship between the mean association rank scores of psi-hitters and those of psi-missers obtained from their unsuccessful ESP trials.   Hitters and missers are defined according to two criteria: (a) According to one criterion, hitters are those who score three or more hits in 25 ESP trials ($p = 1/10$) and missers are those who obtain two or less.   (b) The second criterion defines the hitter as one who obtains four or more hits and the misser as one who gets one or zero hits.   It was planned to test this hypothesis separately for both criteria by means of a two-tailed independent t test for the difference between the mean association rank scores of hitters and missers.

Results of Exploratory Study

The results were analyzed to test the two hypotheses

for each of the series separately. The overall ESP scores
were not significantly different from MCE in any of the sev-
en series. The combined results show that the mean ESP
score per subject is 2.47 hits where chance expectancy is
2.5.

      Correlations of memory and ESP scores of subjects
computed separately for each series were close to chance.
There was also no consistency in the direction across the
seven series. It was not possible to work out a correlation
for the whole group of 150 subjects for two reasons. First,
the memory material for the first two series was different
from that of the other five, and therefore the memory scores
were not comparable. Also since the timing of the test was
somewhat informal, it cannot be assumed that each of the
subjects in the class spent exactly the same amount of time
on the memory task. In Series 4, because of some confusion in the distribution of test materials, some subjects had
slightly more time (less than a minute) than the usual five
minutes to spend on the memory task.

      The association ranking sheets gave information as to
how each subject ranked one word against the others as to
relatedness. For example, if a subject gave the rank of 1
to the word ball and 9 to the word eat against the key word
game it is assumed that for this subject the word ball is
closest to and the word eat is furthest from the word game
in terms of their relative associations. The sum of association ranks given to a subject's response words relative to
target words on all his ESP-missing trials was obtained.
From this, the subject's mean association rank score was
computed. To illustrate this point, let us assume that in a
given trial the target word was dad and the subject responded
with game. Obviously this trial is scored as a miss. Now
we find that in the subject's association ranking sheet he gave
game a rank of 2 against the key word dad. In this case,
the subject gets an association rank score of 2 on this trial.
The lower the association score, the "closer" or more "related" in the mind of the subject is the response word to the
target word. The mean association rank score expected by
chance is 5, which is the midpoint of the 1-9 scale of ranks.

      To test our association hypothesis, the results were
analyzed in the following way: The subjects were divided
into two groups, hitters and missers, on the basis of their
ESP scores. Hitters and missers were defined in two ways
as per the criteria set in advance of the experiment. Ac-

cording to the first criterion, the subjects who scored three
or more hits were hitters and those who obtained two or less
were missers. As per the second, more stringent criterion,
subjects obtaining four or more hits were classed as hitters
while those obtaining one and zero hits were regarded as
missers. The mean association rank scores given to incorrect ESP responses by the hitters were compared with those
given by the missers, separately for each series and for all
the series combined. As planned, the t statistic was employed to test the significance of the difference in the means.

The results showed significant differences in the mean
association rank scores of hitters and missers as defined by
the first criterion in two of the seven series, as well as in
all the series combined. In Series 1, the subjects who
scored three or more ESP hits obtained a mean association
rank score of 1.63 on their misses while the subjects who
scored two or less had a mean score of 5.15. This gives
a t of -2.47 (20 df); p < .05, two-tailed. In Series 4 the
hitters had a mean of 4.61 and missers 5.14 giving t =
-2.50 (17 df); p < .05, two-tailed. In three more series
the results were in the same direction. In Series 7 the
trend was in the opposite direction. In another (Series 5),
both the missers and hitters had the same mean score of
5.00. The data for all seven series were pooled for exploratory purposes and for guidance in the planning of confirmatory experiments. The results show that the hitters averaged 4.83 whereas the missers obtained a mean association
rank score of 5.04. The difference of the means gives a t
of -2.52 (148 df); p < .02, two-tailed.

Since the association values were obtained for response mistakes and since missers, by definition, made
more of these mistakes, there were more trials for the
missers than for the hitters. The mean number of unsuccessful ESP trials for hitters and missers were 21.10 and
23.72, respectively. The t test was considered to be sufficiently robust not to be biased by this small difference in
the number of trials. A chi-square contingency test with
the subject as a unit was also performed so as to ascertain
the overall consistency across the subjects in all seven
series. Among the hitters, 44 had a mean association score
of less than 5.00 and 24, more than 5.00. Forty-two missers had mean association scores of more than 5.00 and 37
had less than 5.00. Three subjects had mean scores of exactly 5.00. Such a distribution gives a chi-square of 4.02
(1 df); p < .05, two-tailed.

A similar analysis of the results using the second criterion (in which hitters have four hits and above, missers, one and below) shows a similar trend, but none of the t's in the seven series is significant. We find, however, that the overall association rank score of hitters according to the second criterion is close to that of hitters for the first criterion (4.86 vs. 4.83). The same is true of the missers (5.07 vs. 5.04). The difference in the overall mean scores of hitters and missers is the same for both the criteria, i.e., .21.

Thus the results of the exploratory study give us some basis for rejecting our second null hypothesis and suggest that hitters and missers differ significantly in the choice of their responses when they miss. It would appear that hitters, unlike missers, tend to respond with words closer in their association to the target words.

Since it was planned to run a confirmatory study, a number of post hoc analyses were made for possible confirmation later. It is obvious from the mean association rank scores of hitters and missers that the effect was wholly contributed by the hitters. The obtained overall mean was 4.83 for the hitters (criterion 1) whereas the mean score for the missers was close to chance. Again, the mean association rank scores of hitters are independently significant in Series 4 and 6. None of the means for the missers is significantly different from chance. This indicates that the tendency to respond with words closer in their association to the targets is a response characteristic of the hitters and that the missers do not show a countertendency to respond with words further away in their association to the targets.

The data were also analyzed for internal psi effects. The recall-ESP sheet had two columns. In the first column there were 1,851 trials and 171 hits, an average of 2.31 hits per 25 trials. In the second column the subjects obtained 199 hits out of 1,899 trials, an average of 2.62 hits. The difference between the two means is not statistically significant.

Results of Replication Study

A second set of tests to replicate the overall findings of the first was carried out in seven separate high-school classes in the Durham area. M.M. was the experimenter in all seven classes. She was assisted by K.R.R. in three

classes and by J. M. H. in the rest. The test materials and
the procedure of testing were identical with those employed
in the last five classes of the first study. By using a stopwatch, better control of the time allotted for subjects to
memorize the list of paired associates was achieved in this
set of experiments.

It was decided, on the basis of pooled results from
the exploratory work, that the seven classes included in the
replication would be considered as a single unit in terms of
analysis. Pooling the findings of the earlier experiments
suggested that the weak but relatively consistent effect evidenced could most reliably be observed in a large group of
subjects. The goal of testing 150 high-school students was
not fully realized since some of the classes involved were
small and several students had to be excluded because of
improperly completed response sheets. No analysis of association rank scores was carried out until the experiment
had ended.

Of the 132 subjects tested, 118 provided acceptable
responses and are included in the analysis reported. (Criteria for inclusion are identical to those described earlier
in reference to the exploratory work.)

The following hypotheses derived from the overall results of the first series of experiments were stated in advance: (1) The psi-hitters would obtain significantly lower
mean association rank scores than the psi-missers on their
ESP missing trials; (2) The psi hitters would obtain significantly lower mean association rank scores than mean chance
expectation. It was determined in advance to test these hypotheses by means of t tests.

The mean association rank scores of criterion 1 psi-
hitters (those obtaining three or more hits) on their ESP
misses was 4.88. The mean for the missers (obtaining two
or less hits) was 4.96. The difference gives a t of -.80
(116 df), which is in the expected direction but not significantly so. The second criterion of hitters (four and above)
and missers (one and zero) yields a t of -1.01 (59 df), with
the hitters having a mean of 4.82 and missers 4.95. Thus,
the results of the second set of tests failed to confirm the
first hypothesis.

The mean association rank score of first criterion
hitters yields a t of -1.42 (49 df), while that of criterion 2

hitters gives a t of -1.81 (26 df).   Again, the two t's do
not reach acceptable levels of significance to confirm the
second hypothesis.   But it is of interest to see that the
means are not too different from the means obtained for hitters in our first set of tests, in which the overall mean association rank score for criterion 1 and 2 hitters are 4.83
and 4.86, respectively, as compared to the mean scores of
4.88 and 4.82 in the second set of experiments.

Since the first hypothesis of our preliminary tests relating to a possible relationship between overall memory and
overall ESP scores did not receive any support from the data,
it was not planned to test this hypothesis in the second set
of tests.   However, a post hoc analysis gave a Pearson's
product moment correlation of -.18, which has an associated
t value of -1.99 (116 df); p < .05, two-tailed.   A Spearman's
rho of -.21 was also computed, with an associated t value
of -2.36 (116 df); p < .02, two-tailed.

Discussion

While the results of the first set of tests gave no
evidence of any relationship between a subject's memory and
his ESP score, there is suggestive evidence in the second
that they were negatively related.   The post hoc nature of
this finding as well as the size of the correlation, which is
quite small though suggestive, led us to be cautious on this
question and reserve judgment until we have more data.   It
should be noted also that there was a good deal of variance
in the memory scores of the subjects which is likely to be
due to the variability of attentiveness with which the subjects
took the memory test.   Very low memory scores on the part
of some subjects indicate that they did not pay sufficient attention to the test.   It is a difficulty that the experimenter
encounters in a group situation which involves testing as
many as 20 subjects in one session.   Therefore, it would
seem more appropriate to administer a memory test of this
sort individually to the subjects rather than to a group.   Perhaps a memory drum or a tachistoscope could be profitably
employed to control the time factor adequately.

The most interesting aspect of the results of the first
set of experiments is the significant difference in the association rank scores of hitters and missers in Series 1 and
4.   This tendency is apparent in five out of the seven series.
The results of the second set of experiments did not confirm this finding, however, even though they are in the same

direction; the same relationship is indicated in five of the
seven classes tested in the replication study. Thus, while
the effect appears to be fairly consistent, it seems to be
quite weak.

The ESP responses of hitters, unlike those of missers, tended to be closer in association to the target word.
This phenomenon is not unlike what happens when we fail to
recall something we have learned previously. We tend to
have a memory response which in some sense has a subjective association with the forgotten word. Thus there is a
suggestion that memory retrieval and ESP response may involve similar processing.

The fact that the observed difference in the association rank scores of hitters and missers is almost wholly contributed by the hitters is relevant to our discussion. We
may assume that hitters generally do not show a tendency to
avoid the target. When they fail to hit, it is more a failure
to get at the right target than an attempt to avoid the target,
a tendency which we may expect to find among psi-missing
subjects. The words that were used in these tests were
chosen on the basis of their similarity rather than opposi-
tion (for example, dad and love, sun and moon, tree and
pine, fish and eat, ball and game). Also, the subjects were
asked to rank in terms of "appropriateness" rather than "inappropriateness." So our association rank sheets are likely
to guide the hitters more adequately than the missers. It
would be interesting to see the results of a test with half
the words selected for their obvious inappropriateness to the
other half and the subjects asked to rank them on the basis
of inappropriateness. If our reasoning is correct, we should
expect psi-missing subjects to show the effect now observed
with psi-hitters. Other possible manipulations of the meaningful words in terms of their interrelatedness are being
considered as ways to maximize the hitter-misser differences
in terms of association rank scores.

If we may further speculate on similarities in the processes of memory and ESP, we may be led to a dual-process
model of ESP similar to the retrieve-recognize model in
memory theory. In memory we retrieve memory images
from the cortical bank where they are stored. We do not
know where the ESP images are stored just as we do not
know how they are invoked in the first place. Insofar as
psi seems to transcend sensory-motor limitations, it is unlikely that ESP images have a cerebral or physicochemical

base.   An ESP image once retrieved goes through a second
phase of processing which may be much the same as the
second stage of memory processing.   The ESP images for
the most part are extremely weak and are often below the
threshold of conscious recognition.   Like memory images of
similar low intensity, ESP may manifest in somewhat unre-
liable and elusive ways unless we become aware of the psychodynamic attributes of processing at this stage.   The association relatedness of the ESP response seems to point out one
such attribute.

Our general survey of memory-ESP research, as
well as our own attempts to study the problem, reveal the
existence of a variety of approaches for studying memory-
ESP interrelations.   Finding a common ground among these
diversities is admittedly difficult; but a synthesis is important
and necessary if this area of study is to yield results that
fulfill the promise it holds for understanding the psi process.

THE ROLE OF ASSOCIATION
IN MEMORY-RECALL AND ESP

K. Ramakrishna Rao, Melissa Morrison,† James W. Davis
    and John A. Freeman (Institute of Parapsychology, and
    Campbell College, Buies Creek, N.C.)

The preceding study by Rao, Morrison, and Davis
suggested that the ESP responses of psi-hitters which did
not match the correct targets tended nevertheless to be more
closely associated in the subject's mind with the correct targets than did similar responses made by psi-missers.   The
degree of association was determined by having the subject
rank each of the 10 target words in relation to the other
nine in terms of how closely associated they were in his
mind.   The mean association rank scores of hitters were
found to be significantly different from those of missers on
incorrect trials.

The subjects in six out of seven series in that study
were high-school students.   In the only series with college
students as subjects, the association rank scores of both hitters and missers were found to be 5.00, which is the same
as mean chance expectation.   This raised the question as to
whether the reported effect is peculiar to high-school subjects

and is not generalizable to others. It also raised doubt as
to whether the test in the form given in the previous experiment was appropriate for older groups, such as the college
population.   Therefore, when J. A. F. expressed interest in
giving the tests to students in his college classes, the opportunity was welcomed.

The objectives of the study were: (1) to see whether
significant differences in the association rank scores of hitters and missers as suggested by the results of the previous
study by Rao et al. would be found among college students;
and (2) to explore whether incorrect memory and ESP trials
involved similar associative processes affecting their responses.

Method

The subjects in this study were 76 students in three
psychology classes taught by J. A. F. at Campbell College in
North Carolina.   They were tested in three separate groups
of 8, 46, and 22.   There were 36 female and 40 male subjects.

The materials and the test procedures employed were
like those used in the last five series of the Rao-Morrison-
Davis (RMD) study.   The test materials were prepared individually for each subject by J. W. D. and M. M.   Briefly, the
test procedure was as follows:

J. A. F. was the experimenter.   The students, who
had already heard J. A. F. lecture to them on parapsychology,
were given a paired-associates learning sheet consisting of
a list of 25 trigrams taken from the same pool of high-association nonsense syllables used in the previous RMD study.
The trigrams were randomly paired with 10 meaningful
words--"ball, dad, eat, fish, game, love, moon, pine, sun,
tree."   The subjects had five minutes in which to learn the
associations.   Immediately after the five-minute learning
period, the learning sheets were collected and the students
were given the target envelopes and recall-ESP sheets to
record their responses.   The recall-ESP sheets consisted of
the 25 trigrams memorized earlier and 25 new ones.   These
50 items were randomly intermized and served as stimulus
words.   The subject's task was to record the appropriate
word beside each of the stimulus words.   The total number
of correct response matches on the pairs the subject had an
opportunity to learn was his memory score and the total num-

ber of correct matches on the pairs he had no opportunity to learn constituted his ESP score. No time limit was set for completing the recall-ESP task. The following instructions were printed at the top of the sheet: "Given below is a list of three-letter words. Please fill each blank with the 'correct' meaning. The correct meaning may be any of the following ten words: ball, dad, eat, fish, game, love, moon, pine, sun, tree. You may remember some of the meanings from what you read a little while ago. Even if your memory does not help, guess it anyway. You may still be right. Please do not leave any blanks."

After all the subjects in a class filled in their recall-ESP sheets, they were given association ranking sheets. These contained the 10 meaningful words written in alphabetical order. Beside each word there were the nine other words, with blank spaces beneath them. The subjects received the following written instructions, which were also orally explained: "For each of the following key words, order by appropriateness the nine matching words by writing the numbers 1 through 9 in the spaces provided (1 for most appropriate, 9 for least appropriate). Each matching word on a line should have a different number."

When the recall-ESP sheets and the association ranking sheets were returned to the Institute for Parapsychology, they were photocopied and the two sets were independently entered in a computer as response files. These two files were then compared by the computer and discrepancies were rectified by the enterers with reference to the data sheets, which were then processed in conjunction with the appropriate key files and target files to produce memory scores, ESP scores, and association rank scores for each subject. In cases where subjects left blanks or made inappropriate responses not exceeding five in a total of 50, random digits were inserted. In cases of two or less errors on the association ranking sheets (ties, etc.) random numbers were used to resolve them. Sheets with more errors were classed as such by the computer and dropped from the evaluation. The computer gave the printouts of memory scores, ESP scores, and mean association rank scores for ESP misses and memory misses separately. The mean ESP association rank scores were computed in the following manner: First the sum of the association rank scores given to each wrong ESP response in relation to the correct target was obtained for each subject and the mean score was computed by dividing the sum by the number of ESP misses. By following a sim-

ilar procedure, mean association rank scores for memory
misses were also computed.

Hypotheses

It was hypothesized in advance that: (1) The psi-hitters would obtain on their ESP-missing trials significantly
lower association rank scores than the psi-missers. Two
separate criteria were set to define hitters and missers.
According to the first criterion, the hitters were those who
scored three or more hits, and missers were those who
scored two or less. In the second criterion, hitters were
defined as those obtaining four or more hits, and missers
as those obtaining one and zero. It was planned to test this
hypothesis using independent t tests. (2) The subjects' mean
association rank score on ESP misses and memory misses
would be in the same direction. It was decided to use a sign
test to test this hypothesis.

J. A. F. , who was experimenter in this study, had
earlier reported in his work significant sex differences.
Therefore information about the sex of the subjects was
solicited. While no hypotheses based on sex were stated in
advance, it was planned to carry out some post hoc analyses
on the basis of the sex variable.

Results

Defined in accordance with the first criterion, hitters
and missers had mean association rank scores of 5.00 and
5.02, respectively. The difference between the means gives
a t of -.11 (74 df). The second criterion hitters and missers averaged 4.90 and 5.06 on their association ranks. The
mean difference of -.16 gives a t of -.88 (29 df). Both the
t's are in the expected direction, but nonsignificant. Therefore the results of this study do not confirm the first hypothesis.

The mean association rank scores of subjects on memory misses and ESP misses showed that 38 subjects obtained
scores above or below 5.00 for both memory and ESP misses.
Twenty-two subjects had scores which were above 5.00 in
memory data and below 5.00 in ESP data or below 5.00 in
memory data and above 5.00 in ESP data. The others had
mean association rank scores exactly at 5.00 in one of the
two conditions. A sign test gives a p of .052, two-tailed,
and provides evidence in support of the second hypothesis.

This result suggests that in a test of this sort, the subjects who respond on the memory task with a word other than the correct word but one which is relatively close in terms of association or "appropriateness" to the correct word will tend to do the same when they miss the ESP target. Conversely, those who respond with a word more remote in terms of association to the correct memory word will do the same with the missed ESP targets.

In addition to the above planned analyses, some post hoc analyses were carried out. To examine further the possibility of similar missing tendencies in ESP and memory, a Pearsons' product moment and a Spearman correlation were computed between mean association rank scores for memory and ESP trials. Each was nonsignificant, with correlations of .16 and .17, respectively.

It appeared to be of interest to go back and check the data of the RMD study as they related to the second hypothesis. Therefore the results of that study were checked to see whether the subjects showed similar tendencies in their memory- and ESP-missing trials. The data from the exploratory study could not be used because of the several differences in the memory test between the series. In fact, the first two series of the exploratory study did not give any evidence of memory at all. In the replication study, 61 subjects had mean association rank scores that were above or below MCE in both memory misses and ESP misses, while 50 had scores above or below, but in the opposite direction. Seven had scores exactly at chance. The sign test gives an insignificant result, as does a correlation between mean association rank scores for memory and ESP trials.

A second group of post hoc analyses of the data of the present study were carried out to look for possible differences in scoring related to the subjects' sex. Criterion 1 male hitters obtained a mean association rank score of 4.84, whereas missers had a mean of 5.07. A t of the difference was -1.28 (38 df). According to the second, more stringent criterion, male hitters had a mean of 4.75 and missers, 5.06. The difference in the means gives a t of -1.46 (18 df). Neither of the two t's reaches an acceptable level of significance. The female subjects, on the other hand, obtained mean association rank scores in the opposite direction. The hitters, according to criterion 1, averaged 5.20 and the missers, 4.97. This gives a t of 1.24 (34 df). The criterion 2 hitters and missers obtained mean association rank scores of 5.23 and 5.04, respectively (t = .59, 9 df).

Almost all the deviation in these four comparisons was contributed by the hitters. The averages of the missers were close to mean chance expectation. When the mean association rank scores of male hitters were compared with the mean of female hitters (criterion 1), there was a suggestive difference between the sexes (t = 1.93, 33 df).

To test further for this apparent interaction between sex and ESP scoring on the mean association scores, these variables were used as factors in a two-way analysis of variance for unequal sample sizes, using the method of unweighted means. The resulting F for the interaction of 3.13 (1, 72 df) lies between p = .1 and p = .05. This interaction is not significant, and it cannot be concluded that males and females made consistently different types of responses on the incorrect ESP trials.

An analysis based on sex was also carried out in relation to the second hypothesis, which predicted that the mean association ranks for ESP and memory misses would vary in the same direction. Of the 38 subjects who scored in the expected way, 20 were males and 18 were females. Among the 22 subjects who scored in the opposite direction, there were 11 males and 11 females. Thus there was no evidence of sex differences here.

Finally, a set of analyses were carried out on just the memory rank scores to see if the data supported the notion that in memory, when we fail to recall a word, we tend to recall a word similar to or associated with it. The mean association rank score for all the memory misses was 4.75. Large differences in the number of memory misses among the subjects made a t test inappropriate for evaluating the significance of these memory mean association rank scores. Instead, a sign test was carried out to compare the total number of scores below vs. those above the theoretical mean of 5.00. This analysis yielded a nonsignificant result.

The memory scores were also analyzed for the sex differences. The mean association rank score of male subjects was 4.52 and that of females, 5.00. When a two-by-two chi-square contingency test with the subject as a unit was carried out, the results were that of the 28 subjects who had above-MCE mean memory rank association scores, 8

were males and 20 were females, whereas 26 males and 10
females obtained memory rank scores of less than 5.00.
Such a distribution gives a chi-square of 10.36 (1 df); p <
.01, two-tailed.

The analyses on memory trials do not directly support the notion that subjects tend to recall similar or associated words when they cannot remember the actual target.
Instead, there is a suggestion that, although males tended
to respond in the above manner, females showed an opposite
tendency to avoid the correct memory target.

Conclusions

While the results of this experiment fail to confirm
the findings of the RMD study, they suggest the possibility
that the sex variable may confound the relationship of association rank scores and ESP, especially in a college-student
population.

An interesting aspect of this study is the suggestive
evidence that subjects' association rank scores on ESP
misses tend to be in the same direction (i.e., either above
or below mean chance expectation) as their association rank
scores on memory misses. Thus there is some indication
that similar processing of information may be involved in
both memory and ESP.

Further credibility is added to the above suggestion
by the fact that similar reversals took place in the memory
and the ESP data: the males obtained lower association rank
scores than females in both tasks. That a similar sex difference might be present in both the memory and the ESP
data is indeed encouraging to us in our attempts to understand memory-ESP interactions.

CONSIDERATION OF INTERNAL PROCESSES
IN USING IMMEDIATE FEEDBACK TO TEACH ESP ABILITY

Charles T. Tart (University of California, Davis)

Some years ago (in 1966), I argued that the standard
parapsychological procedure of a percipient's making repeated
guesses at a multiple-choice target, such as cards, without

the provision of feedback until many trials had passed, constituted an extinction paradigm.   In almost all conventional
learning situations some kind of feedback on performance is
provided almost immediately after each response, and under
these circumstances we usually see an improvement in performance with practice.   Eliminating this immediate feedback
of consequences is a standard way to induce extinction, a
steady worsening of performance with repeated practice.
Thus I argued that the commonness of the decline effect in
psi experiments, where the percipient eventually lost his psi
as he was repeatedly tested, was just what we would expect.
The provision of immediate feedback, on the other hand,
should allow some percipients to improve their performance.

Most colleagues who read the original theoretical
article did not grasp the importance of the prediction stating
that if immediate feedback were given, only some percipients
would show learning.   Rather they mistakenly read it as predicting that all percipients should show an increase, or
groups of percipients, as a sample of a population, should
show an increase.

When a percipient is guessing at a limited set of targets, say five possible cards, he or she will be right by
chance alone approximately one-fifth of the time.   Since the
models of internal processes underlying my original learning
theory, delineated only briefly in the original publication,
was that immediate feedback allows the percipient to compare aspects of his ongoing experience with success or failure in responding, the presence of chance-correct responses
is an important confusing factor.

What a percipient should be doing is learning what
kinds of experiential cues or patterns of cues are associated
with success, so he can learn to call when he recognizes
the presence of that momentary state.   He should also learn
what kinds of cues or patterns of cues are associated with
failure, so he can either pass, wait for that set of cues to
change, or deliberately try to alter his momentary internal
condition to one that has been associated with success cues
in the past.   Because the percipient is sometimes right by
chance alone, this means that he associates particular sets
of internal conditions with being right, but these sets of conditions have nothing to do with learning to use psi.   The
presence of chance-correct successes, then, constitutes a
kind of noise in the procedure or, more precisely, they constitute an inherent extinction procedure built into any repeated

guessing situation.   We shall consider the nature of extinction in detail later.   The balance between the confusion/ex-
tinction induced by chance-correct responses and psi-influ-
enced correct responses will determine whether learning takes
place for a given percipient.

I originally expressed this point in the concept of the
talent threshold: if a percipient was above some minimal
threshold level of psi talent when he began feedback training,
the proportion of correct responses due to psi should be high
enough so that learning would predominate over the extinction inherent in any repeated guessing situation.   If a given
percipient possessed some psi ability, but was below this
talent threshold, we would have a shifting balance between
a possible learning process and an extinction process, so
what we would generally expect would be that decline or extinction would be slowed down, usually to the point of giving
relatively stable psi performance for short to moderate
length experiments where fatigue, boredom, loss of motivation, and the like did not become important factors.   For
percipients with no detectable psi ability to begin with, the
provision of immediate feedback would, in general, have no
effect, although if enough such percipients were tested there
would undoubtedly be some with hidden psi abilities that might
flower in this situation.

These considerations led to another prediction made
in the original publication, namely that the degree to which
a percipient profited from the provision of immediate feedback would be directly proportional to the degree of demonstrable psi ability he had to begin with.

I believe that these three basic predictions, namely
that given some psi talent to begin with, (a) the provision
of immediate feedback should stabilize performance in most
percipients and (b) allow learning in some percipients, and
(c) that the degree of learning will be proportional to the
incoming psi talent level of the percipients, have now received very strong support.   An initial review of the literature and evidence from my first extensive training series
has been presented elsewhere, and generally confirmatory
results from a second major training study should be published shortly (by Tart, Palmer, and Redington).

In the original theoretical article and the subsequent
publications, I deliberately kept theorizing about the internal
psychological processes involved in learning psi performance

to a minimum, preferring to emphasize the importance of immèdiate feedback from a conventional, behavioral point of view.   The purpose of this article is to elaborate my theoretical modeling of the psychological processes involved in learning to use psi under conditions of immediate feedback. Empirical support for the theory is discussed elsewhere. While I shall focus on ESP, this discussion is readily applicable to other aspects of psi, such as psychokinesis.

Background:
Our Ordinary State of Consciousness

I do not consider learning to use psi ability more effectively to be an easy task, even for the highly talented percipient.   A brief look at the nature of our ordinary state of consciousness, which is what we usually try to learn psi ability in, will provide background for this contention.   This understanding of our ordinary state of consciousness is spelled out in much greater detail elsewhere and will be just briefly touched on here.

By virtue of being born human beings, we have a vast range of potentialities that could be developed, including the potential for using various kinds of psi abilities.   There may or may not be some genetic differences among individuals here, but as we have no solid evidence on this, we shall ignore this factor.   What is important, however, is that each of us is born into a particular culture, which is a group of people who, through historical processes, only recognize the existence of a limited number of the total spectrum of human potentialities, and so allow a large number of human potentialities to either remain latent or to become essentially completely unavailable by not being developed within a critical time period.   Further, of those human potentials known, some are labeled "good" and receive active encouragement for development, others are labeled "bad" and are actively inhibited: psi potentials are either unrecognized or are put in the latter category for most of us.

The enculturation process, carried out through selective pressures and guidance, rewards and punishments, from parents, teachers, and peers, takes our unorganized human potentialities of infancy and, in the course of growing up, organizes a much smaller number of these into our "normal" or ordinary state of consciousness, a state that might be more accurately characterized as "consensus consciousness," a habitual and quite restrictive pattern of mental functioning

that reflects the consensus reality, the cultural reality of our
particular society. The fully developed consensus consciousness represents a largely automatic, routinized, habitual set
of psychological structures and operations that implicitly
guides our perceptions, our fantasies, our evaluations, our
feelings, and our actions into channels and patterns that are
approved of by our society. Insofar as psi phenomena have
no valued place within our particular consensus reality, the
immense force of habit and conditioning makes it difficult for
us to make a very wholehearted commitment to attempting to
use or develop such faculties. Thus when we ask a percipient to sit down in the laboratory and attempt to use or develop psi, in many ways we can get only a limited amount of
attention focused on this, and there is a tremendous amount
of implicit mental habit militating against any significant
amount of psi appearing. There are important individual exceptions to this, of course, but this is the social reality that
is a constant background to our work.

Resistance to Psi

Note also that the cognitive conditionings that limit
our range of mental experience and behavior are not simply
cognitive: they have very strong emotional components, such
that if you seriously begin to question the explicit and implicit judgments and limits conditioned into you, you may
start becoming disoriented, experience generalized anxiety,
and have specific guilt reactions ("These powers are from
the Devil, no decent person has anything to do with them!"
or "These ideas are left over from times of ignorance and
superstition, and it is a sign of stupidity or mental instabil-
ity to give them any consideration!"). Mentally deciding
that you will try to use psi does not make this emotional
conditioning go away, so we may have both conscious and emotional resistances to using psi. Again, there are enormous
individual differences in the strength of these factors, but
they are quite common in our culture.

These specific cultural resistances to psi functioning,
which may be specifically activated by deliberately trying to
use psi, are not the only factors that prevent people in our
culture from seriously trying to learn psi. A few minutes'
observation of our own mental processes will demonstrate
that we do not experience a passive state of mind with specific cultural conditionings activated only when the requisite
stimuli come in from the environment. To the contrary,
our ordinary state of consensus consciousness is like a three-

ring circus: We're constantly thinking, fantasizing, remembering, planning, reacting to our own thoughts and fantasies, thinking about our reactions, etc., etc., etc.! Our ordinary state of consensus consciousness is a dynamically active, interactive, exceptionally busy state of affairs. Our ability to pay deliberate attention is, as it were, almost totally used up by the continual ongoing thought and fantasy that is our common lot. Some of the appeal of trying to develop psi ability in altered states of consciousness lies in the fact that the sheer activity level may be reduced in some altered states, thus allowing more awareness to be focused on the psi task. But in the typical percipient who sits down in our laboratories to work with a psi task, there is an incredibly high noise level in the percipient's mind. Further, this is a noise level over which most percipients have practically no voluntary control. Try to not think of anything for five minutes, and the point will be amply demonstrated.

As with the specific resistances discussed above, there are again enormous individual differences, but most people in our culture have an extremely high noise (mental activity irrelevant to psi functioning) level in their ordinary state of consciousness and can do very little, if anything, about it.

Given this brief sketch of the nature of our ordinary state of consensus consciousness, when we ask a percipient to try to learn to use psi, it's as if we walk up to someone who is in the middle of a lively party in a popular tavern. The jukebox is playing loudly, dozens of people are dancing and shouting, others are conversing loudly about all sorts of topics that seem important or are fashionable. Everyone, including our would-be percipient (and possibly our experimenter), is drunk: drunk not only with liquor flowing so freely, but with the social and intellectual stimulation provided by the party. This is not a passing accident that just happened to our percipient, either: he chose (or was conditioned) to come to the "party," he is enjoying it (or has been conditioned to believe he is enjoying it), and doesn't ever want to leave.

We make our way through the crowd and finally get alongside him for a moment and somehow try to persuade him that it is important for him to try to overhear a whispered conversation which is going on outside in the street. We are lucky if we can guide him, staggeringly, over toward the door, closer to where the outside conversation is taking

place. His friends may continually come up and engage him
in loud conversation, ply him with drink, or whisk him away
to the dance floor. The task of getting him to actually leave
the warm, friendly, intoxicating party in the tavern into
(what seems) the cold, dark street outside, to pay prolonged
attention to this hard-to-hear conversation, is a prodigious
one indeed!

I may seem to be sketching the situation in stark
terms, but my studies of the psychology of consciousness
have convinced me that this is indeed a very apt simile for
our ordinary state of consciousness and what we are asking
someone to do in trying to learn to use psi. The simile
should be extended to include insanities and the resistances:
our percipient has probably heard a lot of stories about the
awful things that happen to people who go out in the cold,
dark streets and get involved with people they don't know.
His friends in the tavern (who can represent both other people, who constantly reinforce our consensus state of consciousness, and the existing internal structures in our heads
that carry the consensus reality within them) have similarly
been warned about such encounters, and want to keep our
percipient in the tavern. Or our would-be percipient may
have fantastic ideas about Wise Men from the East waiting in
the street, who are going to shower him with fantastic psychic gifts. He wants to run out into the street shouting "Here
I am, you found me, I'm wonderful, give it all to me,
now!," but this is not very adaptive behavior for accurately
hearing a whispered conversation either.

This three-ring circus of the mind ordinarily constitutes the bulk or often the totality of our experiential field.
Given this incredibly noisy background for listening for the
"still small voice" of psi, let us now model the psi processes,
as I understand it.

Overview of the Psi Process

A series of psychological functions, which I shall call
sensing, evaluation, and decision-making systems--the functions which allow us to detect various kinds of inputs, evaluate their meaning, and decide on some kind of decision--is
central. This is where we find conscious awareness. The
most prominent input to the sensing, evaluation, decision-
making systems, however, is the constant ongoing noise discussed above, irrelevant thoughts, feelings, strategies for
gratification and fantasies, and our cognitive, emotional and

bodily attachments (resistances to altering or giving up) to these things that constitute so much of our consensus consciousness.

The overall process begins with the target about which we wish to obtain information via psi. I assume that this information is continuously available from the target, "passes" through some currently unknown sort of channel, and arrives at whatever process or mechanism functions as a psi-receptor, which converts whatever form psi information in the environment takes into the appropriate mental or neural transforms within the percipient.

I have mentioned noise being carried over a psi channel: noise is any kind of psi information which, given the percipient's task to identify a specific target, is irrelevant to or interferes with this. Further characteristics of psi noise, including whether it is random or introduces systematic bias, have been discussed elsewhere. We shall not consider aspects of the target or the channel further in this paper, but simply assume that psi information about targets is continuously available.

Intermittency

Whatever the nature of psi-receptor (or receptors) may be, it probably operates only intermittently in the vast majority of cases. More precisely, percipients respond in ways that manifest psi only intermittently, and while the intermittency might occur in a process that may be labeled "psi-specific information processing," or in further unconscious processes, in this modeling we shall assume intermittency occurs independently in the psi-receptor, in psi-specific information processing, and in relevant unconscious processes.

Looking at this another way, most percipients are simply guessing most of the time, i.e., whatever determines their particular calls of the target, there is no psi-relevant information detectibly influencing it. I shall discuss guessing in detail below. Sometimes a percipient may be "hot," i.e., he may make a long run of psi-related responses. Considerable "psi-bursting" of this sort is apparent in data collected in my laboratory on learning to use psi, and will be treated in future publications.

Information Flow Routes

The psi information may sometimes proceed directly from the psi-receptor into awareness (as associated with the sensing, evaluation, decision-making systems). Insofar as the process of psi reception may not have been very selective up to this point, i.e., there may be a lot of information coming in by psi other than that pertaining to the desired target, this direct information output from the psi-receptor may be only partially useful: it contains irrelevant as well as relevant information. The percipient may or may not be able to discriminate the relevant aspects of this by means of the ordinary kinds of psychological functions available in the sensing, evaluation, and decision-making systems.

An alternative route of psi information flow, perhaps operating instead of or sometimes simultaneously with the previous one, is from the psi-receptor to psi-specific information processing. These are postulated mechanisms not used in sensory information processing, but which work specifically with psi information. Their function is to enhance the detectability or discriminatability of the relevant target information. Their internal functioning is ordinarily not accessible to awareness. An example of such a mechanism (resulting in psi missing of immediately past and future targets), is one I have termed "trans-temporal inhibition," which is analogous to lateral inhibition in ordinary sensory systems, whereby (irrelevant) background activity of receptors laterally adjacent to the stimulated one is actively inhibited in order to sharpen perception. The output of such psi-specific information processing is shown as going into the sensing, evaluation, decision-making systems, where it may receive further processing that we can be consciously aware of.

We also know that psi information often undergoes processing by those aspects of the human mind we call the unconscious, those inferred, but not directly accessible to ordinary consciousness aspects of personality which show dynamic qualities of emotional significance to the percipient. I have shown psi information going from psi-specific information processing into unconscious processes, and the output of the unconscious transformations of the information being presented to awareness in the sensing, evaluation, decision-making systems. Psi information passing through unconscious processes is more likely to undergo transformations or distortions which fit in with a particular percipient's individual needs than information which comes directly from

the psi-receptor or the psi-specific information processing
mechanisms.

Operating Signals

In addition to the psi information that is about the
identity of the relevant target, I have shown what I call an
"operating signal" going from the psi-receptor, psi-specific
information processing, and unconscious processes into
awareness, into the sensing, evaluation, and decision-making
systems. By operating signal I mean a quality or pattern
of qualities (which may vary over time) that does not convey
target identity information itself but merely serves to indicate that a particular mechanism is operating. This might
manifest itself as, for instance, a feeling of confidence, or
a feeling of "energy" in a particular part of the body, or a
particular quality of imagery or mental functioning that is
distinctive from ordinary functioning. When one or more
such operating signals are present in the experiential field,
they can be used as an indicator that other contents of the
experiential field which seem target-relevant may indeed be
influenced by psi information or be psi information. Such
operating signals are the basis for successful confidence
calls.

The psi-receptor, psi-specific information processing,
or unconscious processes systems may each have only one
signal associated with its operation, or a combination of
operating signals. If more than one operating signal is perceived simultaneously in the experiential field, a percipient
could be even more certain that psi-related information was
also present. If there are always operating signals created
by one or more of these mechanisms or processes operating
(even if it takes a lot of training to detect them in the experiential field), then, in theory, a percipient could learn to
use psi whenever the relevant mechanisms were operating.
Then the ultimate level of psi functioning would be determined by the proportion of the time we could learn to stimulate these mechanisms to operate (the control strategies,
discussed below). If operating signals are only intermittently or unreliably associated with the operation of these
mechanisms, or are not strong compared to the noise level
in the percipient's mind, that could create an inherent limit
on the maximum level of psi functioning.

Control Strategies

I have also shown a "control signal" going from the

percipient's sensing, evaluation, and decision-making processes to each of the three lower processes. In one or
more ways, we deliberately attempt to make these necessary
processes operate. Such control signals may take the
vaguest form of simply hoping that psi will occur, or they
may involve an elaborate behavioral or mental ritual on the
percipient's part that he hopes will make psi manifest. The
provision of immediate feedback ought not only to allow a
percipient to determine what sort of operating signals he
should use as a basis for response decisions, but also to
determine what sorts of control strategies reliably yield
relevant psi information. A percipient might for example believe that "not trying" might facilitate psi: feedback training
will allow him to compare that strategy with a more active
one.

This is a basic model of psi-relevant information making its way into awareness, where it can be detected and
evaluated so the percipient can decide how to respond. The
percipient should also try to control and inhibit the irrelevant thoughts, feelings, strategies, fantasies and attachments
which, as noise, flood the sensing, evaluation, decision-making systems and impair their efficiency. Note also that
sensory input that comes into awareness constitutes noise,
since, by experimental specification, any sensory input must
be irrelevant to the task of detecting the target by psi.
Such noise reduction seems to partially underly success with
Ganzfeld techniques. One exception to this is the specific
sensory input, controlled by the overt response of the percipient, that brings in feedback information. Finally, storing strategies in memory, and drawing such past memories
back into awareness, is extremely important, as we shall
see when we consider the specific trial by trial process of
learning to use psi.

Learning to Use Psi: The First Trial

Assume our percipient is given some multiple-choice-
type psi test to work with, such as trying to guess which of
ten unlit lamps on a panel in front of him has been randomly selected as a target. His task is to push a button beside the lamp which he thinks has been selected as the target for this first trial, and the machinery is wired in such
a fashion that he receives immediate feedback. The correct
target lamp comes on as soon as he makes his response.
He will know instantly if he was right or wrong and, if
wrong, in exactly what way he was wrong, such as displacing
quite close to the correct target.

On this very first trial, the percipient must consciously or semi-consciously decide on some kind of strategy
for coming up with a response.   This strategy may be a
relatively articulated, conscious strategy, or a relatively
non-conscious strategy.   He might, for example, decide to
wait for a visual image of the correct target number to appear, or he might try to instruct some non-conscious part
of his mind to deliberately make an especially vivid image
appear.   He might decide to run his fingers around the
circle of lamps to see if there is any kind of "feel" to the
correct one, or he might try to think about how the random
target selection process might work and what it might likely
determine as a target, or he might call on his memories for
ideas he has about what sorts of numbers generally "come
up first."

The Guessing Process

An important input to (or aspect of) the sensing, evaluation, decision-making systems is what I shall call the
guessing process.   The percipient sits down at his psi task
and is asked to produce a long series of responses in the
absence of sensory information about the target identities.
While we would like him to use psi, we can hardly expect
him to do so on every trial, so part (usually most) of the
time the percipient is under pressure just to guess: it is
generally not socially acceptable in the experimental situation for a percipient to sit for long periods of time and give
no responses at all!

The percipient, consciously or semi-consciously,
starts a relatively mechanical and irrelevant process going
in his mind that continually throws up mental calls, the
digits one through ten in our particular case.   In the absence of a target identity that comes along in some obviously
novel way (such as a vivid visual image), or is associated
with a discriminable experiential quality that might be an
operating signal, the percipient can always respond with
whatever call the guessing process is throwing out at a particular time.

The guessing process is not, however, a good random
number generator in a statistical sense.   It is usually a
very biased source.   Even though we almost always have
our actual targets generated in such a way that each is equally probable and each target is independent of the previous
targets, the percipient's guessing process will probably have

definite biases that over-generate some calls and under-generate others, as well as definite sequential dependencies. An example of the latter is the well-known habit of not generating enough XX doublets, repeating the same call twice in a row, when people are asked to generate random numbers. This non-randomicity of call generation by percipients can be turned into an advantage, however, as it offers a possibility of separating responses produced by the guessing process from responses produced as a result of other mental processes. The psychological literature on response bias should be of value here.

    Cognitive/emotional/habitual attachment to the output of the guessing process is a major obstacle to using and learning psi. Suppose a percipient has guessed a nine on the previous trial, and he has a very strong habit of guessing a one after a nine. Now his task is to attend to his experiential field for any contents that might be psi related, but the psychological pressure to respond with a one is strong, and can keep him from adequately attending to his experiential field.

    In a situation where we have immediate feedback, another problem created by the guessing process occurs. The guessing process is probably not "free-running" in most percipients, i.e., uninfluenced by knowledge about previous targets, but is to varying degrees influenced by such knowledge. Although we design our target randomizing process to have serial independence, and although we may inform our percipients of this, many percipients (consciously or non-consciously) spend some time trying to "figure out the random number generator," i.e., they keep track of what past targets have been and modify guessing accordingly. A percipient is likely to strongly believe, e.g., that XX target doublets are extremely unlikely. Thus if a 5 has been the previous target, the percipient may modify his guessing process so he will guess almost any number but a 5. If the current target is again a 5, however, this guessing strategy will again make it very difficult for the percipient to pick up any psi-related aspects of his experiential field that could inform him that the target is a 5: he has too strong a bias against it.

    Elsewhere I have shown how a measure of this kind of maladaptive guessing process, which I call strategy boundness, is indeed significantly and negatively related to present-time hitting, trans-temporal inhibition, and short-term learning.

Note that the number of alternatives in a guessing task will have some effect on how much a percipient is bound by maladaptive guessing processes. If there are only a few choices, say four targets, it is relatively easy and thus more tempting to try to keep track of what targets have occurred on previous trials and so try to "figure out the random number generator." If there are many choices, as in our ten-choice task, keeping track is more formidable and so less tempting, and is less likely to be engaged in for long. This is one reason I think a ten-choice training task was superior to a four-choice training task for eliciting psi in my first major study of learning. The extreme of this dimension is a free-response GESP task, where the well nigh infinite number of possible alternatives on every trial discourages guessing processes based on "figuring out" the random generator or keeping track of previous trials. This may be an important reason for the high level of success often found with free-response psi tests. Braud and Wood (in press) have found that feedback training increases success in a free-response Ganzfeld study.

Ideally, our percipient should never initiate these sorts of maladaptive guessing processes, but only pay attention to his experiential field on each trial and make a deliberate, conscious "estimate" of what the target may be. But, since I assume that the psi-receptor and other relevant information processing mechanisms that pass the information into awareness may not be functioning at all on many trials, the percipient's "estimate" is then based only on noise, so he will likely use a simple guessing process. If he can inhibit the guessing process on trials when his experiential field may contain psi-relevant information, that is fine, but the compulsion of guessing processes, discussed above, can make this difficult.

The provision of a pass option on any psi training device is probably helpful here, as the percipient can just pass when he feels he has no real cues to the target. I have not yet investigated the usefulness of the pass option empirically.

Deciding on a Response

Whatever strategy he consciously or semi-consciously uses, the percipient finally gets some kind of output from it that he attends to, senses, and then is led by to decide to make a particular response.

Our percipient has (irrelevant) guessing strategies affecting him.   He has all sorts of experiences that, given
our psi task, are noise affecting him, including the com-
pelling, constant thinking and fantasizing along consensus
reality lines discussed earlier.   Some of this activity is
random noise, simply distraction from the task at hand, but
some of it may amount to systematic noise that biases him
away from successfully using psi.   Our percipient may also
have to deal with external noise from sensory input in terms
of the effects of the experimental situation, including experimenter biases.   Hopefully, on this first trial the psi-receptor and subsequent, relevant information processing mechanisms are also functioning and producing operating signals as
well as the psi information.   For the reasons discussed
above, it may be a "still small voice" that is totally drowned
out in the internal mental noise.   But it might be heard, and
might have some specific sorts of experiential qualities, operating signals, associated with it.

Our percipient may try to sort out and categorize
this mass of ongoing experience and base his overt response
on some quality (or pattern of qualities) of it that he hopes
is relevant.   Or he may try to ignore most or all of his
experiential field and try to produce some form of control
signal, engage in some sort of mental strategy, that he hopes
will make the target-relevant information clearly appear in
his experiential field.   He may combine these two strategies.
He finally makes a decision and pushes a particular response
button.   Immediately the correct target is indicated and so
he has feedback as to the correctness and usefulness of his
first strategy.   In order to consciously learn to use psi, he
must attend to both this feedback information about correctness and to his immediately available memories of how he
went about making this particular decision.   He is still being
subjected, in most cases, to considerable noise of the sort
discussed above at this time.

Making Use of the Feedback

If the percipient wishes to profit from receiving feedback, he must now somehow categorize in partial detail, or
remember in full detail, what his response strategy was on
this first trial and what the outcome of it was in terms of
success or (various degrees of) failure and store this information in his memory.   This can become a highly complex
process.

Ideally, the percipient should store all data about his experience at the time of making a decision as to what his response should be, and he should store all feedback information, whether he was right or wrong and exactly how he was right or wrong, to take partial successes, such as close spatial displacement, into account. In reality, most percipients in our culture have had very little practice with and have seldom been rewarded for paying such close attention to internal processes, so our percipient may not have had very good awareness of his own processes that led to his response. He may, to varying degrees, simplify the details and overall Gestalt of his experience into just one or a few concepts that he stores, such as "Had a visual image of the correct target and feet felt warm, I was successful." The conceptualization process, then, might have included relevant information about operating signals or control strategies for learning to use psi and will probably also have included some of the noise, the irrelevant information that occurred either during the response process or the evaluation of the outcome.

For simplicity I've assumed above that this was the first time our percipient had ever attempted to make any psi response, so we did not have to consider any past experience of this task. Let us also assume he is successful in calling the target on this first trial.

The Second Trial

As we consider internal psychological processes on the percipient's second and subsequent trials, past experience becomes quite important. He may have a deliberate response strategy as before: it may be the same response strategy he used on the first trial or he may decide to use a different one. Or he may just guess. Noise, irrelevant information is again present, although it may not have the same configuration as before. He might have been distracted by, or worrying about, an impending examination on the first trial, but as a result of the feedback he recognized that the previous target number was exactly the same as the number of dollars he owes to a friend, so now he is (semiconsciously) worrying about his inability to pay back the money today as he promised. Psi information may or may not actually be reaching awareness on this second trial: we cannot assume that the aspects of the mind which receive the psi information work on every trial, so on some trials there is nothing but noise to work with. For simplicity, we

will assume the psi-receptor and psi-specific information processing are working on this trial.

    To make his decision on trial two, our percipient
must again try to separate the psi signal from the noise.
That is, he must try to attend to and discriminate the psi
signal and any identifying experiential characteristics it might
have (i.e., operating signals) from all his other ongoing experiences. As a new and important part of this, he may
consult his memory as to what he did on the previous trial
and the consequences of it. If his experience is somewhat
similar he might repeat that previously successful strategy,
or he might feel that his momentary constellation of experiences has changed in a way that makes the previous strategy
irrelevant. However he does it, he makes a decision as to
how to respond, makes an overt response, and again must
attend to his decision-making processes, his response, and
the consequences of this in terms of feedback as to correctness or incorrectness. He must also evaluate how well
whatever strategy he used seemed to work this time. Insofar as he used the previous strategy that was stored in memory, he must re-evaluate how well that previously successful
strategy worked when it was applied in this second trial.
Again, he would ideally store all of the experiential information about this trial (possible operating signals and control
strategies) and the previous one, but in practice he will
probably store only parts of the information available to him.

Later Trials

    Let us now skip ahead some number of trials, say a
couple of dozen, and look at the internal psychological processes now on trial N. This is like trial 2 except that the
information which is now available to be consulted from memory is far more complex than it was earlier. Results (ab-
stracted and schematized to varying degrees) of a variety of
potential operating signals and control strategies and their
successful and unsuccessful outcomes are stored (with varying degrees of fidelity) in memory. Some of these, if our
percipient has been relatively successful, are relevant to the
genuine use of psi ability. Some of them may seem relevant,
but, as they were involved with chance-induced successes,
are actually a confusing form of noise.

    To make his response now, our percipient must try
to ignore (or try to lower) the irrelevant noise that is stead-
ily going on in his mind and use an optimal response strategy

to identify the signal which might come from the psi aspects of his mind.   If he has been fairly successful up to now, he may continue to repeat whatever strategy he has used before. If he has not been very successful, he may wish to use his memory of previous strategies in a negative way to deliberately try to devise some entirely different strategy.   If he has been fairly or partially successful, he may still want to try modifying some previous successful strategem, or he may decide to stick with one of them, even if it's only partially successful.   To illustrate, he might wish to try a sort of motor automatism for responding instead of waiting for some kind of inner visual image to appear.

He finally makes an overt response for trial N and receives immediate feedback.   He must again attend to this information in order to store the consequences in memory, but by this time, there is already so much information stored in memory, and so much more information is going to come along to be stored, that he must, consciously or semi-consciously, start working out strategies to store information more efficiently.   He simply can't carry everything in memory.   How useful these simplifying schemes will be is an important question: he may work out an esthetically satisfying scheme, but it may not encode the really relevant portions of his experience.   His long-term results with the immediate feedback should enable him to eventually evaluate his mnemonic strategies, assuming he has not become too confused or given up by this time, or become rigidly attached to non-adaptive response or mnemonic strategies.

The Importance of Memory

This need to store a great deal of information in memory in a useful form is an exceptionally important part of the learning process, and should eventually be the subject of much research.   Given that we can only remember so much, we not only need to work up an abstracting system for our experiences in order to put simpler information in memory, but the percipient may need to figure out what kind of information he can stop storing in memory, or what kind of information already stored in memory he can deliberately forget.   He might make decisions, for example, to try to clearly remember only trials on which he was successful and ignore the ones on which he failed.   Perhaps another percipient might decide that some of the trials on which he failed were as or more instructive than some of those on which he succeeded.   A great deal of internal experimentation

must go on over the course of training for a given percipient to work out a memory strategy that is optimal for him;
individual differences are important here, but immediate
feedback should allow any individual percipient to learn what
does and doesn't work for him.

Any factors which interfere with the efficient use of
memory input, organization, or retrieval are detrimental to
learning to use psi more effectively. The sheer load on
memory is per se detrimental, so we would expect to see
learning over relatively short, psychologically homogeneous
periods, such as a single run. Such learning would usually
fall off over a longer period, as memory becomes over-
loaded. Any distraction or interruption could be detrimental.
Certainly the time intervals between training sessions would
be detrimental, especially in the early stages of learning,
when it would be difficult to hold a subtle, poorly-learned
memory strategy over that time and insulate it from other
psychological processes and real-world events which might
disrupt or confuse it. As adaptive psi strategies become
more consolidated, of course, they should be better able to
withstand the disruptions between sessions, so there should
eventually be an overall increase from session to session,
as well as within sessions.

A promising line of research to help percipients learn
psi will center around techniques for helping them to clarify,
organize, and retain their memories.

Immediacy of Feedback

The importance of storing multiple aspects of the experiential field in memory in order to devise discriminative
and response strategies, as well as storing these strategies,
is the reason why immediate feedback is so important. The
longer the interval between the various internal events that
are scanned and the feedback about success or lack of it,
the greater the opportunity for relevant aspects of memory
to lose sharpness or for intervening events (external or internal) to interfere with and confuse these memories. A
particular source of intervening events that can be highly
confusing if feedback is at all delayed is that of memories
of previous experiential scans and/or operating strategies
which become confused with the current memory. If psi-
associated operating signals were very clear to begin with,
they could be stored in memory in a distinctive fashion that
was resistant to interference, but, especially in the be-

ginning of training, the operating signals and other psi-asso-
ciated cues may be quite amorphous and subtle. Ideally, a
percipient would "stop" his mental activity between his last
scan of his experiential field and the feedback, so there was
no intervening, potentially interfering activity. In such an
ideal case feedback could be considerably delayed. In most
cases, however, feedback should be given as rapidly as possible, and electronic devices make it possible for feedback
to be (in terms of human time) instantaneous.

Wholistic Processes

I have talked about the process of storing relevant
information and evaluation/response strategies in a linear,
sequential kind of way, as that is the style I am most familiar with, but I should note that we are not just linear, sequential beings but also wholistic, pattern-sensing beings.
We engage in the kind of sensing and thinking now popularly
associated with research on right-hemisphere functions of the
brain, and we will eventually have to deal with these more
wholistic pattern kinds of sensing, storing, evaluating, and
responding.

Successful Psi Performance

Assuming a percipient whose psi-receptor and relevant information processing mechanisms bring him psi information a fair amount of the time, and that there are experiential qualities associated with the operation of these
parts of the mind, operating signals, that can be eventually
discriminated, we can see now how conscious use of psi
must be learned. Over a number of trials with immediate
feedback, the percipient must gradually build up a set of
conceptualizations about generation of control strategies and
discrimination of operating signals, leading to various response strategies, that he stores in memory. On any given
trial he must then compare the components and pattern of
his ongoing experience at that time with his conceptualizations
of discrimination and control strategies, and make one of
several kinds of decisions. One decision might be that the
idea he has of the correct target is associated with experiential qualities that have been frequently associated with success in the past, so he should respond with this particular
idea of the target. A second decision might be that the experienced conditions of the moment have been routinely associated with failure, so he should not make any response at
the moment, but either wait for a new impression to arise

that might be associated with experiential qualities associated
with success, or perhaps deliberately try to alter his momentary mental state into one associated with success.

Altering Strategies

These are not the only kinds of decisions a talented
percipient might have to make. He might, for example,
have worked out a strategy that produces a fair degree of
psi success, but continued repetition of that strategy does
not produce any further improvement in performance. Now
our percipient must decide: Should I stick with this safe
strategy that does produce results, or should I try modifying it or perhaps discarding it altogether, and experiment
with new strategies that might lead to a higher level of performance? If he does decide to experiment, this may mean
a percipient who has been responding at a high, successful,
rather steady rate may suddenly drop back to chance-level
performance (or even psi-missing). We would see great
variability in his performance as these new strategies are
tried out.

Although I have not yet had a chance to review the
relevant literature in detail, there is a clear parallel here
with some of the findings in biofeedback research. A subject is asked to try to gain voluntary control over some
bodily function for which he has no clear experiential representation (at the beginning). By means of immediate feedback, through appropriate instrumentation, he learns what
value that bodily function takes from moment-to-moment,
and then must try to search within his (noisy) experiential
field for particular cues (operating signals) which are associated with manipulations (control signals) that are successful in effecting that bodily function. For some tasks, such
as modifying brain waves, subjects frequently find a strategy
which gives them some degree of success, but after sticking
with that strategy for a while, they find they simply can't
go very far with it, and so must abandon it in order to try
new strategies. Thus performance curves in biofeedback
frequently show runs with increasing levels of success, leading to stable performance, and then a sudden loss of success
and great variability for subsequent runs.

Stabilization of Psi Skill

Although one of my main interests in teaching psi
ability is in pushing such learning as high as it can go, it

is important to recognize that people like success and dis-
like chancing failure. When they have found something that
is successful to a satisfying degree, they are often very
hesitant to risk tampering with the successful strategy in
order to try something else. I would expect that as we
study the process of learning with immediate feedback more
extensively we shall find a fair number of percipients who
hit upon some reasonably successful strategy and stabilize
at fairly high levels of psi performance, but who, for various reasons, will not seriously risk tampering with that
strategy in order to try something that might (but might not)
be more successful.

If this strategy has included learning to discriminate
against some experiential cues that indicate the psi process
is working and these experiential cues are experientially
clear, or if he has found a clearly successful control strategy, such a percipient might be able to maintain his level
of psi performance without further immediate feedback training, or with only occasional refresher training. My understanding of the mental processes of some successful psychics
reinforces this view. They originally learned some sort of
special psi ability under naturalistic conditions that seem to
have involved some degree of feedback, they learned to identify some cues (a special state of consciousness, a certain
kind of bodily quality, etc.) that indicated when they were
"hot," when they were using psi, or they learned a successful ritual, and they became attached enough to the rewards
resulting from this partially successful performance that they
simply do not tamper with it. They may actively resist attempts to explore the mechanisms of their success, their
belief systems, through fear of undermining their effectiveness. They are then able to keep this strategy psychologically isolated enough from other mental processes that it
does not get blurred by the noise of the rest of experience.

The functional isolation of a (partially) successful
strategy can thus be highly important. If the successful
strategy is not isolated, then other kinds of experiences will
be mixed with it, and it may become unclear just when the
proper cues are present to act on an impression that will
turn out to be based on psi. This can explain why many
psychics and many traditional rituals for evoking psychic
powers involve complex, but very stylized and rigid psychological processes. They are designed to produce a state of
mental isolation, as it were, around the particular psi functioning, to keep it from coming in touch with ordinary mental
processes that might confuse the issue.

An example of temporary stabilization of psi ability
in the course of immediate feedback training is provided by
Kanthamani and Kelly. Working with B.D., an exceptionally
talented percipient, they reported that his performance in a
single card clairvoyance test seemed to be superior when
immediate feedback of results was, at B.D.'s own request,
withheld. Specifically, for 86 trials in which immediate feedback was withheld, B.D. scored 11 exact (suit and number)
hits plus 8 number hits. These no-feedback trials were in-
termixed with the feedback ones. For 122 feedback trials,
he obtained only 5 exact hits and 13 number hits. A parallel
finding was reported in an earlier study with B.D. These
results are illustrative of how successful immediate feedback
learning of psi can be: after some feedback trials in which
B.D. learned to develop a good strategy, he would know that
he was "hot," i.e., he could apparently detect operating signals associated with high success and so would deliberately
request that feedback not be given on a forthcoming trial.
Perhaps he wanted time to internally consolidate his mental
state/response strategies without the distraction of processing
further feedback information, or needed the absence of distraction from feedback to encapsulate his successful states/
strategies from interference.

The Nature of Extinction

As a result of our discussion of learning, we can now
look in detail at a phenomenon we have been taking for
granted, extinction. In my original presentation of the learning theory application I used the term extinction in a be-
havioristic style, meaning by it a decrement in performance
with continued practice that leads to disappearance of the
response. A rat, for example, may have learned to press
a lever when a green light is on, and this resulted in an
immediate food pellet reward. We now change the situation
so pressing the lever when the green light is on no longer
activates the food dispenser. The rat still presses the lever
frequently at first, then slows down, and finally stops pressing it altogether. We say the rat's lever pressing behavior
has been extinguished.

We could just as well argue, however, that this extinction represents new learning: the rat gradually learns
that there is no point in pressing the lever. The response
contingencies have changed. The rat has not lost his ability
to lever press.

Suppose we have run a percipient through many psi trials without immediate feedback and find that his scores hold steady for a while and may sometimes be increased by upping his motivation, etc., but then gradually decline, until he is eventually scoring at chance expectation. Behavioristically this is extinction, but it is not the same phenomenon as with the rat, for the percipient seems to have lost his ability to use psi, even though we offer him inducements and rewards to manifest psi again. What has happened?

I suggest that the percipient had some native psi talent to begin with that was occasionally activated under the conditions of our experiment, but this ability had been functionally isolated from the rest of his mental processes, in the manner we discussed above. That is, his ordinary mental life seldom or never activated control strategies that might be (partially) successful in activating psi processes, and seldom brought much awareness to possible operating signals associated with psi functioning.

When we put the percipient in the psi experiment, however, even without feedback, his attention is repeatedly directed toward trying various kinds of control strategies and examining his experiential field, out of both a natural curiosity and the task demands of the experiment. Gradually this breaks down the functional isolation of his psi processes, but for lack of immediate feedback, there is no efficient way for the percipient to constructively control this breakdown of and tampering with subtle and delicate mental processes, nor to devise new and effective control strategies and sense new operating signals to replace his original mental processes for manifesting psi. We get extinction through a confusion procedure.

Depending on the degree of functional isolation of psi-relevant processes, the time for extinction will vary across individuals. In the extreme case of a percipient whose psi-relevant processes are very isolated, this can take a long time, especially if the percipient uses them in a relatively automatic, non-conscious way, rather than subjecting them to conscious scrutiny. In this respect it is interesting to note the trend that developed along with the widespread use of card-guessing tests to deliberately try to keep percipients from being "self-conscious," a strategy that unknowingly would help maintain the functional isolation of the psi processes. Few people have any mental process existing in total isolation from all others, however, so eventually just about every talented percipient we repeatedly worked with got so confused about the delicate processes involved in using psi that he lost his ability to use them.

Level of Psi Talent and Learning

In any repeated guessing task, the percipient is right a certain proportion of the time by chance alone. As discussed earlier, the occasions when a percipient is right by chance alone constitute a kind of systematic noise which will confuse him, so this constitutes an extinction procedure built right into any repeated guessing task even with the provision of immediate feedback. The ratio of psi-produced hits to chance-produced hits will determine the balance between learning and extinction processes. In the original presentation of the theory, I expressed this dilemma in two ways. One was the idea of a "talent threshold," above which learning would predominate over extinction. The second was as a prediction that the degree of learning manifested under conditions of immediate feedback would be positively correlated with the degree of psi talent the percipient brought into the training situation. Let us consider these ideas in more detail.

The kind of relationships I would predict for different categories of percipients depends on the level of psi talent a percipient brings to the training situation (not the level he develops as a result of the training) and on the measure of learning in the training, such as the slope of the performance curve over time. Two important assumptions occur here, namely, (a) that whatever processes in a given percipient lead to psi performance are not totally isolated from other mental processes, so he will actively investigate and experiment with them, and (b) that each percipient is not only reasonably motivated to learn psi but will stay reasonably motivated throughout the experiment. The second assumption thus restricts the following discussion to "short to moderate" length experiments that are not likely to lead to boredom and loss of motivation. "Short to moderate" needs to be determined empirically, although existing literature suggests it may run as high as ten thousand or more trials.

High Talent Percipients

Consider highly talented psi hitters as our first category--percipients who are above the postulated talent threshold.

These percipients show strongly and individually significant
psi hitting prior to starting training. The theory predicts
that the learning process will outweigh the inherent extinction due to chance-produced hits, so we would expect to see
these high levels of psi associated with significantly positive
measures of learning. While the relationship between psi
talent level and measures of learning might be linear for
part of the range for these highly talented percipients, it
may very well be that above some high talent level learning
becomes extremely rapid, and so their regression line would
flatten out.

Moderate Talent Percipients

A second category of percipients is moderately talented psi hitters. Immediate feedback should stabilize performance for these percipients, that is, eliminate significantly negative measures of learning and stabilize psi hitting at
a moderate level.

Low or No Psi Talent

In a third category are percipients with no manifest
individual psi talent at all and percipients who have only a
small degree of psi talent. Those with none would probably
show extinction; the preponderance of chance-produced hits
would make the extinction process predominate over the possibility of stabilizing due to the immediate feedback. The
longer the length of the experiment, the greater the likelihood of significantly negative learning measures for these
low talent percipients. The shorter the experiment, the
more this combined group will tend not to reach either significant psi scores or significant learning or decline measures. For the three categories considered so far, the "rich
get richer and the poor get poorer" with the "middle class"
holding its own!

Motivated Psi Missers

The fourth category is that of moderately talented
motivated psi missers who are, to varying degrees, statistically naive. These percipients have some conscious or
unconscious motivation to prove psi doesn't exist, and have
some psi talent operating in the service of this desire. For
the least statistically naive such percipients, we would expect
scores clustered around the origin, neither significant hitting
or missing nor significant positive or negative learning

measures. For more naive motivated psi missers, who interpreted significantly negative psi scoring as supporting their beliefs, and getting worse as further supporting their beliefs, we would see significantly negative hitting scores and significantly negative slopes.

Malfunctioning Psi Missers

A fifth category of percipients can be distinguished, namely moderately talented, malfunctioning psi missers who make use of the immediate feedback to correct their malfunctioning and thus improve their scoring. These percipients do not have any emotional or cognitive need to prove that psi is not real, so they can profit from the feedback to correct the malfunctioning of their psi-receptor, psi-specific information processing, or unconscious processes responsible for the distortion. Depending on the length of the experiment, their average psi level might be somewhat above, somewhat below, or even at chance, since the early psi missing can negate the later hitting. But they may have significantly positive measures of learning as a result of going from missing to hitting. For a given length experiment then, we might have percipients who showed no significant psi scores, but significant learning. In a longer experiment, they presumably might then go on to show significant psi hitting, assuming, as in all the above discussions, that they remained motivated.

There is a sixth category of percipients. These are highly talented, motivated psi missers. I would think that exceptionally strong psi missing by a percipient and/or obvious decrements in performance, when the percipient had consciously agreed to participate in a study designed to produce psi hitting and learning, would rapidly produce a conflict in the percipient. What the outcome of this conflict would do to psi performance is not clear.

It is clear that we would expect a roughly linear relationship between overall psi level brought into the training and our measure of learning. The high psi-talent hitters should contribute the most toward making this correlation significant, ignoring possible nonlinearity induced in very high ranges. The moderately talented, statistically naive, motivated psi missers, and the other low psi-talent percipients should also contribute toward bringing out a significant linear relationship. The percipients with no obvious individual psi and the moderate-talent psi hitters would tend to create a lot of variability and this will tend to obscure the relationship of psi-talent level with learning. This possible obscuration is particularly serious in a study which uses percipients whose range of psi talent is limited, although in studies using large numbers of such percipients, the relationship should still be statistically detectable.

Interaction of Other Factors with Talent Level

I want to stress again that the talent threshold is not an absolutely fixed entity. It is not the case that percipients with only a low psi level can never hope to do more than stabilize their performance. Having a high psi talent at the beginning of training will make learning much easier, but learning is affected by other things than just the frequency with which psi-related cues are present in the percipient's experiential field.

One psychological factor which is likely to be related is motivation. If a percipient is only mildly motivated to learn to improve his psi ability, he simply will not work hard at the demanding tasks of discriminating psi-related information, operating signals, successful control strategies, cutting down the noise from irrelevant mental processes, etc. A percipient who is strongly motivated to learn will work harder at this task and be able to compensate for a lower psi-talent level. We should be aware of possible non-linearities here. Too strong a motivation, too strong an attachment to success, might introduce psychological difficulties of a different sort that would detract from the learning process.

A second psychological factor which will also probably be related to ability to learn improved psi functioning is general learning ability. We have psychological measures of general learning ability, but probably need more specific measures of such as (a) the ability to inhibit extraneous internal noise, quiet one's own mind; (b) the ability to ignore sensory input which might be distracting; (c) the ability to organize one's memory efficiently while building up a catalog of successful strategies; and (d) the ability to introspect and make fine discriminations among aspects of the experiential field. Other psychological factors will also probably turn out to be relevant. In initial research our prime goal will usually be training a few percipients to show very high, reliable levels of psi, so other aspects of the nature of psi

may be investigated. As a practical measure, we shall want
to confine our training efforts to moderate and high psi-talent
learners with high motivation, and make all experimental
conditions, such as positive encouragement from the experimenter, as supportive as possible.

Miscellaneous Considerations

Immediate Feedback as a Reinforcer. In the psychological literature on learning, the term "immediate reinforcement" is frequently associated with the term "immediate
feedback," and while they mean quite different things, it becomes easy to confuse the two. Immediate feedback, as discussed in this paper and my earlier writings on the application of learning theory to psi performance, is conceived as
purely informational feedback to the percipient which he may
make use of to modify his internal strategies which are relevant to manifesting and learning improved psi performance.
This assumes, of course, that the percipient wants to learn
to improve his psi abilities. If he is unmotivated to improve
his psi ability, he will probably pay little attention to the informational feedback and show very little profit from it.

Reinforcement refers to a process designed to elicit
or strengthen motivation to perform on a task. If a hungry
rat must learn to press two levers in a particular sequence
in order for a dispenser to drop a food pellet, the appearance of the food pellet is not only informational feedback, it
is also reinforcement, it satisfies the rat's hunger need and
so strengthens its motivation to perform the lever task
properly. A similar thing may happen with the provision of
immediate feedback for psi training. The feedback that the
percipient is correct, may, in addition to its informational
function, serve cognitively and emotionally to reward the
percipient for attempting to learn to use his psi abilities
more effectively, and reinforce his longer-term motivation
to continue trying to do so. Thus immediate feedback can
also constitute immediate reward or immediate reinforcement, to varying degrees, for some percipients.

There is clearly room for great variability here. If
a percipient is already highly motivated to learn to use his
psi better when he begins the training procedure, the reinforcement aspect of the feedback will be relatively negligible.
If his existing motivation is low, or if his motivation tends
to disappear rapidly and needs repeated encouragement from
the feedback of being correct, then the reinforcement aspect
of the feedback is much more important.

This reinforcement aspect of immediate feedback creates an important factor which should be explored empirically as well as theoretically. One aspect of it is the optimal number of choices to be used in a repeated guessing task. In my own research to date, my multiple-step selection procedures have pretty well insured that only highly motivated percipients made it into the training studies, so I believe the reinforcement aspects of the feedback were not too important there. Based on the cognitive considerations discussed earlier, as well as results to date, I also believe a large number of choices is more effective in training psi as it keeps the noise level down. The proportion of times you are right by chance alone is low in, for instance, a ten-choice task. At the other extreme, a binary guessing task, the percipient would be right for psi-irrelevant reasons 50 per cent of the time, and I think this would be very confusing.

For a percipient who had low motivation to begin with, or whose motivation needed to be strengthened frequently, a smaller number of choices in the repeated guessing task might lead to better results by keeping motivation up. For any individual percipient, there might be an optimal number of choices for getting the best balance between strengthening motivation versus minimizing confusion due to chance-induced hits. This factor needs empirical exploration. My guess at the present time is that the confusion induced by many chance-induced hits will be a much bigger detrimental factor than the strengthening of motivation produced by increasing the reinforcement ratio, and I would prefer to use other means, such as (genuine) encouragement from the experimenter, to keep motivation up in those percipients who need such assistance. Also, if each percipient can choose the number of target choices for his training task, after some experience with different numbers, he might select the best balance on his own.

Psi-Conducive Procedures. Over decades of research we have discovered a number of general procedures which are generally (i.e., over groups of percipients) conducive to better psi manifestation. These include such procedures as physical relaxation, friendly and relaxed experimenter-percipient relationships, reduced attention to sensory stimuli, hypnosis, Ganzfeld procedures, White's "waiting technique," game-like procedures, and a "don't try, just let it happen" attitude. While my theoretical approach is aiming toward deliberate, conscious control of psi, it is not contradictory to any of the above procedures, but complementary.

The point of providing immediate feedback of results
is that a unique, individual percipient can find out what does
and doesn't work for him.   While all of the above sorts of
procedures may be helpful to some percipients, none are
helpful to all.   Immediate feedback training gives each percipient the opportunity to try one or several of these strategies, or strategies unique to himself, and develop or dis-
card it on the basis of actual results.

In research to date I have generally allowed individual
percipients to originate strategies and try them out, but it
would also be worthwhile to obtain descriptions of mental processes and strategies from the more successful percipients
and then deliberately inform new percipients of these, so
they can try out more strategies than they might think of on
their own.

I would guess that a combination of hypnosis, for
quieting the noise of ordinary consciousness and producing
increased attention to the experiential field, combined with
White's "waiting technique," would be particularly fruitful
additions to immediate feedback training.

Momentary vs. Longer-Term Operating Signals.   I
have discussed operating signals that indicate that a useful
psi-reception and/or information processing mechanism is
working on a particular trial, in order to emphasize that the
operation of these processes is intermittent and can vary
rapidly.   Both the experience of talented percipients and the
fact that we often see fairly long bursts of psi functioning
should remind us, however, that the appropriate processes
can function for relatively long periods.   We may see total
success on several (two to a dozen, sometimes) consecutive
trials, or a high (albeit not 100 per cent) level of success
for even longer periods.   We can take these to represent
the temporary existence of a "psi-conducive state," a constellation of psychological processes in the percipient that
is relatively stable over a period of time, a period that is
long compared with the length of the individual trial.

We may have operating signals (qualities of the state)
that indicate the presence of a psi-conducive state, rather
than the momentary functioning of relevant psi information
gathering and processing mechanisms per se.   Immediate
feedback training thus might allow some percipients to learn
to recognize when they were in a psi-conducive state and respond rapidly, as opposed to not being in such a state and
waiting for one to appear or trying to induce it.

Experimental Situation and Experimenter Effects. It is important to recognize that a percipient neither manifests nor tries to learn to use psi more effectively in a vacuum. He works in a particular experimental/social situation, set up by a particular experimenter or experimenters. As White aptly put it, "... it is difficult to see how the experimental situation can be separated from the experimenter, for in a sense it can be viewed as a trap which the experimenter has devised with the intention of catching a particular finding which will fulfill his hopes and expectations." Experimenter and situational influence can reach the percipient through sensory input, or as a kind of systematic noise conveyed by psi. Conditions that increase the likelihood of psi manifestation in the first place are generally likely to increase the likelihood of learning improved psi performance.

While particular effects of the situation and experimenter bias on possible learning could be discussed at length, I want to emphasize only one thing here. Given that learning to use psi, as modeled above, is a subtle and difficult process, it is rather easy to interfere with it. Until our understanding of the learning process is much better, I think the experimenter should give all possible support to the percipients.

Predictions

By way of summary, listed here are the main predictions resulting from my application of learning theory to psi (specifically those predictions dealing with: adequately motivated percipients who have a fair to high degree of psi talent at the start of immediate feedback training, and who train for short to moderate periods):

(1) The vast majority of such percipients will show relatively stable psi performance, neither significantly inclining nor declining.

(2) Some percipients will show significant learning.

(3) The degree of improvement of psi performance will be positively correlated with the psi talent level at the start of training.

These are the three predictions from the original presentation of the theory. Given the great importance of memory processes in building up adaptive response strategies:

(4) The early stages of training will be characterized by learning over short, homogeneous time periods, such as the run, with decrements associated with interruptions of training such as breaks between runs or sessions, interpolated activities that interfere with memory consolidation, and the like.

(5) Sufficient training in the more talented percipients should allow learning to occur over longer time periods.

Since the percipient must be manifesting psi at least occasionally for the feedback to have something to operate on, we generally predict that:

(6) Procedures and factors which have generally been found to be psi-conducive will generally facilitate learning.

More specifically,

(7) The following factors will be positively correlated with improved psi performance: (a) high (but not excessive) motivation; (b) high general learning ability; (c) absence of specific conscious or (inferred) unconscious resistances to psi; (d) good ability to discriminate contents of the experiential field; (e) good ability to separate experience-as-perceived from experience-as-interpreted; (f) good memory skills; (g) ability to quiet one's mind; (h) non-attachment, ability to drop strategies that are not adaptive in spite of emotional investment in them; (i) low levels of maladaptive strategy boundness, in the specific sense of not guessing what has just come up as the previous target; and (j) ability to ignore sensory distractions.

In conclusion, it is well to remind ourselves of a prime problem of parapsychology: we want to study the nature of psi, but it usually works so unreliably and at such low levels that productive study of its nature is very difficult. The results obtained to date with immediate feedback training strongly suggest that it is a valuable tool such that we can train reliable, high-level psi performance in many percipients, and so open a door to productive studies of the nature of psi. I hope others will join me in further elucidating the nature of this promising tool.

ALLOBIOFEEDBACK: IMMEDIATE FEEDBACK
FOR A PSYCHOKINETIC INFLUENCE
UPON ANOTHER PERSON'S PHYSIOLOGY

William Braud (Mind Science Foundation)

In a typical biofeedback experiment, some aspect of
an individual's physiological activity is detected, amplified,
then transduced into an easily recognized exteroceptive signal, usually a light or a tone. Such immediate, sensory-
augmented feedback allows the individual to become aware of
the activity being monitored and bring it under control. The
procedure might be termed "autobiofeedback," since an individual receives feedback about and attempts to influence
his own physiological activity. There is another feedback
possibility, however, and this possibility suggests an interesting design with which to explore psychokinetic (PK) influences upon living target systems. In this new procedure,
some aspect of the physiological activity of Person A is
monitored, but feedback for changes in this activity is provided not to Person A but to another person, Person B, who
is attempting psychokinetically to influence Person A's physiological functioning. We suggest the term "allobiofeedback"
to describe this variation (allos is the Greek word for other)
since someone receives feedback about and attempts to influence another's physiology. The procedure may be quite
useful in that the "agent" who is attempting psychokinesis receives instantaneous analog feedback for his successes and
failures. Tart has made a case for the importance of immediate feedback in psi experiments.

Related experiments may be found in the experimental
parapsychological literature. Schmeidler provided analog
feedback to her subjects in a successful study of PK on in-
animate targets (thermistors). Two experiments have been
published in which subjects attempted to psychically influence
the movements of another person. Vasiliev reported successful attempts to induce muscular sway (recorded kymo-
graphically) at a distance. Dean reported successful attempts to influence the direction of eye movements (recorded
electrophysiologically) in dreaming "target persons." In
neither of these two studies was feedback provided while the
influence was being attempted. The experiments which are
most comparable to the ones to be described in this paper
were performed by Brier. Brier's subjects were successful
in influencing the bio-electrical activity recorded from the

leaves of plants. In a pilot experiment and in five confirmatory series, the subjects did not watch the polygraph readout of the plant's activity and thus did not receive feedback. In some preliminary tests, the subjects appear to have had feedback since they were "seated in front of the polygraph."

In the present experiments, an "agent" attempted to influence the ongoing spontaneous galvanic skin response (GSR) activity of another person while watching an analog recording (polygraph tracing) of that activity, thereby receiving instantaneous and continuous feedback. The allobiofeedback procedure was embedded within a receptive-psi (clairvoyance) experiment. In the pilot study, the attempted PK influence occurred without the "target person's" knowledge. In the confirmation study, the target person was informed that a PK influence of his or her GSR activity would be attempted but no details were provided about when or exactly how this attempt would be made.

The paper also includes observations of some possible novel instances of "conformance behavior" (Stanford) which occurred during the course of the experiments.

Pilot Experiment: Method

The subjects for the pilot investigation were six female and four male volunteers from the San Antonio area. The volunteers had previously contacted Mind Science Foundation to express an interest in participating in the Foundation's psi experiments about which they had learned through local newspaper advertisements and articles, notices posted throughout the city, lectures given by Foundation staff at local colleges and universities, and comments from other persons who had already participated in the Foundation's experiments. All of the participants could be classified as "enthusiastic sheep." They were very interested in the experiment and were highly motivated to participate. Three of the volunteers had participated in previous experiments of the author; seven volunteers had not participated previously in any of W.G.B.'s experiments. The subjects were selected from a pool of names of volunteers, were telephoned by the Foundation's secretary and asked if they were interested in participating in a clairvoyance experiment. If a volunteer expressed interest and his or her schedule permitted, an appointment was made for an experimental session. The person serving as "agent" in these experiments was the author, W.G.B.

When the volunteer arrived at the laboratory, W. G. B. interacted socially with him or her for a few minutes in his office, then escorted the volunteer to the experimental room where he described the work of the Foundation in general and the present experiment in particular. The experiment was introduced as a study of the effect of a combination of relaxation techniques upon clairvoyance. The volunteer was told that galvanic skin response (GSR) activity was to be recorded throughout the session in order to measure the effectiveness of the relaxation procedures.

The experiment was conducted in two rooms of the suite of rooms that comprises the Foundation. One room housed the volunteer's reclining chair, an adjustable floor lamp containing a red 25-watt incandescent bulb and positioned two feet directly ahead of the volunteer's eyes (for Ganzfeld stimulation), a Sony TC-440 reel-to-reel tape deck, a Schmidt binary random event generator (REG), and a Sony TC-110A cassette tape recorder. Another room, 70 feet and two closed doors away, housed a six-channel polygraph (Stoelting Multigraphic Recorder, Model 22656), a Realistic stereo cassette tape recorder, and an armchair.

When W. G. B. was satisfied that the volunteer clearly understood the experimental protocol, he attached two electrodes (silver/silver chloride, each embedded in a plastic insulator disc, Autogenic Systems) to the volunteer's right palm, using adhesive electrode collars (Beckman Instruments) and Spectra 360 electrode gel (Parker Laboratories). He then placed translucent acetate hemispheres (halved ping pong balls) over the volunteer's eyes, moved the chair to a semi-reclining position, turned on the red Ganzfeld light, placed headphones over the volunteer's ears, then left the room.

In the agent's room, W. G. B. started a cassette tape recorder which played instructions through the volunteer's headphones; these instructions could also be monitored through headphones in the agent's room.

During the initial three-minute music section of the tape, W. G. B. recorded the volunteer's basal skin resistance (BSR) and adjusted the sensitivity of the GSR amplifier (Stoelting Model SA 1473) so that the internal calibrating signal of 1 K ohm resulted in a 10-mm. deflection of the recording pen. The amplifier was then set for the automatic self-centering mode of operation, at which setting it remained until the end of the impression period. W. G. B. then

occupied himself by reading and writing, listening occasionally to the instruction tape and marking the onsets of the different instructional segments on the polygraph chart. At the
time of the beginning of the Ganzfeld instructions, W.G.B.
quietly entered the volunteer's room to turn on the REG and
the two tape recorders. On his way back to the agent's
room, he turned on a paper tape punching recorder which
was housed in still another room in a sound-attenuating box
and which provided a permanent record of the output of the
REG. The recorder-REG-recorder system, with associated
timing and relay devices, was allowed to run for a 32-min-
ute period, overlapping the Ganzfeld instructions, Ganzfeld
stimulation, impression instructions, impression period, con-
cluding remarks, and rest periods of the instruction tape.
The reel-to-reel recorder continuously played a tape with two
monoaural tracks, one containing "relaxing" natural environmental sounds and music and the other containing "activating"
sounds and music. Every 30 seconds, the REG was automatically triggered randomly to select one of these two
tracks and record a 30-second segment from the selected
track onto the second (cassette) tape recorder which could
be monitored in the agent's room. It was not possible for
the volunteer to hear any of the selections of either tape.
In fact, the volunteer was unaware of the recorder-REG-
recorder system and its function in the experiment, which
was to provide a random sequence of relaxing and activating
sounds. Which REG output resulted in the selection of a
relaxing soundtrack and which resulted in the selection of
an activating soundtrack was randomly determined by a coin
toss accomplished before each session.

Six minutes (timed by stopwatch) after the start of
the Ganzfeld instructions, W.G.B. plugged another set of
headphones into a jack in the agent's room, permitting him
to monitor the cassette tape containing the random sound
sequence for a ten-minute period. This was the allobiofeedback period. Throughout this period, W.G.B. listened to
the 20 sound segments which were being randomly generated
by the REG system, while watching the polygraph tracing of
the volunteer's GSR activity. The volunteer himself received
no exteroceptive feedback regarding his own GSR activity.
Whenever W.G.B. heard a relaxing 30-second sound segment, he attempted to relax his own body and mind, intended for the volunteer's autonomic system to relax, visualized the volunteer relaxing, and "wished" for the GSR
tracing to evidence little activity--i.e., to approximate a
straight line. Whenever W.G.B. heard an activating 30-

second sound segment, he attempted to activate his own body
and mind, intended for the volunteer's autonomic system to
become active, visualized the volunteer becoming activated,
and wished for the GSR tracing to evidence much activity--
i. e. , to yield frequent and large deflections.   Thus, the
sounds provided cues to W. G. B. as to the direction of his
attempted PK influence upon the volunteer's physiological
activity.   The analog tracing provided immediate feedback to
the agent for successful influences.   W. G. B. marked a
shorthand code for the content of each selection above a second (30-second) event-marking channel on the graph.   At the
end of the twentieth influence period, W. G. B. disconnected
his headphones from the jack so that the random sequence
tape would no longer be audible to him.   W. G. B. then busied
himself again with other matters and paid no attention to
the instruction tape or polygraph other than to sample it now
and then and mark the onsets of the different segments on
the chart paper.

      The five-minute impression period was signaled by
the sound of a bell on the instruction tape.   During this period, the volunteer had been instructed to gain clairvoyant
impressions of a 35-mm. slide (from the Maimonides binary
target system) concealed inside of a No. 000 "jet-pak"
(Jiffy bag) envelope.   The target slide had been randomly
selected, from the pool of 1024 slides comprising the target
system, by an assistant just before the experimental session.
The assistant secured the target slide inside of the envelope
with staples and tape and left the target envelope at an
agreed-upon location without contact with either the volunteer
or the experimenter; even the assistant did not know the content of the target slide, since he selected it by number only
and handled it, in placing it into the opaque envelope, in
such a way that he did not notice its contents.   Before the
volunteer arrived, W. G. B. sealed the envelope over the tape
and staples with sealing wax and a special seal in such a
way that the envelope could not be opened by anyone without
leaving evidence of tampering.   While describing the experiment to the volunteer, W. G. B. had placed the target envelope on the volunteer's lap, where it remained until the
end of the experiment.

      At the end of the final two-minute rest period, W. G. B.
determined the volunteer's terminal BSR level, turned off all
apparatus in the agent's room, and went to the volunteer's
room to remove the headphones, eye covers and electrodes.
W. G. B. then reminded the volunteer to write and draw any

impressions that had occurred during the five-minute impression period and, when this had been completed, assisted the volunteer in coding impression content according to the system described by Honorton. Following this, the volunteer completed a brief questionnaire assessing degree of relaxation and focus of attention (internal/external) during the impression period, instantaneous mood, and confidence about the accuracy of impressions. Finally, W. G. B. opened the envelope, revealed its contents to the volunteer, determined the number of correspondences between the impression and target codes, and debriefed the volunteer about all aspects of the study, including the allobiofeedback portion, about which the volunteer had been unaware. Before leaving the laboratory, the volunteer was once again thanked for his or her cooperation and was told that he or she would be telephoned and would be given additional information about his or her allobiofeedback results as soon as the GSR tracings had been measured and the data reduced. This phone call was usually made the following day.

Tests of the randomness of the REG were conducted immediately following each experimental session. For these tests, the REG was allowed to run for 32 minutes, making a "decision" every 30 seconds; however, the two tape recorders were turned off and no one was present in the room with the REG. W. G. B. started the REG, left the room, and occupied himself with other matters; he attempted not to think about the REG until a timer indicated that the randomness run of 64 trials had been completed. W. G. B. then entered the room in which the REG was housed and recorded the scores from the two counters which would normally indicate the number of relaxing and activating segments, respectively, the REG selected. Scores were recorded from the electromechanical counters rather than from punched paper tapes in order to prevent delayed trial-by-trial feedback (which would have resulted from counting the individual punched holes in the tape) and to reduce the experimenter's involvement in the randomness test runs.

Pilot Experiment: Results

The allobiofeedback data were quantified in the following manner. The target sequence (random sequence of relaxing and activating periods) written above the event-marker channel of the chart paper was hidden by means of two layers of duct tape. The amplitudes of all GSR deflections greater than 1 mm. were measured, recorded, and

summed for each of the twenty 30-second influence periods.
Next, the tape was removed and the target sequence determined; this target sequence was confirmed by comparison
with the punched paper tape record of the REG's output.
The mean GSR amplitudes for relaxation (decrease) and for
activation (increase) periods were then calculated, and a
paired t test was used to compare these scores. In the
absence of a paranormal influence, one would expect 50 per
cent of a volunteer's GSR activity to occur during the decrease periods and 50 per cent to occur during the increase
periods. In fact, 58.78 percent of the total amount of GSR
activity occurred during periods in which W. G. B. was attempting to increase this activity. Nine out of ten volunteers evidenced greater GSR activity during the increase periods than during the decrease periods, and the GSR amplitude difference between these two periods was significant
(t = 3.07, p < .02, two-tailed).

The REG functioned randomly during the randomness
test runs and during the ten-minute allobiofeedback period;
in the course of the latter the sounds selected by the REG
were audible and used as cues for W. G. B. However, during
the 22 minutes for which the selected sounds were inaudible,
the recorder-REG-recorder system exhibited a significant
bias in favor of generation of relaxing sounds (t = 5.83,
p < .002, two-tailed). The system's relaxation-sound bias
was also evident in the data for the 64 trials of the entire
period during which the REG system ran (t = 6.86, p <
.002, two-tailed); this period includes both audible and inaudible segments.

A single mean t test was used to compare the clairvoyance scores (number of correspondences of impression
and target binary codes) with chance expectation (five out of
ten matches). The mean number of correspondences was
5.1, which was not significantly different from chance expectancy (t = 0.25, p = n.s.).

Confirmation Experiment: Method

The volunteers for the confirmation experiment were
selected from the same pool and in the same manner as
those of the pilot study. Five volunteers were female, five
male. Three volunteers had previously participated in one
or more of W. G. B. 's psi experiments; the remaining seven
had not.

The procedure was identical to that of the pilot experiment, with a single exception. In the confirmation, the volunteers were informed about the allobiofeedback portion of the experiment. After the general procedure was described, the volunteer was told that at some time during the experiment, W. G. B. would attempt to influence his or her GSR activity, sometimes attempting an increase, sometimes a decrease. The volunteer was not told when or in exactly which manner the attempted influence would occur. The volunteer was asked to make himself or herself receptive to this influence, to allow himself or herself to be open to the influence, but not to try to guess when or how the influence would occur nor to try to work with or against the influence. W. G. B.'s subjective feeling was that all volunteers seemed curious and excited about the possibility of such a PK influence and none appeared threatened by the possibility. As in the pilot experiment, no mention was made of the recorder-REG-recorder system or its function.

Confirmation Experiment: Results

The pilot results were replicated in all respects. Eight out of ten volunteers evidenced greater GSR activity during the activating (increase) periods than during the relaxing (decrease) periods, and 57.50 per cent of the total GSR activity occurred during increase periods. A paired t test indicated a significantly higher mean GSR amplitude during increase than during decrease periods ($t = 2.96$, $p < .01$, one-tailed).

As in the pilot experiment, the REG functioned randomly during the randomness test runs and during the audible period. During the entire and inaudible periods, the REG evidenced significant biases in favor of selecting relaxing sounds ($t = 3.04$, $p < .01$, one-tailed and $t = 3.41$, $p < .005$, one-tailed, respectively).

The binary coding scores for the clairvoyance portion of the experiment gave a mean score of 5.8 correspondences which was not significantly different from chance expectation by a single mean t test ($t = 1.63$, $p < .2$, two-tailed). However, the scores are considerably higher than in the pilot study and would reach an encouraging probability level if a one-tailed test were used.

Discussion

Allobiofeedback.   The volunteers in these experiments

exhibited significantly greater GSR activity during activation (increase) influence periods than during relaxation (decrease) influence periods. The most direct interpretation of this finding is that the agent exerted a systematic psychokinetic influence upon the ongoing physiological activity of the volunteer, as indexed by the autonomic measure. If this interpretation is correct, the present findings would be consistent with those deriving from other studies of PK influences upon living target systems. In this case, the "allobiofeedback loop" would be "closed" via PK. An observation which lends some support to this PK hypothesis is a comment which was made spontaneously by the volunteer showing the greatest per cent increase score (71.16 per cent) in the pilot study. Before being told about the existence of the allobiofeedback portion of the experiment, he asked if I had been present in his room just before the impression period (I had not). He remarked that he had felt my presence in the room and at times almost physically felt me shaking him and his chair, as though I were attempting to rouse him. Further research is needed to determine whether immediate analog feedback, of the type provided by the polygraph tracing in the present study, is a necessary condition for an effective PK influence.

Another interpretation of the findings, which is still consistent with the allobiofeedback view, is that the feedback loop was closed by the volunteer via either telepathy (of the agent's relaxing and activating mental contents and his perceptions of the GSR polygraph tracing) or clairvoyance (of the relaxing and activating tape segments themselves and of the polygraph tracing itself). Sensory cues could not have been responsible for the differential ANS reactions of the volunteers since the tape recorders and REG ran continuously and switching from track to track (selection of relaxing and activating sounds) was accomplished electrically. No speakers or headphones in the volunteer's room were connected to the recorder-REG-recorder system, and the electrical signals for the selection of the two tracks could not be sensorily discriminated by the volunteer.

A less parsimonious interpretation of the GSR findings is that the agent precognized the volunteer's GSR pattern and psychokinetically influenced the REG system to yield a target sequence which would correspond maximally with the GSR pattern. This notion could be tested through the use of a more deterministic generation of the target sequence, e.g., through use of a quasirandom sequence derived from a random number table. A related possibility--that the agent

precognized the GSR pattern and the random target sequence
and maximized correspondences between these by beginning
the sequence of influence periods at the optimal time--was
controlled for, since the experimental protocol required that
the influence periods always begin at a fixed time (precisely
six minutes) following the start of the Ganzfeld instructions.

If attempts to replicate the allobiofeedback effect continue to be successful, the procedure may be useful in in-
vestigating a number of interesting issues. Four of these
follow.

(1) The use of a living target system should facilitate PK phenomena since such a target is exceedingly complex and labile--characteristics believed by several recent
theorists to increase the likelihood and magnitude of observed PK effects. (2) The findings of the new research
area of "autobiofeedback" indicate that one can "mentally"
influence one's own physiological reactions; what are the
limits to which one can "mentally" influence another's physiological reactions in an allobiofeedback paradigm?

(3) The outcome of such experiments may have implications for the areas of medical and psychological healing.
Can a therapist or physician correct problematic physiological
functioning psychokinetically? How important to such an effort is immediate sensory feedback of his successes and
failures, with resultant changes to more effective strategies?
How important is the attitude of the person being "healed"--
is conscious cooperation necessary for success? The results of the pilot experiment, in which the volunteers were
unaware of the attempted influence, suggest that conscious
cooperation with the specific attempted influence may not be
necessary. Could the well-known "placebo effect" include,
as a component, just such an effect as we are suggesting
here? The role of the importance of the expected physiological changes (to the target person as well as to the in-
fluencer) could be assessed by selecting target persons with
excessively high physiological activity in certain "channels"
--e.g., those with high blood pressure, tension-induced head-
aches, excessive anxiety, excessive hyperactivity, etc.--and
attempting physiological changes in a beneficial direction only.

(4) Positive findings in this area may have implications for the social-psychological area of "emotional con-
tagion." Can the emotions, positive or negative, of one or
more persons in a group or meeting or mob be "transmitted"

to other group members in a psychic manner? If so, how
might the likelihood of such influences be increased or decreased?

The REG Effect

In both experiments, the recorder-REG-recorder system generated significantly more "relaxing" than "activating"
sound segments. This occurred when the sound segments
were inaudible to both volunteer and agent, but not when they
were audible to the agent. In Stanford's PMIR model and in
its later elaboration as a "conformance behavior" model it
is assumed that individuals may scan their environments unconsciously, psychically, to detect circumstances that may
satisfy their needs or predispositions. When such "incen-
tives" are detected, the occurrence or timing of instrumental
acts may be altered so that the probability of encountering
the incentive is increased. Psychokinesis may also occur,
unconsciously, in the service of needs. It may be the case
that, in the present experiments, our volunteers psychically
detected events, namely recorded relaxing and activating
sounds, which were potentially conducive to or disruptive of
the relaxed atmosphere which was encouraged in the experiment. Activating sounds (if heard) would disrupt, while relaxing sounds (if heard) would be congruent with the volunteer's disposition (encouraged by the experimental protocol)
to be quiet, relaxed, and inactive. If the volunteer could detect these potentially congruent and incongruent sounds (unconsciously, psychically) he or she might "influence" the
REG (unconsciously, psychokinetically) so that a greater number of congruent sounds were selected. It is conceivable
that all of this could occur without any form of conventional
sensory feedback. An everyday life analog would be successfully avoiding a potential accident situation (perhaps even
via an unconscious PK influence) about which one never
learns sensorily. Alternatively, the necessary feedback, if
any, may be psychically mediated. During the period in
which the sounds were audible to the agent and used as cues
by him, the agent's predisposition to have an approximately
equal number of relaxing and activating influence opportunities may have predominated. A similar disposition would
have existed during randomness tests. If some sort of ultimate or overriding motive or predisposition must exist and
eventually be satisfied in order for these hypothesized events
to occur, it may be something as simple as the disposition
of both volunteer and experimenter to have the experiment
succeed in the most direct manner possible.

An alternative interpretation of the REG effect is that the experimenter-agent unconsciously exerted a contemporaneous PK influence upon the REG during the appropriate periods of the experiment, without feedback, or exerted a time-displaced (retroactive) PK influence upon the REG allowed by the delayed, trial-by-trial feedback about the activity of the REG which he received later when he scored the individual "relaxing" and "activating" holes in the punched paper tape record of the REG's output. Schmidt has recently discussed the possibility of such time-displaced PK effects and has provided some experimental evidence consistent with his retroactive PK hypothesis. It is also possible that the volunteers contributed a time-displaced PK influence upon the REG, since they too received delayed feedback about the activity of the REG. This feedback to volunteers consisted of overall scores only and was not of a trial-by-trial nature as it was for the agent-experimenter who scored the paper tapes.

Obviously, much further research will be needed to attempt to determine which of these various interpretations is most appropriate.

Clairvoyance. The clairvoyance scores (correspondences between impression and target coding binary content) of the volunteers in these experiments were not significantly above chance expectancy. This is the first time we have employed a very complex "induction procedure" consisting of progressive relaxation exercises, autogenic phrases, suggestions for mental stillness and quietude, and Ganzfeld stimulation; this sequence of preparatory exercises was also quite lengthy, approximately 70 minutes. Perhaps either the particular combination of techniques or the length of the entire procedure was not conducive to the manifestation of psi. We might note, however, that we have observed significantly high clairvoyance performance following exposure to a tape-recorded sequence of exercises including those mentioned above as well as others, but without concurrent Ganzfeld stimulation and lasting only 45 minutes. In that successful experiment, clairvoyance was measured by means of a target-ranking procedure ($p = 1/4$) rather than the binary coding method used in the present experiments.

The complexity of the present experiments and the fact that the experimenter was most concerned with the allo-biofeedback and REG portions and least concerned with the clairvoyance portion may have contributed to the obtained pattern of results, to the extent that experimenter motivation and interest are important to specific outcomes.

PSYCHOKINETIC EFFECTS UPON A RANDOM EVENT
GENERATOR UNDER CONDITIONS OF LIMITED
FEEDBACK TO VOLUNTEERS AND EXPERIMENTER

Lendell Braud and William Braud† (Texas Southern University and Mind Science Foundation)

In this paper, we report the results of the first phase
of a three-phase series of experiments, the ultimate purpose of which is the study of remote, nocturnal psychokinesis.
A relatively strong case has been made that nocturnal dreaming (or, more accurately, nocturnal sleep, since dream sleep
vs. nondream sleep comparisons have not yet been made)
may be accompanied by dramatic instances of receptive psi.
Can dreaming (or sleeping) also be accompanied by dramatic
instances of "active" psi, i.e., PK? One would expect an
affirmative answer based upon (a) indications that receptive
psi and PK may be two aspects or manifestations of the
same "process" and (b) the suggestion that emerges from
Stanford's recent review of the experimental PK research
that PK manifestations may accompany a reduction in "egocentric striving"; dreaming and sleeping would seem to be
"ego-alien" conditions.

While nocturnal dreaming PK studies could be conducted with volunteers spending nights in the laboratory, we
are more interested in designing experiments that may be
carried out with volunteers remaining in their own homes,
some at considerable distances from the lab. Thus, we
have planned a three-phase experimental series. In Phase 1,
we determine whether sufficiently impressive PK results can
obtain under conditions in which volunteers receive no immediate, trial-by-trial feedback. In Phase 2, we determine
whether promising results continue while volunteers are at
locations remote from the random event generator (REG)
used to assess PK. In Phase 3, we determine whether
promising results obtain when volunteers in their own homes
attempt to influence a remote REG in our laboratory while
dreaming (sleeping) and receiving no concurrent, trial-by-
trial sensory feedback regarding their PK success.

In Experiment 1, a within-subjects design is employed. A volunteer attempts several runs of PK on a
Schmidt REG, some with and some without concurrent trial-
by-trial sensory feedback. In this instance, immediate visual feedback is provided by the direction of "movement" of

illuminated lamps in a circular, "clock-face" array. For
the nonfeedback condition, the visual display is disengaged
and neither the volunteer nor the experimenter receives trial-
by-trial feedback. The experimenter receives delayed,
gross feedback at the end of each run as he records scores
from the REG's electromechanical counters. The volunteer
receives delayed, gross feedback at the very end of the experiment when he or she is informed of the number of "successful" runs (those in which hit scores are greater than
miss scores).

Experiment 1: Method

        The subjects for this experiment were six female and
four male volunteers from the San Antonio area. The volunteers had previously contacted Mind Science Foundation to
express an interest in participating in the Foundation's psi
experiments about which they had learned through local newspaper advertisements and articles, notices posted throughout
the city, lectures given by Foundation staff at local colleges
and universities, radio and television appearances by Foundation staff, and comments from other persons who had already participated in the Foundation's experiments. All of
the participants could be classified as "enthusiastic sheep."
The subjects were selected from a pool of names of volunteers, were telephoned by the Foundation's secretary and
asked if they were interested in participating in a psychokinesis experiment. If a volunteer expressed interest and
his or her schedule permitted, an appointment was made for
an experimental session.

        The apparatus consisted of a Schmidt binary random
event generator (REG). Internal circuitry allowed trials to
be programmed at a rate of one trial per second. A run
was automatically terminated after a preset number of trials.
The REG was attached to a visual feedback display consisting of 12 small lamps in a circular "clock-face" array. The
REG's binary "decisions" (hits and misses) were automatically recorded on punched paper tape by a device housed in a
sound-attenuating enclosure in another room. The apparatus
has been described fully by Schmidt. The circular lights
arrangement seemed a psychologically optimal one since the
visual feedback was binary, yet variable enough to maintain
attention.

        When the volunteer arrived at the laboratory, the ex-
perimenter (W. G. B.) interacted socially with him or her for

a few minutes in his office, then escorted the volunteer to the experimental room where he described the work of the Foundation in general and the present experiment in particular. The experiment was introduced as the first of a series of three experiments. The volunteer was told that he or she could participate in one, two, or all three of the phases of the series, as preferred. The volunteer sat in a comfortable desk chair approximately 30 cm. from the REG as W. G. B. explained the operating principles of the REG and demonstrated its action for 16 trials in the feedback mode. The volunteer was told that feedback runs would alternate with nonfeedback runs. During feedback runs, the volunteer was instructed to watch the "clock lights" display while intending for the lights to "move" always in a clockwise direction. It was suggested that the volunteer "wish" for the light to move appropriately, imagine it moving properly, attend to it strongly when it moved correctly, and ignore its incorrect moves. No mention of "effort" was ever made. During nonfeedback runs, the volunteer was instructed to attend to the darkened display while imagining a light moving from bulb to bulb always in a clockwise direction and at the same rate as in the feedback runs. The experimenter explained that both the volunteer and the experimenter would listen to loud white noise during each run (a) to eliminate distracting environmental sounds, (b) to prevent hearing of any auditory feedback provided by the operation of the electromechanical counters of the REG, and (c) because the acoustic Ganzfeld created by the white noise may itself be PK-conducive. The experimenter then attached his own and the volunteer's headphones and started the REG for the first run. The REG stopped automatically at the conclusion of each 256-trial run. Feedback and nonfeedback runs were alternated according to an ABBA or BAAB counterbalanced design (to control for any time-dependent effects), with the nature of the first run being determined by a coin toss accomplished immediately before the first run. The clock-lights display was inactivated and the counters of the REG were covered with an opaque card (to prevent visual feedback) during nonfeedback trials. The experimenter and the volunteer removed their headphones between runs to minimize sensory adaptation to the white noise. The inter-run interval was 30 seconds. At the conclusion of each run, the experimenter notified the volunteer (by means of a prearranged signal) that the run was over and recorded the hit (clockwise moves) and miss (counterclockwise moves) scores from the counters. Each volunteer completed 12 runs of 256 trials each--six with and six without immediate visual feedback.

Throughout the session, the experimenter sat next to the volunteer and the REG and allowed his mind to be as blank as possible. He attempted to allow his sole thought about the experiment to be: "may this experiment yield useful results."

At the very end of the session, gross delayed feedback was provided the volunteer in the form of information about the number of successful runs (hit score greater than miss score) out of a possible 12.

Experiment 1: Results

Single mean t tests were used to compare the number of hits (clockwise moves) with mean chance expectation, separately for feedback and nonfeedback trials. The mean number of hits for the feedback condition did not differ significantly from chance ($\overline{X}$ = 771.8, t = .56, df = 9, p = n.s.). The mean number of hits for the nonfeedback condition was significantly greater than chance ($\overline{X}$ = 784.1, t = 2.70, df = 9, p < .05, two-tailed). Hit scores for the two conditions did not differ significantly from each other, as assessed by a paired t test (t = 1.64, df = 9, p < .20, two-tailed).

Experiment 2: Method

Since significant PK hitting occurred under the nonfeedback condition of Experiment 1, a second experiment was designed in which the absence of feedback was enforced even more strictly. Several procedural changes were made in Experiment 2. All trials were run without feedback, the volunteer reclined throughout the session in a comfortable reclining chair, a "passive volition" or "effortless intention" attitude toward the PK task was encouraged, the actual PK trials were preceded by tape-recorded exercises for progressive muscular relaxation, autogenic phrases, suggestions for mental stillness and quietude, and suggestions for success at the PK task, and the experimenter attempted to remove himself and his influence from the experiment as much as possible.

The subjects for Experiment 2 were three male and 17 female volunteers from the San Antonio area, ranging in age from 26 to 73 years, with a mean age of 41.3 years. Volunteers were selected from the same pool of names and in the same manner as in Experiment 1.

The apparatus was identical to that described in Ex-

periment 1, with the addition of a reel-to-reel tape recorder
for the playing of the induction tape described below.

After greeting the volunteer and chatting socially with
him or her, the experimenter (W. G. B.) escorted the volunteer into the experimental room and asked him or her to sit
in the recliner. The proposed series of experiments (PK
without feedback, remote PK, remote nocturnal PK) was explained and the volunteer was informed that he or she would
be participating in the first phase of this series. The REG
was demonstrated as in Experiment 1. Next, the purpose of
the tape recorded exercises was explained and each exercise
was described briefly. The "passive volition" attitude was
explained. When the experimenter was certain that the volunteer understood the nature of the experiment, he placed headphones over the volunteer's ears, reclined the chair to a
45-degree position, started the instructional tape recorder,
started the REG, then left the room, busying himself with
other matters until a timer signaled the end of the session.

The instructional tape played for a total of 57 minutes
and included the following contents: (a) a two-minute mu-
sical introduction, (b) two minutes of introductory comments
about PK and the procedures which follow, (c) 17 minutes of
progressive muscular relaxation exercises, with alternate
tension omitted, (d) six minutes of autogenic exercises,
(e) four minutes of suggestions for mental stillness and
quietude, (f) two minutes of task-orientation ("effortless intention") instructions, and (g) a 24-minute period of soft
white noise, signalling the actual PK period. Parts (c) and
(d) were mixed with a barely audible, slow heartbeat sound
of 48 beats per minute (Environments Disc 5, Ultimate Heartbeat, SD 66005).

The volunteer was asked to allow the REG to generate more "hits" than "misses." For this experiment "hits"
were described as events which would advance the right
hits counter and move the lights in a clockwise direction (if
these were not disengaged) and would be indicated by holes
in the hit column of the punched paper tape, a sample of
which was shown to the volunteer.

The PK task itself consisted of ten runs of 128 trials
each, generated at a rate of one trial per second. There
were 20-second rests between runs. During the experiment,
neither experimenter nor volunteer received trial-by-trial
feedback. The "clock lights" display and the electromechan-

ical counters were disengaged and the REG outputs (hit and miss counts) were recorded remotely on punched paper tape by a device housed in a sound-attenuating enclosure in another room. The punched paper tapes were later scored by another person who counted the holes while unaware of which were hits and which were misses. At the end of the experiment, the scorer gave a list of total counts (of holes in two positions on the tapes) to the experimenter who decoded these numbers into total numbers of hits and misses. Thus, the experimenter received only very gross, delayed feedback. When the experiment had been concluded, the volunteers were notified by telephone about the outcome of the experiment as a whole; not even their individual total scores were revealed to them.

Experiment 2: Results

A single mean t test was used to compare the hit scores of these twenty volunteers with mean chance expectation. The scores were significantly greater than chance (μ = 640, $\overline{X}$ = 646.95, t = 1.89, df = 19, p < .05, one-tailed). A one-tailed test was used on the basis of findings for the nonfeedback condition of Experiment 1.

Randomness Tests

Randomness test trials were accumulated throughout the course of the two experiments in order to determine whether any "side bias" existed in the REG. As recommended by Davis and Akers, for each experiment, the total number of randomness trials collected was four times the number of trials collected in the actual experimental series. Randomness test trials were accumulated before and after the experimental sessions of each of the volunteers. The REG was allowed to run under conditions identical to those of the PK sessions, with two exceptions: volunteers were absent and the experimenter left the room and attempted to busy himself with other matters and not think about the REG, and scores were read directly from the electromechanical counters, rather than from punched paper tape, which was not employed at all.

The 122,880 randomness test trials collected during Experiment 1 indicated that the REG had no detectable side bias (61,383 hits, 61,497 misses, CR = -.32, p = n.s.); nor was there any indication of bias in the 102,400 randomness trials accumulated during Experiment 2 (51,241 hits, 51,159 misses, CR = .26, p = n.s.).

Discussion

Marginally significant PK effects occurred under the "nonfeedback" conditions of these experiments. These conditions could more accurately be called "limited feedback" conditions. The importance of these findings lies in the suggestion that immediate, trial-by-trial feedback does not appear essential to the occurrence of experimental PK. Schmidt has already provided evidence, in his "time-displaced" or "retroactive" PK experiments, that feedback need not be immediate for successful PK to occur; in fact, significant PK effects obtained even when feedback to the volunteer was delayed for as long as days or weeks. What the present findings suggest is that feedback need not be of a trial-by-trial nature to be effective. In these experiments, the only feedback received by the volunteers was information about the number of successful runs (in Experiment 1) and information about the outcome of the experiment as a whole (in Experiment 2). The only feedback received by the experimenter was individual run scores (in Experiment 1) and total run scores (in Experiment 2). While immediate, trial-by-trial feedback may augment PK performance (as Tart has suggested), it is not necessary for the simple occurrence of PK; gross, delayed feedback seems sufficient for a PK manifestation. This finding is consistent with Cox's "blind PK" results and with the results of several other "nonfeedback" or "limited feedback" studies reviewed by Stanford.

There are reasons to expect that, under certain conditions, the absence of feedback may actually facilitate PK performance. Especially early in a session or on other occasions when PK phenomena are not yet in evidence, feedback might be discouraging to an individual attempting PK. The discouragement resulting from the conflict between the intention for an event to happen and the perception of the event not happening would be minimized by eliminating feedback and hence knowledge of the event not happening. "Imaginary feedback" (as in the present experiments), in which the volunteer imagines a reality congruent with his intention, would seem psychologically more optimal for success. In fact, several of our volunteers, in Experiment 1, spontaneously commented that the visual feedback seemed to interfere with a PK effect and that PK seemed "easier" when the intended outcome was simply "imagined." Similar views have been expressed by Padfield and by Brookes-Smith. A second consideration that suggests the usefulness of the absence of feedback derives from Stanford's suggestion that "egocentric effort" may disrupt PK performance. It would appear that feedback would increase egocentric involvement in a PK task.

In the foregoing paragraphs, we have of course been discussing sensory feedback. There is no reason to believe that feedback need be sensory. Psi-mediated feedback may be sufficient for the activation and "reinforcement" of psi and PK effects. Please note that by that statement, we are not committing ourselves to a "cybernetic" model of the type discussed by Stanford; our position regarding a cybernetic model is identical to Stanford's. We would argue, however, that "feedback" and "contingency" need not be as sensorily-bound as Schmidt and Stanford seem to imply in their theoretical statements.

An unexpected finding remains to be discussed, and that is the absence of a PK effect in the feedback condition of Experiment 1. Such a finding is inconsistent with a substantial body of experimental PK results as well as with the expectations of the experimenters that PK effects would occur in both conditions but would be of greater magnitude in the feedback condition. It should be noted, however, that for the experimenters, the most important outcome of these experiments was that PK be evident in the nonfeedback condition. This finding would be essential if we were to progress to phases 2 and 3 of the planned series. It may well be the case that experimenters obtain the results that are most important to them, but sometimes at a cost. This "cost" may be the disappearance or reduction of psi effects at other "places" in the experiment. Palmer has made a similar observation in discussing the results of an experiment by Smith, Tremmel, and Honorton. In that experiment, psi occurred in a new and important experimental condition (tachistoscopic presentation of a target to an agent), but not in one (long duration exposure to the target) in which psi had been occurring in many previous experiments in the Maimonides laboratory. Similarly, in an experiment by Braud and Wood psi effects occurred in a new and important condition (following feedback training in a free-response context), but not in another condition (Ganzfeld stimulation tests without feedback) which had been yielding consistent psi effects in prior experiments. We have already raised this issue elsewhere and space does not permit a lengthy discussion of the notion here. Briefly, the hypothesis is that there may be a definite "quantity" of availability of psi. Psi "expended" at a certain place, time, or to obtain a certain effect may no longer be available for use elsewhere. Additional evidence suggesting this hypothesis and some suggested tests of its validity may be found in the Wood, Braud, and Kirk paper.

Practically, the present Phase 1 findings are encouraging enough for us to proceed with Phase 2 of the planned experimental series described in the Introduction to this paper.

FREE-RESPONSE ESP TRAINING
WITH FEEDBACK TO AGENT AND RECEIVER

Robert Morris,† Peter Robblee, Richard Neville and Kathleen Bailey (University of California, Santa Barbara)

Very little research has studied the effect of short-term feedback to agent or receiver upon free-response GESP performance. Last year we presented a preliminary paper [RIP 1976, pp. 50-2] on research with a selected receiver using a procedure for providing the receiver with feedback following the completion of each imagery period. The present paper represents a continuation and extension of this research. Two separate projects are involved.

Project I: continued research with Richard Neville. The present study arose as a result of several preliminary series with R. N. as receiver and R. M. as agent. In earlier work both Maimonides slides and photographs from National Geographic were used as targets. It was noticed, however, that the slides differed greatly in thematic cohesiveness and that R. N. had a bias toward selecting the slide with greater cohesiveness. Thus it was decided to focus upon the photographs as targets, and to use target pools of four rather than two items.

A formal series of 20 sessions has been completed. Targets were drawn from a pool of over 500 color photographs from National Geographic. Before each session, four target pools of four photos each are prepared by someone not otherwise involved and placed in a packet. During the session, the agent (R. M.) is two rooms from the receiver (R. N.) and experimenter (P. R.). An intercom allows the agent to hear the receiver's imagery, but the receiver can hear nothing from the agent's room.

The receiver starts the session with five minutes of relaxation, then signals the agent to select a target and
concentrate on it.   The agent checks an agent's console
to see which of four lights has been lit by a random
number generator.   This tells him which target in the
first pool of four to send.   All four are in folders; the
target folder is opened face up, the others face down.
Thus no targets are handled, yet all four folders have been
handled.   The agent then concentrates on the target, drawing
it, and generating other relevant mental images, body ges-
tures, and so on.   During this time the receiver speaks his
images out loud and the experimenter records them.   When
he is done, generally about four minutes later, he tells the
agent to stop sending.   The agent then records the identification numbers of all four photographs, closes the folders,
places them in their original order, goes out into the hall
and slides them under the receiver's door, then returns to
his room.   The experimenter records the four identification
numbers and shows all four to the receiver.   The receiver
reviews his imagery and then ranks the four photos as they
correspond with his impressions.   He then underlines the
imagery that in his opinion resembles his first choice.   The
experimenter then registers the receiver's preference on a
receiver's console, and presses a confidence call button if
the receiver felt especially good about his choice.   A central
processing unit (described in RIP 1976, pp. 38-40) then
registers the trial, whether or not it was a hit, and with or
without confidence, displays the correct choice on the receiver's console, and selects a new target to display to the
agent.   The receiver can then check his imagery against the
actual target, to assess which of his impressions if any
were accurate, and what feelings were associated with those
impressions.   This procedure is repeated for three more
trials, with brief rest periods between each trial.   At the
end of the session, all three participants go over the imagery
and targets to see if additional insight can be obtained.

        Project II: developmental work with pretested sub-
jects.   The basic procedure in this project is very similar
to that described above, except that target pools may be
either pairs of photographs or pairs of Maimonides slides.
When the targets are slides, the receiver is shown a duplicate set of slides already in the experimenter's possession
for rating purposes.   This eliminates any exposure to the
agent's slides, one of which would be warmer than the other,
having just been projected on the agent's wall via carousel
projector.   The target pool type is chosen independently for

each trial via RNG by the person who prepares the target pools, such that there are generally but not always both kinds in each session.

For this study, R.M. still serves as agent and K.B. is the experimenter. Subjects are drawn mainly from R.M.'s students, but may include other members of the UCSB community. All go through a two-session screening test conducted as described above. Those who show promise in terms of imagery ability, psi ability and general attitude towards the project are invited to participate in a followup series comprising four additional sessions at the rate of one a week. The project was originally designed to be continued until eight subjects had completed all four followup sessions. Unfortunately only six were found who qualified.

The judging target pool for each trial is as follows: the target itself, the non-target, and two additional control pictures never seen by the subject. For those trials in which the target was a magazine picture, the non-target was a picture just before or just after the target picture in our consecutively-numbered target pool of 500 photos. The additional control pictures was a couplet just before or just after the target-nontarget couplet. A system based on the last digit of the target picture but unknown to the judges is used to determine whether the couplet before or after is used. The system, a simple procedure involving no further decisions, guarantees that, from the judge's standpoint, each of the four pictures is equally likely to be the target. For those trials in which the target was a Maimonides slide, the non-target was the slide coded as the exact opposite from the target in categorical content. The two additional slides were the same in content as the target and control with the exception of the "activity" category. Once again, this should provide a judging pool of four slides with no cues to the judge as to which slides were which. Judges compare a transcript of subject's imagery with each member of the judging pool, in counterbalanced order. Judges were blind and were student-researchers not connected with this project in any other way.

Results and Discussion

The Neville series had a total of 80 trials. For his own choices, Neville got 19 direct hits, one below chance and clearly nonsignificant. Six occurred during the first ten sessions and 13 during the last ten. This difference, although in the expected direction, was not significant (z = 1.70, p = ns). The judges' ratings were also nonsignificant, and in the opposite direction. Target pictures were rated slightly lower than the nontarget pictures (t = -1.04, 79 df, p = ns), and this difference was insignificantly stronger during the second ten sessions than the first ten (t = -.966, 78 df, p = ns).

The pretested subject series had a total of 96 trials (four per session, four sessions for each of the six subjects). Subjects made choices in 93 trials (three had to be removed because the subject's target pool inadvertently had been improperly prepared). Of these 93 trials, subjects' choices produced 58 hits, which was statistically significant (z = 2.385, p < .02, two-tailed). The hitting occurred during the first two sessions for each subject (34 of 47 for 72.3 per cent) rather than the second two (24 of 46, for 52.2 per cent); this difference produced a z of 2.074, p < .05, two-tailed). This apparent decline effect was contrary to what would be expected had subjects been learning from the feedback they received. Judges' ratings produced nonsignificant results in the opposite direction. Ratings for the target were slightly lower than those for the non-target pictures (t = 1.53, 95 df, p = ns); ratings for target pictures were almost exactly the same as those for control pictures (t = .37, 95 df, p = ns); ratings for non-target pictures were slightly higher than those for the control pictures (t = 1.89, 95 df, p = ns). The difference between target and non-target ratings was essentially the same for the first two sessions and last two sessions (t = .446, df = 94, p = ns). Thus there was no evidence for improvement as a result of feedback, although subjects' own choices did indicate that the general procedure was psi-conducive.

MULTIPLE CHANNELS
IN PRECOGNITIVE REMOTE VIEWING

Brenda J. Dunne† and John P. Bisaha (University of Chicago and Mundelein College, Chicago)

The present investigation of precognitive remote viewing is an extension of earlier research in this area by Puthoff and Targ and the authors. Subjects are asked to generate a 15-minute description of a target site where the ex-

perimenter will be 35 minutes before the experimenter arrives at the target location and 20 minutes before the target
is selected. The present study follows the established protocol of our earlier experiments but includes an additional
variable, by testing two subjects simultaneously. Seven such
double trials were conducted.

Method

Each pair of subjects, spatially separated from each
other, was asked to describe, over the initial 15-minute
period of each trial, the location where the experimenter
would be during the 15-minute period beginning 35 minutes
later. The target was not selected until five minutes after
the subjects had completed their descriptions.

The judging procedure which was followed to determine the significance of the results consisted of three separate analyses, each by two separate judges: (1) a comparison of the A subjects' descriptions with the targets;
(2) a comparison of the B subjects' descriptions with the targets; and (3) a comparison of the A subjects' descriptions
with the B subjects' descriptions. The first two procedures
tested for evidence of psi communication between each subject and the appropriate target. The third procedure provided a check on the first two by attempting to ascertain
whether there was sufficient information in each transcript
to confirm its accuracy in describing the correct target.

Seven inexperienced and untrained subjects were selected on a volunteer basis, none of whom claimed any extra-
ordinary psychic ability. The only requirement was that they
hold a positive, or at least open-minded, attitude toward the
phenomenon being tested. Two males and five females,
ranging in age from 24 to 37, were tested in four different
subject pairs. The subjects in each pair knew each other
prior to the experiment, but were not related either by blood
or marriage.

A target pool of over 100 locations in the city and
suburbs of Chicago had been compiled by an independent person who was the only individual familiar with the targets and
who had no other association with the experiment. The targets were printed on index cards, sealed in envelopes, and
kept in a locked file cabinet.

The nature and protocol of the experiment were explained to subjects before the trials began. They were told that they would have sufficient time to relax, make themselves comfortable, and allow their minds to become as blank as possible. They were then instructed to try and visualize where the experimenter would be between 35 and 50 minutes after the trial began, and to describe whatever images or thoughts came to mind during the initial 15-minute period of the trial aloud into the tape recorder and to make any drawings if they so desired. Each subject was provided with a tape recorder and paper and pencils. Subjects were advised not to try specifically to define or identify their impressions (that is, name the target they thought they were seeing), but to describe them generally with as much detail as possible, even if the images appeared to make no sense or have no continuity. The time at which the trial was to commence was agreed upon by both subjects and experimenter, and subjects were then separated with instructions to have no communication with each other until after their parts in the trial were completed. In four trials the subjects were in the same building, but in separate rooms on different floors. There were observers stationed with each subject in three of these trials. In the remaining three trials, subjects were in different locations, separated by approximately ten miles.

When subjects began generating their descriptions, the experimenter left the area with ten envelopes which had been randomly selected from the target pool by the second experimenter, the contents of which were unknown to either experimenters or to the subjects. Driving continuously for 20 minutes with no particular direction, or until five minutes after the subjects had completed their descriptions, the experimenter then randomly selected a number between one and ten, counted down to the chosen number of envelopes, opened that envelope and proceeded to the location indicated on the enclosed card, arriving at the target 15 minutes later, or 35 minutes after the subjects had begun recording their descriptions. The experimenter remained at the target for 15 minutes, photographed the location and made notes as to her impressions of the site, then returned to the point of origin. Typed, unedited transcripts were made of subjects' recorded responses and attached to any associated drawings which the subject may have made.

Seven trials of this sort were performed, resulting in a set of seven photographs with accompanying notes, and 14 transcripts which were randomly divided into two sets so that each set contained one description for each of the seven targets. The transcript sets were labeled Group A and Group B. Six persons, not otherwise affiliated with the experiment, were asked to be judges. Two judges blind rank ordered Group A transcripts against the target photographs and notes; two judges blind rank ordered Group B transcripts against the photographs and notes; and two judges blind rank ordered Group A transcripts against Group B transcripts. In this manner each judging procedure was independent from the others, avoiding the possibilities of cueing from one set of descriptions to the other, or fatigue on the part of the judges if they were required to match all 14 transcripts. It also provided six separate sets of scores for evaluation from six separate and impartial individuals. Each set of rankings was made on a scale of 1 to 7; 1 being the best match and 7 being the worst. Seven was the lowest possible rank sum for each set, 49 was the highest.

Results

Statistical analysis of the obtained results was performed using Robert Morris' method for evaluating preferentially matched free-response material. The sums of the ranks assigned by the two judges matching Group A transcripts against the targets were 15 and 13 ($p = 0.01$ and $p = 0.005$, respectively). The sums of the ranks assigned by the two judges matching Group B transcripts against the targets were 15 in both cases ($p = 0.01$). Of the total of 28 rankings which were made in these two procedures (four judges ranking seven items each) there was a total of 11 direct hits (matches ranked as 1) and 7 rankings of 2. The mean of all ranks assigned was 14.5, a figure significant at $p = 0.009$.

The rankings of the third pair of judges matching A transcripts against B transcripts were also significant. The sums of ranks were 12 ($p = 0.001$) and 14 ($p = 0.005$), indicating that the descriptions of both subjects in each trial were found to be significantly descriptive of the respective target.

Discussion

The significant results of this series of trials lend further support to the hypothesis that the extrasensory channel of communication and/or perception utilized in precognitive remote viewing is a widespread and relatively common faculty which can be exercised without extensive training or experience when the environmental conditions are favorable. These results confirm the successful findings of our earlier trials with a single subject. Distance and time appear to pose no barriers to its effectiveness. The present results are in keeping with those of other studies testing remote viewing in individual and group settings, and provide evidence that even the precognitive aspect of this phenomenon operates on an open channel which can be "tuned into" by a variety of "consoles" with differing genetic and cognitive structures.

By using separate pairs of judges in the ranking procedures, the possibility of the matches of Group A influencing those of Group B was eliminated. Each set of transcripts was thus matched against the targets in two independent procedures and the significant results which emerged from these rankings are independent of each other.

While the results of the A matches and the B matches were both statistically significant, the possibility of ৳ stacking effect must be acknowledged. Although the two subjects in each trial were separated from each other by up to ten miles, this arrangement modified the possible influences of stacking, but did not eliminate them entirely. Also, the procedure followed for target selection does not exclude the possibility of experimenter clairvoyance in choosing the number which yielded a target which best matched the subjects' descriptions, presenting a difficulty in specifically demonstrating the locus of the psi process.

In future experiments of this type, it has been suggested that the rankings for each transcript against the pool of targets be made by a separate judge to control further for independence in the ranking procedure.

It should be noted that although there was enough information in each transcript to provide a significant cross correspondence between subjects on the same target, no telepathic indication between subjects can be deduced. The reports of the subjects in each pair differed enough to make it obvious that, while both subjects were perceiving the same target, the perceptions reflected individual differences in cognitive processing of information and interpretation.

The principle factor which appears to be operating under the conditions of these experiments is a situation where normal modes of rational thought or communication are inoperable, thus sufficiently reducing the internal noise and external stimuli to permit the weaker psi signal to be distinguished and recognized. Subjects have discovered (particularly those who have performed more than one trial) that they are capable of screening out the noise, sensory and cognitive, and perceiving the information being transmitted, in spite of the logical impossibility of such an accomplishment. When subjects are given permission and encouraged to explore their psychic abilities in an environment where these abilities are the only possible ones which can produce results, they discover that such abilities do exist and are relatively reliable.

The positive results obtained from the various experiments in precognitive remote viewing attempted to date indicate that the overall protocol of this experimental design is generally a useful and effective tool for additional research into the nature of non-ordinary information transfer in "ordinary" people.

MEDITATION AND E S P: REMOTE VIEWING

Gerald Solfvin,† William G. Roll and Joan Krieger (Psychical Research Foundation)

During the past three years, the Psychical Research Foundation (PRF) has conducted a series of experiments exploring meditation and ESP in group situations. The general format of the studies has remained essentially the same throughout the period, with each study changing in relatively minor ways according to the nature of the group and as a result of the findings of the previous studies. Each group has been trained in Eno meditation, a technique developed at the PRF, and each person has been asked to practice the technique twice a day on his own during the period of the study. The group meets daily or weekly to meditate together with an opportunity for a psi input (clairvoyant or GESP) during the session.

In the first experiment of this series we found a relation between success on the ESP task (during the meditation) and the self-rated quality of meditation (nine pre-meditation and 37 post-meditation items); that is, we isolated a subset of the questionnaire items by which we could classify

meditators into "hitters" and "missers." In our second
study, in order to avoid the statistical limitations of multiple calling (a single ESP target for the group), each meditator was randomly assigned an individual target within a
daily theme (e.g., William Blake paintings). The only significant psi scoring emerged from the separation into "most
liked" versus "least liked" themes. There was psi hitting
on individual targets with themes that were liked (ranked in
the upper half) and psi missing with themes that were disliked (ranked in the lower half). We also noted significant
individual scoring by a meditator who was emotionally close
to the agent.

The first study spanned ten weeks with one session
per week, while the second study had daily sessions and
lasted ten days. We attribute the lack of correlations with
the meditation responses in the second study to the shorter
exposure to meditation.

Each of the experiments has been time consuming
and the analyses limited by small sample sizes. We have
therefore kept the general format of the experiments, the
meditative technique and the personality, attitudinal and mood
questionnaires constant from experiment to experiment in
order to build a larger pool of data for future analysis.

In the present experiment we met with a group of 16
juniors and seniors at Durham Academy, a private school in
Durham, N.C. The students had chosen a course on psi
and altered states of consciousness as a "mini-term" lasting
nine consecutive school days. Six of these days included experimental sessions, usually taking up about one-half of the
two-hour class, the other being devoted to lectures and discussions. We wanted to explore the liking-disliking aspects
of the psi production and we also wanted to make the psi
task exciting for this age group to maximize the possibility
of results. We therefore chose a remote viewing situation
where one of the students would leave the classroom to visit
a randomly selected location in Durham while his classmates
meditated.

Procedure

During the first two class sessions, the 16 students
(11 males, 5 females) were instructed in Eno meditation by
W.G.R. Each student was given a parental consent form,
Personal Orientation Inventory (POI), Taylor Manifest Anxiety

Scale, Sheep-Goat questionnaire and a Betts QMI Vividness
of Imagery Scale (shortened form) to be completed and returned prior to the beginning of the experimental sessions.
They were also given a copy of the class list and asked to
rank their 15 classmates according to how much they liked
being with them. The Harvard Group Scale of Hypnotic Sus-
ceptibility (Form A) was administered by G. F. S. after three
experimental sessions had been completed.

Each experimental sessions lasted about one hour.
After an initial period of settling down, the students were
given a meditation questionnaire booklet and responded to the
nine pre-session questions dealing with their individual medi-
tations and current moods. An agent was then randomly selected and left the room with G. F. S. The group would meditate for about 20 minutes and then attempt to experience what
the agent was experiencing for another five minutes. Each
meditator would then complete the 37 post-session questions
dealing with the quality of their meditation and then indicate
how emotionally close or friendly (on a 1 to 9 scale) they
felt about the day's agent. Finally, they were shown photos
and instruction sheets (described below) of the four possible
target locations. These were pinned on the bulletin board
in random (shuffled) order, and the students were asked to
rank them according to their own impressions of where the
agent visited.

A target universe of 28 locations was selected and
photographed prior to the beginning of the class. Seven
pools were formed with each pool consisting of four dissimilar locations. Instruction sheets with the name and address
of the location, directions to drive there from the school,
and brief instructions to the agent (suggesting what he or
she might do there) were sealed in identical individual envelopes. Each day an assistant (not otherwise involved with
the experiment) randomly selected one of the pools by drawing a numbered coin from a container. There was also a
duplicate set of the instruction sheets with attached photos,
in a larger envelope for the meditators to rank. The four
target envelopes and the larger envelope containing the duplicate set and photos were given to G. F. S. who brought them
to the school at the beginning of the class and handed the
duplicate set to W. G. R. After G. F. S. and the agent left
the classroom they went to the car where the agent was
given the four sealed envelopes with the following instructions:
"Here are the four envelopes containing the possible target
locations for today. Choose one and give me back the other

three." G. F. S. then drove one block away from the school parking lot, the target envelope was opened by the agent, and the two proceeded to the target location. On the trip back to the school the agent recorded his experiences during the visit in his own words. G. F. S. and the agent did not return to the classroom until the meditators had completed and turned in their questionnaire booklets.

Analysis

A majority vote procedure was used to assess the group ESP scores. The mean and mode of the ranks were calculated for each location for each day. The mean was used to establish the group ranking with the mode as a tie-breaker.

We then formed subgroups of the meditators based on how they rated the agent (liked, disliked) and how the agent ranked them (liked by, moderate, disliked by). For the former we calculated the median rating from all the meditators for all six days. This was used as a cut-off point to assign the meditators to the "liking" or "disliking" subgroups. We then applied the majority vote procedure described above to the target responses of these subgroups.

From the agent ranking of his 15 classmates we categorized ranks 1 to 5 as "liked by agent," ranks 6 to 10 "moderate" and ranks 11 to 15 "disliked by agent." The majority vote procedure was also applied to target responses of each of these subgroups for each day.

To examine for individuals who may have achieved individual significance on their target responses, we used the sum-of-ranks statistic for preferentially ranked data developed by Solfvin and Kelly.

The rest of the data collected in this experiment will be used in the series analysis and was not planned for use in the present study.

Results

No significant psi scoring was evident in the group majority vote rankings. This was true also of the majority vote rankings of the various subgroupings--liked agent, disliked agent, liked by agent, moderate, disliked by agent. The target rankings of these subgroupings did not differ sig-

nificantly from one another nor from the rankings of the entire group.

None of the meditators showed individually significant
psi scoring, although several of them showed tendencies towards psi-hitting over this small number of trials (six or
less).

During the calculation of these statistics it was noted
that a measure of the group feeling towards the agent was
available in the proportion of meditators who liked the agent
during each experimental session. This was decided after
the experiment had been conducted but before we had decoded the remote viewing targets. A statistic was formed
by subtracting the number of meditators who disliked the
agent from the number who liked the agent and dividing this
difference by the total number present. This statistic varies
between -1 and +1 with a positive value indicating a majority
of likers and a negative value reflecting a majority of dislikers while zero indicates a 50-50 split. The absolute value
of the statistic indicates the strength of the majority. The
results show that in the two sessions with negative scores
for the like-dislike statistic, there were two direct misses
(fourth place) on the group target response. The remaining
four sessions, all with positive like-dislike scores, showed
two first-place and two second-place hits. The Pearson correlation between the majority vote rank assigned to the target and the like-dislike statistic is significant ($r = .91$,
$t = 4.417$, 4 df, $p < .02$, two-tailed).

Discussion

We have used the term "remote viewing" in the title
of this paper. It should be pointed out that this refers only
to the procedure that was utilized. We made no attempt to
categorize the kind or origin of the psi but rather concerned
ourselves with how extra-chance target correspondences may
emerge from a group situation.

Indeed, a group effect did seem to emerge in the
post-hoc correlation between the relative abundance of meditators who liked the agent and the majority vote target rank.
This is especially interesting in this study since there were
no significant psi scores for any of the individuals or subgroups (likers, dislikers, etc.).

This group effect brings to mind many parallels in

reports of spontaneous cases. The elicitation of seance
room phenomena is commonly reported to be dependent upon
the group interactions. Sensitives often speak of the "vibra-
tions" of the group situation as a major factor in their own
production of psi.

On the experimental side we are reminded of experimenter effects which imply that psi may emerge from the
characteristics of the group (experimenters, subjects, scor-
ers, etc.) rather than the characteristics of the individual.
Recently, Charles Thomas Cayce (Association for Research
and Enlightenment) visited the PRF and told us of the success of some informal experiments with group dreaming.
This developed from his introductory lectures on parapsychology to school groups where the students are asked to recall and write down their dreams to bring to class the following day to look for correspondences with a free-response
GESP target. While Cayce has found little evidence of any
striking individual correspondences, the group selection of
the target (group discussion and voting) has been very successful. Cayce speculated on the possibility that each member of the group may supply one piece of the puzzle that becomes meaningful only when put together with the other
pieces. He is currently designing an experiment to explore
this. The same concept proved successful also for Patricia
Barker who evaluated the group majority vote for the presence or absence of mentation in each of ten categories
(color, activity, etc.). She found significant correspondence
in a pilot study involving sensory relaxation procedures
(Ganzfeld and relaxation) which may be beneficial in establish-
ing a group feeling similar to that which seems to emerge
from our own meditation sessions.

In the present study the liking-disliking separation
was made on the basis of the median of this daily rating
over all meditators and all sessions. The group liking-
disliking statistic may therefore reflect other factors such
as daily mood. It does, however, seem more meaningful
in view of our previous result where individual preference
for the target theme was accompanied by psi-hitting. In
that study the meditators knew in advance that they were
responding to an individual target. Meditators in the present
study had a person for a target and they knew in advance
that the entire group was focussing on the same target person. In both studies the disliked themes or persons produced
psi-missing rather than chance scoring, a fact which further
strengthens the consistency of the results.

Conclusion

The remote viewing task was a stimulating one for this high-school group and we did not detect any decline in interest over the six experimental sessions. The students, primarily from upper-middle-class families, had a stimulating school environment. We hope to use the remote viewing task with other groups to see if this interest level is maintained.

The liking-disliking separation has been a fruitful one in both of our studies where this information has been collected and it may prove an interesting parameter for other researchers. Although the possible influence of other factors needs to be weeded out in future research, this effect appears to be sound and consistent.

The group aspect of the effect is a first in this series, although it has been frequently noted by meditators that group meditation is qualitatively different from individual meditation. The simple group liking-disliking statistic may reflect one dimension of this qualitative difference and we will seek further evidence for group effects in our analysis of the questionnaire data across studies.

COMPUTER CONTROLLED RANDOM
NUMBER GENERATOR PK TESTS

Roger Lee Jungerman† and John A. Jungerman (University of California, Davis)

The use of an on-line computer offers many advantages in random number PK experiments. Since little is known about psi functioning, it is desirable to design considerable flexibility into parapsychological experiments. In this way, any promising leads found in preliminary experiments can be followed up. Computer software provides this flexibility. By use of different programs it is possible simultaneously to engage in several experiments with the same physical apparatus. For example, in the system described below, three experiments are being conducted. Two involve testing for real time PK on numbers generated by two different methods, while the third tests for PK on pre-generated targets.

Another use of the computer is in the management of large amounts of data. In the above three experiments, close to a million random bits have been generated. Programs sort and store this data with a minimum of confusion. Real time analyses are also performed to provide both subject and experimenter with rapid statistical feedback.

Yet, unfortunately, the present computer-based experiment has several disadvantages. The computer is located in the counting area of a cyclotron laboratory. This environment is noisy and rather "sterile." Schmidt has suggested that a more comfortable environment might lead to improved scoring. The computer is only available for limited periods on weekends, which makes it difficult to run or rerun subjects. When the subjects do arrive they tend to be serious and feel a need to perform.

On a few occasions several subjects have worked together in a friendly competitive spirit. In these runs the scoring tended to be higher. In fact, it is these runs which give the positive results quoted later in this paper. To investigate this effect a new program, "Psychic Pong," is being implemented. It is hoped that in this experiment subjects will relax, be less serious and score better.

We will next consider two of the experiments in detail. The first is a pilot study, and is used to select the data analysis method. The second, followup study applies this analysis to new data. Since the two experiments differ in some respects, the experimental apparatus and protocol common to the two will be discussed first.

Experimental Apparatus

Testing is conducted on a PDP 15-40 computer. Attached to the computer via CAMAC interface is a random-number generator. The device consists of a white noise source from a voltage-regulator tube from which all pulses greater than a certain amplitude are counted in a scaler. The pulses are counted at a rate of approximately 10 kHz. Under program control, this scaler is interrogated at 60 Hz and the least significant bit is taken as a binary-random variable. The bit is then compared with a bit generated by a pseudo-random number algorithm. If the two match a 1 is produced, if the two bits differ a 0 is output. It is hoped that this generation method will insure random output of the random-number generator in control runs. For non-random behavior there needs to be a correlation between the pseudo-random and random sequences, which is unlikely, neglecting PK effects. The output of the random-number generator is stored in computer memory. A moving average is then constructed of the last 20 trials. This moving average, representing the hit rate during the last two seconds, is displayed to the subject on a graphics teletype. The subject sees an oscillating hit rate versus time plot forming about a stationary chance level axis.

After a predetermined number of trials the run is completed. The results are printed on the subject's terminal, on a hard copy experimenter teletype about ten feet away, and recorded on magnetic tape. Additional information including the date and time of the run, the subject's name, and the unanalysed data are also recorded on the tape. Other programs sort the data and give cumulative subject totals on a line printer.

Standard Protocol

There was no subject selection used in these studies. Anyone interested in the experiment was given a chance as subject. These people included those interested in parapsychology, friends and physicists passing through the lab. It is our intention to return talented subjects. This has not yet been done because many of the talented subjects have left the area, while others are occupied during the limited time that the computer is available. It has been reported by Schmidt and others that subject selection yields much improved results.

A typical series of runs for a subject are conducted as follows. After being shown the apparatus, the subject seats himself before the video terminal. The experimenter then initiates the program by typing in the subject's name at his teletype. The computer responds by typing a message at the subject's teletype identifying him by name and instructing him as to the exact task to be performed. The experimenter insures that the subject has no further questions and then, in most cases, leaves the room. When the subject feels confident to begin the run, he types a key at his terminal. This initiates the run which lasts about one minute. His only task during this time is to try to move the line up. At the conclusion of the run the results of various statistical analyses are outputed to his terminal. These include the percentage of hits in the run and the normal deviation (Z

score) of the run. The subject is then free to type the key
again and begin a second run.

At the early stages of experimentation, it was observed that there was a strong decline effect in later runs.
This effect has been commented on before. Eve André noted
that most significant runs occurred during the first four
runs of a session. Those experiments also used a similar
random-number generator.

To counter this problem, we decided to limit sessions to two or three runs. Yet many times subjects would
get "locked in" and insist on doing many more runs. Not
surprisingly there were few significant effects in these cases.

The results from about 40 subjects are considered in
the following sections.

Preliminary Experiment

This experiment is used to determine the analysis
method to be used on the independent followup experiment.
Except for slight differences in run length and feedback, this
experiment is a close duplication of Schmidt's work. There
are 1024 random trials in each run. The probability of a
hit for each trial is $1/2$. The significance of a deviation of
H hits from the mean value of 512 can be evaluated as fol-
lows: $Z = (H-512)/(1/2 \cdot 1/2 \cdot 1024)^{\frac{1}{2}}$, where Z is a normal
random variable obtained by approximation to the binomial.

The analysis method must account for two characteristics of the data. First, it must avoid losing significant
first-run effects in a large number of later runs which show
poor scoring due to decline effect. Second, it must treat
each subject, on each day that he attempts the apparatus,
as a separate event and not average them together. Two-
tail tests must be used for all these events so as to ac-
commodate psi missers. In this way psi missers will not
negate the effects of psi hitters, even if it is the same subject who hits on one day and misses on the next.

The method which gave the best results with this data
is the following: First a composite Z, Z', is made from
the first two runs on each day for each subject, $(Z' = Z_1 + Z_2)/(2)^{\frac{1}{2}})$. If there is only one run for the subject on a
given day, the run is discarded. It should be noted that
this guarantees that a subject will not stop after a few good

runs and thus make his score artificially high.   The number
of runs is predetermined.

The significance of the distribution of Z' is determined
by counting the number of cases N, where $|Z'| > z$, where
z is some cutoff value.   Reasonable value of z are found to
be 2.5 or 3.0.   The probability of N or more cases out of n
is then easily evaluated using a binomial distribution, where
n is equal to the total number of subject-days and p is equal
to the two-tailed probability of z from the normal distribution.

An alternate method is to evaluate the distribution of
subject Z's.   These are obtained from all of the subjects'
runs.   The distribution is then evaluated with a binomial cut-
off method as described above.   This analysis method is prone
to criticism in that it ignores both decline effect and the
problem of an arbitrary number of runs per subject.

The results for the two methods are similar, $p < .01$
and $p < .04$ respectively.   This is due to the fact that the
significant Z's occurred with subjects who completed only two
runs.   The analysis method is next applied to an independent
experiment.

The Followup Experiment

This experiment is similar to that just described.   Instead of generating 1024 trials with a probability of 1/2, 500
trials of probability 1/8 are used.   The subject's task of
moving the line up is the same as described above.   The
feedback appears slightly different because of the 1/8 instead
of the previous 1/2 probability.   The run length is half that
of the preliminary experiment, 50 seconds instead of 102
seconds.

Each trial is produced by generating six bits on the
random number generator.   If the sequence of the first three
bits matches the second three than a hit is scored.

Out of 39 subject-days, two subject-days had an absolute value of their first run Z' of more than 3.0.   This
corresponds to a binomial probability of $p < .005$.   Considering all subject runs, the results for the two high-scoring subjects remains the same because they completed only
two runs each.   The resulting binomial probability for these
two subjects out of the total of 25 subjects is $p < .002$.

Thus the results seem reasonably independent of the analysis method used. However, it is essential in this experiment to avoid summing the scores of all subjects, and instead use some type of binomial test. For example, if the first-run Z scores for all subject-days, Z', are combined into a grand total Z, Z_g, then: $Z_g = \sum_{1}^{39} Z_i' / (39)^{\frac{1}{2}} =$ 0.81 (not significant).

One hundred and fifty controls of two runs each were performed by the experimenter. For these runs attention was diverted from the PK task (by reading a book) except when a new run was initiated.

Another analysis was used to get some insight into the nature of the PK effect. A chi-square test was used to determine if the distributions of the two octal numbers (determined by the sequences of three bits) which are matched to determine if a hit has been scored, were altered. For example, one way a subject might get a good score would be to cause the random number generator always to produce 0's. In this case, when three bits were combined to form the first and then the second octal numbers, the result would be 0 in both cases and a hit would be scored. If a chi-square test is constructed for the number of 0-7's in both the first and second octal numbers for the 500 trials, such non-randomness would be apparent. None of the chi squares are close to being significant ($p < .6$) for the high-scoring runs. This indicates that the PK effect is subtle. It involves a correlation between the two octal numbers rather than a distortion of the distributions of each.

Conclusions

This experiment constitutes a confirmation of earlier random-number generator PK work by others. It also provides a method for analyzing such experiments to get reasonably significant results without preselection of subjects.

The goal-oriented nature of PK is dramatically shown. A subject is able to effect a blackbox RNG so that its output matches that of a pseudo-random sequence. He is then able to group the output bits into matching octal numbers. All this is done without a knowledge of the inner workings of the apparatus.

Finally, it is shown that a computer system can be successfully used in PK studies. This opens the way for a simpler manipulation of more sophisticated experiments.

A TEST OF THE SCHMIDT MODEL'S PREDICTION CONCERNING MULTIPLE FEEDBACK IN A PK TASK

James W. Davis† and Melissa D. Morrison (Institute of Parapsychology, FRNM)

Schmidt has proposed a model for psi interactions which predicts increases in scoring rates when the outcomes of PK trials are presented repeatedly to subjects. He has confirmed this in one experimental series, though the experiment confounds the conditions of single versus multiple feedback with the conditions of delayed versus contemporaneous target generation as pointed out by Stanford. There have been some attempts to confirm Schmidt's findings (without matching Schmidt's success, however) in Scotland by Millar and apparently in Amsterdam by Houtkooper, but it seemed appropriate to try some of the feedback methods employed by Schmidt which he had found successful. We report four series of experiments which represent our approach to the problem.

Series I and II: Procedure

The method used in Series I and II was patterned after Schmidt as to feedback presented to the subject, which was a dot of light moving in a circle in random clockwise and counterclockwise steps with the subject trying to influence the dot to move clockwise. In the first series, each of 40 subjects were run for a single 120-trial run, the subjects divided into four groups of ten, each group receiving a different trial rate, the rates being four trials per second, two trials per second, one trial per second and one trial every two seconds. The duration of the run therefore varied from group to group, ranging from two minutes for the slow rate to 30 seconds for the fast rate. After the run the subject completed a questionnaire which asked, among other things, whether the trials came too fast, too slow or neither, and whether the session lasted too long, too short a time or neither. From these it was determined that the optimum trial rate was two trials per second for two minutes, which resulted in a run length of 240 trials for Series II. The subjects in Series II also received the questionnaire.

The trials themselves were from three categories representing the three feedback conditions of the experiment. One-third of the trials were generated at the time of feed-

back presentation, these corresponding to Schmidt's single
feedback condition (direct trials), one-third were generated
immediately before the subject began the test, and were presented to the subject one at a time (delay one trials). The
remaining one-third of the trials were multiple feedback
trials in which previously generated targets were presented
to the subjects four times (delay four trials). For the first
series with 120 trial runs, there were actually 40 direct
targets, 40 delay one targets, and ten delay four targets,
and in Series II, twice as many in each category. The feedback trials were presented from each of the categories sequentially on a trial by trial basis.

The 40 subjects for Series I were primarily laboratory personnel at the Institute for Parapsychology and other
parapsychologists from the area, and a few visitors. For
Series II the subjects were for the most part visitors and
area high-school students. All testing was done by J.W.D.

I and II: Results

The purpose of Series I was more to determine favorable run lengths and trial rates, to test out the computer
program and work out the details of presenting the task to
the subjects. As such no formal expectations were held regarding the outcome of the psi task. Series II was a pilot
study, with expectations of overall psi, with significant differences between the delay four trials and the pooled result
of the direct and delay one trials, with no significant difference between the direct and the delay one trials. Analysis
was performed by dependent t tests, with probabilities to be
evaluated with two tails. No results whatever were found
in either study, nor were differences noted between any of
the categories. Post-hoc analyses based on the possibility
that some subjects might be hitting while others missed were
attempted, both by correlating scores in the categories and
by separating subjects on the basis of a category and looking
for significant differences in other categories. These results
were all nonsignificant, none even being of any interest.

Since the questionnaire was given after the psi task,
it could not be used formally as a predictor of psi performance (nor was it meant to be). This was demonstrated
in Series I where the question of how well the subject thought
he performed significantly separated hitters from missers
(t = +2.33, df = 21, p < .05). Series II however did not
show any such effect, so it was felt appropriate to see if

any separation would occur on the question "Do you think this experiment can show PK?," which is closest to Palmer's Criterion 2, which appears to be the strongest predictor of success. No significant differences were noted among response categories.

I and II: Discussion

The utter failure of the study to produce any evidence of psi along with the lack of any leads to follow led us to think that major modifications in the procedure were in order. The first decision was to pattern the manner of feedback much more closely after Schmidt's 1976 experiment using continuous visual feedback instead of discrete trial visual feedback, and an audio tone. The second was to employ a motor-skill task as a means of introducing the subject to the test environment. As a third measure, another experimenter would test at least some if not most of the subjects as J. W. D. felt his interactions with them in the past had been less than satisfactory.

Series III: Procedure

The experimental program was modified for Series III so that visual feedback was provided by a short vertical red line on the screen that would move from left to right with hits and right to left with misses. Additionally, an audio tone which rose in pitch with misses and fell with hits was supplied to the subject through headphones. The run length was set at 600 trials and the trial rate at ten per second. Subjects did three runs. The categories of target selection and their order of presentation remained the same. Overall scores were printed out and given to the subject by the experimenter following the session, and the questionnaire was eliminated.

The motor skill task was added to provide the subjects some experience with the display and the headphones (to give them an opportunity to set the volume at a comfortable level) and to look for any possible correlations between motor skill and PK, an area of interest to J. W. D. which has received very little attention from experimenters in the past. The task itself was a critical tracking, or "drunk driving" test which involved keeping the small vertical red line in the center of the screen by means of a control knob as it became increasingly unstable in its position. Each subject made three attempts. The score printed out for each attempt was proportional to the time elapsed before the red line hit either side of the screen when the subject lost control.

In this pilot series three categories of sessions emerged. J. W. D. and M. M. both ran various people as demonstrations of the two programs in an informal manner. Some of these were equipment tests; others, J. W. D. showing M. M. how to run the program. A second category consisted of subjects formally run by J. W. D., who were given instructions and handled in a uniform manner. The third category were those formally run by M. M. usually after being tested by her in another computer-based parapsychological study. These latter two groups were almost entirely composed of high-school students in the 11th and 12th grades.

III: Results

While this series was going on, J. W. D. and M. M. both received the impression that M. M.'s formal subjects were performing differently from the others. Additionally, J. W. D. was able to run only three subjects formally. It therefore seemed prudent to look at the data as two groups, J. W. D.'s subjects and the demonstrations in one (comprising nine subjects), and M. M.'s formal subjects in the other (another nine). No overall scoring trends were evident in either group. Applying the technique used in the first two series, categories were divided at their means and used as predictors of scoring in other categories for both groups. M. M.'s group separated delay one successfully on the basis of direct and separated direct on the basis of delay one. Additionally, a rank correlation between these categories is quite high ($r = 0.82$, $t = 3.78$, df = 7). It would thus appear that there are possible psi effects in both the direct and delay one categories, while they appear absent in the delay four category.

The three motor skill scores from each subject were considered in the following manner. The best score of the three was noted, the last score for each (which was not always the best), and the average of all three. Pearson product-moment correlations were run on the motor skill scores and the scores from the three PK trial categories. Only six subject motor skill scores were available. Here there may be some indication of psi operating in the "J. W. D. and demonstration" group, though it is at best tentative, based on only six samples. The "M. M." group also appears

to show a correlation though the same caution applies. It
is interesting to note that in the PK categories the correlations are in the same direction for all three between the
two groups, and that the last score correlations appear to be
the best discriminators.

III: Discussion

The motor skill correlations support to a degree the
conclusion that psi may be present in at least the direct
trials of the "M. M." group, and possibly also the delay one
trials. The size of the delay four correlation in the
"J. W. D. and demonstration" group may be due to a set of
high scores in the demonstration group ($Z = 1.9$). It was
therefore decided by J. W. D. that a confirmation series with
30 subjects run by M. M. should commence, the motor skill
measure to be the last score, which would be correlated
using the Pearson against the three PK categories, with a
prediction of a negative correlation with direct and possibly
delay one as well. It is also predicted that direct will successfully separate delay one scores and vice versa, this to
be evaluated by independent t test.

Series IV

For Series IV the exact same testing procedure was
employed as in Series III except that only M. M. ran subjects,
who were 30 high-school students in the 11th and 12th grades.
All subjects were tested by another experimenter as part of
a study unrelated to this one before being introduced to
M. M.

IV: Results

Unlike the first study there was no relation noted between motor skill as measured by the last score and the
predicted PK categories. The direct scores do not significantly separate the delay one scores, but the results are
suggestive. The delay one scores do successfully separate
the direct scores. Additionally the delay one and direct
scores are significantly correlated (Pearson $r = -0.44$, $t =
-2.60$, 28 df, $p < .02$, two-tailed). As in the first study,
there are no effects related to the delay four trials.

An examination of the motor skill and PK scores revealed an interesting post-hoc result with the best motor
skill scores and the average scores correlating negatively

with the delay one scores. This is in the same direction as
in Series III. Another completely unanticipated result was
an apparent sex interaction with scoring over the direct and
delay one conditions. Though the differences are not significant, it would seem appropriate to look for this result in
future studies.

IV: Discussion

The results of Series IV support the notion that scoring can occur in the direct and delay one categories. There
is no evidence of a meaningful difference between these categories which would confound the results of Schmidt's 1976
series. Our lack of results in the delay four category is
puzzling, given the feedback model, but may relate to the
differences between the implementation of multiple feedback
in Schmidt's experiment and ours. We are also intrigued
by the apparent sex differences shown by our subjects.
These might somehow relate to a difference in the experi-
menter-subject interaction affecting the subjects' performance
due to differing expectations regarding the two conditions,
but to proceed beyond tentative speculation would be premature. It is interesting to note that the significant t test results are all negative, indicating psi missing.

The post-hoc motor-skill findings do suggest some relationship between PK and motor skill, though only in the delay one category. It is probably the case that the average
score more accurately reflects the subject's performance in
the motor skill task, and this measure should be used in the
future.

Conclusions

It would appear that the results of Series II and IV
support Schmidt's finding that unselected subjects can induce
PK effects under conditions of time displacement and that the
effects produced are of the same order as under a direct
PK condition. It does not support an enhancement effect
through multiple feedback of the sort found by Schmidt, but
the lack of evidence for psi in the multiple feedback condition
and differences in procedure lead us to conclude that it does
not refute an enhancement effect. It would appear that the
next steps are to bring the multiple feedback procedure more
in line with Schmidt's, refine the motor skill measure, and
analyze for a possible sex interaction in future experiments.

PLANT P K ON AN R N G AND THE EXPERIMENTER EFFECT

Hoyt L. Edge (Rollins College, Winter Park, Fla.)

In a series of experiments I tested the possibility of
plant PK on a random number generator (RNG). To guard
against experimenter influence on the RNG, I introduced into the experimental procedure a time period, unknown to the
experimenter, in which the plant is removed from the proximity of the REG.

Plant PK

There have been a sufficient number of experiments
with animals using the RNG to conclude that animals have
the ability to exhibit PK in situations of positive or negative
reinforcement. One may ask whether any other living organism might not elicit PK in the same kinds of situations.
We know, for instance, that plants react to light and will
turn toward the sun to seek out this energy source. What
reasons might one give for the possibility of plant PK?

Cleve Backster has purported to show that there is
a primary perception in all living organisms. Much of his
work has been with plants trying to show that they produce
responses analogous to human emotions as well as display-
ing ESP. Without evaluating the adequacy of Backster's
work, which is certainly disputed, I cite it as a source for
believing that plants may display some kinds of ESP functions.
At least the evidence seems to give enough incentive for
setting up well-controlled experiments to further test this
possibility. If we accept that there may be some reason to
think that plants display ESP, then it is possible that plants
may also display PK.

Further, there are some theoretical considerations
that are relevant. Stanford has proposed a new model for
understanding psi, which he has designated "conformance behavior." Three criteria describe the necessary conditions
for the occurrence of conformance behavior: a disposed
system, i.e., an organism that is in a need situation; a
random process, usually a random event generator in a PK
experiment; a situation in which the random process will
produce an event which will fulfill the need of the organism.
The plant PK experiment fits this model exactly. The organism in need is the light-starved plant, which is placed in

relationship to the RNG, which is producing the light which the plant needs for growth. An interesting thing about Stanford's model is that it is expressed in terms of an "organism," which leaves open the possibility that plants may respond in a need situation. In fact, Stanford may have had this in mind when he wrote: "A lower organism is a disposed system, and with the abandonment of the cybernetic view of PK, there is no reason why conformance behavior cannot occur in a RNG which is contingently linked to that organism's dispositions."

Experimenter Effect

As Stanford has pointed out, it is not altogether obvious whether the PK found in animal PK tests can be attributed to the animals or to the experimenters. This question is particularly meaningful when one considers Schmidt's experiment with cockroaches, where he found psi missing. It may be that, since cockroaches are such detestable creatures, the experimenter may have been using his own PK to produce an abnormally high number of shocks. To alleviate to some degree the experimenter effect as a problem, many of these animal PK experiments have been done with the experimenter at another location, which, of course, does not eliminate distance PK. A fairly simple method of taking even more precaution is to set up the experiment so that the experimenter does not know when it is taking place, as opposed to other times when the REG is running to test its randomness. The most foolproof way of doing this would be to automate the experiment using a computer where the agents (animals or plants) are introduced and withdrawn mechanically from the experimental situation on a schedule determined randomly by a computer. The computer would monitor the trials and hits in two situations: when the agent was present and when the agent was absent. Unfortunately, I did not have such sophisticated equipment available for my research, so I followed the next best procedure. An individual who knew nothing about the experiment was asked to remove the plant in the course of the time set for the experiment to run. At what time and how long he removed the plant was determined by the individual and not communicated to the experimenter until after the experiment.

Method

On the advice of a biologist, I selected corn plants as the agents because the seeds are easy to germinate. They

were germinated by soaking them several hours in water and
then they were planted in a small pot of soil and vermiculite.
From that point on, the plants were kept in a closet which
was light secure.   In this way, it was assured that the
plants would be "light starved" and that light would serve as
a positive reinforcement.

A 60-watt incandescent light bulb was hooked up to
modified Paratronics equipment.   A trial was made approximately every 18 seconds.   This allowed time for the light
source to initiate the development of the photosynthetic apparatus, which begins well within five seconds of contact
with the correct light.   A 60-watt incandescent light bulb
was used initially because it emits a variety of waves including blue and red.   The red light is needed for active
growth and the blue for photosynthesis and phototrophism.
During the later confirmation studies, fluorescent bulbs were
also introduced to increase the amount of blue light offered
to the plants, which increased the efficiency of the photosynthetic capacities of the red light.   In both situations
enough light is produced without too much heat, which would
injure the plants.

Three pieces of equipment from Paratronics were
used: (1) An ESP-2, which contains the randoming device.
The randoming source is white noise.   I modified the ESP-2
by adding a rheostat, which allows one automatically to produce trials in as long as 18 second intervals.   (2) The Stimuli Module, which turns the light on for just under 18 seconds when there is a hit.   (3) The XY Module which drives
the counters that record the number of trials and hits.

When the corn plants were two to three inches high
and after a test of randomness was made of the RNG, two
corn plants were taken to the darkened experiment room and
placed in front of the light source.   They were placed about
a foot from the light and the binomial RNG was started at
8:25 p. m.   The experimenter and an assistant left the room
and made sure that the individual whose job it was to remove the plants understood the job.   During the experiment,
he removed the plants for a total of almost two hours, reading the trial and hit counters when he removed and replaced
the agents.   Since he was blind to the purpose of the experiment, I felt that it was safe for the same person to read the
counters as well as remove the plants rather than complicate
the procedure by introducing another sub-experimenter.   The
RNG was working during the whole time of the experiment,
which lasted almost seven hours.

Under Condition 1, when the plants were absent, there were a total of 207 "hits" out of 391 trials.   Therefore 52.95 per cent of trials were hits, yielding a CR of 1.16, which is insignificant.

Under Condition 2, when the plants were present there were a total of 465 hits out of 999 trials.   This means that 46.55 per cent of the trials were hits, yielding marginally significant results (CR = -2.18, p < .03, two-tailed). This lends support to the hypothesis that the REG is being affected, although not in the direction anticipated.

Another hypothesis was that there should be a difference between the two conditions, thus giving support that it was the plants that affected the REG and not the experimenter. This hypothesis was borne out to a marginally significant degree, the difference between the two conditions yielding a CR = 2.13, p < .03, using a Standard Normal Test.   This figure should not be taken as seriously, however, as the results of Condition 2 so long as both Condition 1 and randomness tests before and after the experiment are within standard deviations, as they were in this experiment.

Confirmation Studies

Four confirmatory studies were done.   In Series I the conditions were the same as before except that six plants were used.   Series I, Condition 1, with the plants absent, had a CR of 1.01, which is insignificant.   Likewise, Condition 2 yielded insignificant results with a CR of -.86.   In Series II, the corn plants were grown in light until they had reached a height of two inches and then they were light starved for 48 hours before the experiment.   Also in Series II neither condition was significant, with Condition 1 yielding a CR = 1.04, and Condition 2 yielding a CR = 1.18.

In Series III, the original conditions concerning growth of the seeds in darkness were followed.   However, in addition to the 60-watt incandescent bulb, I added one 40-watt Cool White fluorescent bulb (added more red) and 40-watt Daylight fluorescent bulb (added more violet blue).   In addition to the six "new" plants, I used two plants from the previous experiment.   In Series III, Condition 1, when the plants were absent, there was a total of 206 hits out of 405 trials.   This yields a nonsignificant CR = .25.   However, highly significant results were found under Condition 2, when the plants were present.   There were 1073 hits out of 2355 trials, yielding a CR = -4.3, (p < .000017, two-tailed).

In Series IV, the conditions were the same as in Series III, with the plants grown in darkness and the addition of the fluorescent bulbs. Series IV, Condition 1 yielded a nonsignificant CR = 1.69. Under Condition 2, when the plants were present, there were 1052 hits out of 2010 trials, which yields a marginally significant CR = 2.10, p < .036, two-tailed.

Discussion

The results of this experiment are encouraging and might point to a new field of research in parapsychology-- plant PK. In three of five tests, at least marginal significance was achieved, and in one of them, the results were highly significant. As with most phenomena in parapsychology, there does not seem to be great consistency.

Could the results be due to artifact? For instance, could the randomizing device "drift" enough to give these results? My tests with the ESP-2 make this possibility unlikely. First, a randomness test was performed before and after each experiment with the length of the randomness test being between two and four times the length of the experiment, and none of these randomness tests approached marginal significance. In addition, I ran a series of randomness tests to see if there might be drift within a run, but, again, the results did not approach marginal significance. Because of these two kinds of randomness checks, it looks as if the results are not due to malfunction of the randomness device.

In any test in which the results are surprising, the experimenter effect must be considered as an explanation. I have, of course, attempted to eliminate it through the design of the experiment, but it may have been at work. The experimenter may have known through ESP when the plant was removed and affected the RNG only in this one condition. It would be possible to further reduce the experimenter effect as a likely explanation by having the experiment automated so that the time of the beginning and termination of the experiment are unknown to the experimenter.

If the experimenter effect is at work, it may be explained in one of two ways. The first is a straightforward explanation of the experimenter's unconsciously monitoring through ESP the removal and subsequent reintroduction of the plants and using this PK ability to affect the REG only when he "perceives" the plant to be present. The other way to explain the experimenter effect is more unusual but more consistent with Stanford's conformance behavior model. In this interpretation it is enough for the experimenter merely to wish for a result and, without his monitoring the conditions or continually using his PK, the world conforms to the experimenter's wishes. In another paper, I plan to explore this possibility further and give a theoretical justification for this interpretation of PK.

An unexpected result was the psi-missing on two of the significant experiments. How can this be explained? The usual explanation of psi-missing stemming from the sheep-goat effect does not seem to apply since we normally would not want to attribute belief or nonbelief to a plant. Nevertheless, however odd this explanation may sound, I am prepared to maintain it as an option among others that are more probable at this stage. Just as we must not lightly accept such a wild claim like plant needs or beliefs that would call for a radical revision of our world view, so also we must not be stubborn about it.

Another possible explanation is that the stimulus was not a positive reinforcer as had been thought. However, after the experiment, it was noticed that the plants had tilted slightly toward the light source and had become greener, which indicates to me that the light source was beneficial (at least the blue end), in addition to the theoretical considerations for its positive value. Also, marginal significance in the positive direction was found under similar conditions on the last confirmation study.

One experiment, even with confirmation studies, is not enough to establish conclusively the reality of plant PK, particularly since two of the positive tests were only marginally significant. However, significant results have been found. This should merit further exploration, particularly because of the enormous practical and theoretical implications for parapsychology if plant PK is the case.

THE PEARISBURG POLTERGEIST

J. G. Pratt (Division of Parapsychology, University of Virginia)

A case of recurrent spontaneous psychokinesis (RSPK)

occurred in December 1976 in the small town of Pearisburg,
Va., population about 1500 and the county seat of Giles
County. In spite of my efforts to the contrary, the story
about the disturbances was released to the public media.
The matter attracted attention over a large area--at least
from Germany to Japan--for an unusually long time. Many
of the journalists and broadcasters who wished to cover the
story got in touch with me, but I did not share with them
the information I obtained in my study of the case, on the
ground that my investigation was not yet completed. However, the popular accounts written by the journalists who
went to Pearisburg and talked to the witnesses agreed closely with the accounts I had already heard from the same persons in my own interviews.

       The Pearisburg case is by no means the strongest
evidence we have for the reality of RSPK. If it stood alone,
therefore, it would not, in my opinion, enable us to reach
any conclusion on whether RSPK is a psi phenomenon. But
that issue has already been settled affirmatively on the basis
of a number of earlier investigations, so we are justified to
attach greater scientific importance to a new case that ex-
hibits many of the features of a genuine poltergeist outbreak.
In my judgment this case has scientific value because of the
similarities as well as the contrasts that it shows when compared with other cases.

       Let me say at the outset that I personally have no
doubt that this case was paranormal in nature. In this paper
I will first give a chronological account of the disturbances,
with emphasis upon the main storm of events that occurred
over a period of about 45 minutes on Sunday evening, December 19, 1976. The main actors in the drama will be introduced as they enter upon the stage. After relating the
events themselves, I will consider the case in relation to
several questions that are important for investigations of
RSPK cases and for which the Pearisburg case appears to
be particularly relevant.

The Paranormal Events

       Mrs. Beulah Wilson is a widow who was, at the time
of the disturbances, 65 years of age. She lived in the family home on the outskirts of Pearisburg, a cottage with four
rooms and a bath on the first floor and a finished sleeping
area in the attic. Her husband died in the house of a heart
attack about 14 months earlier, and inasmuch as some of the

Wilson sons and daughters were married and living in their
own homes in the region Mrs. Wilson chose to continue living in her own home. But she took in a foster child, a boy
of nine, to provide her company, purpose and a small amount
of income. This youngster had become a ward of the state
on the ground that the natural parents' alcoholism made them
unsuitable custodians for their son. His name was kept out
of the news stories about the case, and this good precedent
will be followed in this report.

Over a period of about two weeks prior to December
19, 1976, isolated single disturbances occurred. Flower
pots fell from the windowsills onto the floor and were broken.
These events occurred mostly at night and Mrs. Wilson assumed that the pots were pushed off by the cat. To Mrs.
Wilson this explanation seemed reasonable because of the
fact that the cat was very frisky and the animal showed some
unusual behavior such as walking on its two hind legs.

The real trouble started shortly after 8 p.m. on that
Sunday night. Mrs. Wilson had made the boy's bed on the
couch in the living room, and he had gone to bed while Mrs.
Wilson was still working in the kitchen. Behind Mrs. Wilson, a banana and an orange fell from the top of a tall cabinet that stood in the corner of the kitchen toward the living
room. Mrs. Wilson again thought it was the work of the
cat, and she picked up the objects and put them back on top
of the cabinet. Shortly thereafter the two objects fell again.
Things then began to happen in both the kitchen and the living
room too fast and too numerous for the two occupants to keep
track of what followed what. Early in the onslaught the
Christmas tree fell over in the corner of the living room.
Mrs. Wilson set it back up, and later it fell over again.

It was no longer possible for Mrs. Wilson to blame
everything on the cat, and she picked up the phone and rang
her son Edward who lived in a small town about six miles
away. (Donald, another son who lived in Pearisburg, was
out of town at the time.) Mrs. Wilson said to Edward that
things were falling down at her house. Edward answered
that he knew something was happening because he could hear
it. He told his mother to hang up the phone and call the
police; he would get there as soon as he could.

When Mrs. Wilson reached the police station and
asked for help, the dispatcher said that he would contact one
of their cars and tell them to come to that address as soon

as they could. Things were still falling, and Mrs. Wilson
decided to call her next-door neighbor, Mr. Marvin Cardwell.
He is a retired utility linesman and he had an understanding
with Mrs. Wilson that she could call upon him whenever she
needed his help. On this occasion when he answered the
phone Mrs. Wilson asked him if they were having an earth-
quake at their house. He answered that nothing unusual was
happening there, and Mrs. Wilson said that she was having
some kind of trouble and would Mr. Cardwell please come
over. He said it took him about fifteen minutes to get into
his walking clothes and reach the Wilson house. He was the
first one to arrive on the scene.

Mr. Cardwell walked into the kitchen through the back
door, and he said that the room was a total wreck. For a
few minutes he stood near the back door and talked to Mrs.
Wilson who was at the other end of the kitchen, and the boy
was in the diagonally opposite corner near the living room
door. While they were telling what had happened and Mr.
Cardwell was trying to take it all in, he heard a "rumble"
in the living room. He asked in surprise: "What was that?"
The boy looked through the open door and answered: "That
old rocking chair just turned over." Mr. Cardwell said that
he was sure there was nobody in the living room, so this
event really shook him. Then, he said, something caught
his eye through the open door to Mrs. Wilson's bedroom,
and he turned his eyes to the left in time to see an old-
fashioned Singer foot-treadle sewing machine falling down in
the middle of the room. Mr. Cardwell was sure that there
was no one in that room, and he was genuinely frightened.
Shortly he said that he had better go down to the end of the
drive and direct the police.

Outside the house in the sideyard, Mr. Cardwell met
Eddie coming in. He told him: "I don't know what it is,
but there's something going on in that house and you better
get inside. I'm going down to guide the police."

During the next few minutes, with Eddie in the house,
things continued to move and some of them overturned. But
Eddie, like his mother, never happened to be looking in the
right direction to see anything start to move. The last thing
disturbed inside the house was the corner cabinet beside the
stove, which moved out from the wall about ten inches without turning over. The last event took place on the back
porch: A carton of six Pepsi-Cola bottles moved from its
position at the back of a table and landed in front of the table

on the floor. There were other objects in front of the bottles, and they were not disturbed. Thus it seems that the
bottles must have moved upward far enough to clear those
objects before moving forward and falling to the floor.
Shortly after the bottles fell, the police car arrived with
deputies Niece and Pritchett.

The sight that greeted the police investigators inside
that house completely baffled them. Not only were they unable to imagine why Mrs. Wilson and the boy, one or both
of them, would have wanted to wreck the place, but also they
were unable to believe that Mrs. Wilson was lying when she
told them that everything just happened by itself. After siz-
ing up the situation as best they could for about an hour,
Deputy Niece took a number of Polaroid pictures, each one
showing the date and hour on the back and signed by him.
Mrs. Wilson and the boy walked out of the house with Eddie
as the police left. She locked the doors and handed the keys
to the police in case they needed to come back later. Mrs.
Wilson said she was never coming back there to live.

Deputy Niece went back to the station and immediately
got on the telephone in search of expert assistance in the investigation of the case. His first call was to Virginia Poly-
technic Institute in Blacksburg where he drew a blank. Then
he called the University of Virginia, where he was put in
touch with the Department of Psychiatry. The caller was so
persistent and persuasive with the resident on duty that he
telephoned Dr. Ian Stevenson at home even though it was
near midnight. After giving a brief description of the situation, the resident emphasized the caller's desire to have
someone come down to look into the matter. Dr. Stevenson
told me the next morning that it sounded as if the police of-
ficer expected him to jump into his car immediately and get
on the road to Pearisburg.

I telephoned the Pearisburg police station shortly after
Dr. Stevenson had informed me of the situation. When I
first talked to Mr. Niece, he said that he and Mr. Pritchett
wanted to have a further talk with all of the witnesses and see
if they stuck by their stories after the several hours that had
elapsed. About an hour later he called back and said that
they had talked to all the witnesses, including the boy whom
they had to call out of school. The witnesses still stood
firmly by their statements that the happenings were unexplain-
able from the physical point of view, so would I please come
on?

Shortly after I reached Pearisburg around 6 p.m. the
police called Donald Wilson, and he agreed to bring his mother and meet us at the house.   This was the first time the
house had been opened since it was closed and locked the
previous night around 10:30.   The view that greeted me inside the house is shown on the color pictures that I took,
which do not differ in any essential respects from the black
and white pictures taken the night before by the police.

Two "Aftershocks"

By late Tuesday afternoon, December 21, I had completed interviews with those who were present in the house
during the disturbances, except for Eddie whom I reached by
telephone later.   The members of the family obviously did
not wish to invite a recurrence of the events.   They assumed
that they had left the trouble behind when they vacated the
house, and I accepted their statement that they did not intend
to return there.   Even if I could have persuaded them to allow me to take the boy and Mrs. Wilson back there for a
visit, I would have hesitated to accept the responsibility for
precipitating further disturbances.   I decided, therefore, to
terminate my first visit and to return later if there should
be a further outbreak of the disturbances.   Before my departure, however, I told Deputy Niece that there might be
further unexplained events in Donald's home.   I asked him
to keep my statement confidential, since I did not wish to
upset the family over something that might prove to be incorrect.

The next day Donald took Mrs. Wilson and the boy
back to the house to collect the Christmas things and to do
a bit of straightening up.   While they were there they had
all gone upstairs and had started back down again.   The boy
was near the bottom of the steps and Mrs. Wilson was behind him when a small cabinet turned over in Mrs. Wilson's
bedroom, the one where the sewing machine had fallen over.
The boy said: "Granny, it's starting again."   Donald immediately ordered everybody out of the house.

That evening Donald and Deputy Niece called me from
the police station to tell me of this experience.   I suggested
that it was so near Christmas that we should let the matter
rest over the holiday weekend and that I would drive down
with my colleague, Dr. David Barker, on Monday.

Before starting our trip at that time, we telephoned to

find out if there had been any further developments. Indeed
there had been. On Friday, Christmas Eve, the Donald Wilson family decided that they would have their celebration and
open their presents in the afternoon. In the evening when the
boy and the 15-year-old Wilson son were in the room they
were sharing, a small bookcase turned over. A short time
later a statuette fell from its place on a ledge at the head of
the stairs and was smashed. Mr. Wilson said he did not
see the object fall but he was situated so that he could have
seen anyone who had been in a position to have thrown it.
When the 13-year-old daughter went into hysterics, Mr. Wilson took the boy outside to the car while his wife called the
police station to come and get the boy. He spent that night
in the police station and the next two days with the case worker, and on Monday he was placed in another foster home.

So much for the facts of the case. Beyond providing
us with one more instance of poltergeist phenomena, does
this case exhibit any special features that make it stand out
among RSPK occurrences or that may throw some light upon
the nature of RSPK?

Discussion

The first point worthy of note is the alacrity with
which the police sought professional assistance on the case.
Recent cases have given us, I believe, good reason to feel
encouraged that the police are becoming better educated to
recognize when they are confronting a paranormal disturbance
rather than a police matter. Not long ago I wondered if the
cases that come to our attention might be only the tip of the
iceberg, and I sought unsuccessfully to obtain support for a
research project that would survey all the police stations in
the U.S.A. regarding their experience in this area. Because
of this case and other recent ones, I have now come to doubt
that the vast majority of poltergeist outbreaks are bottled up
by the police, perhaps because they are embarrassed to ad-
mit their inability to deal with them. The prospect remains,
however, that alerting the police in advance about our existence and where we can be reached if the need should arise
would be a valuable aid to scientific investigations.

The outstanding feature of the Pearisburg case was the
intensity and short duration of the main onslaught of the unexplained events. At the start Mrs. Wilson picked up the objects that fell from the cabinet and she set up the Christmas
tree the first time it toppled over. But then things happened

so fast and furiously that she and the boy simply let everything lie where it landed.   Thus the sum total of the devas-
tation was still there by the time the police arrived about
45 minutes later.   It was their inability to believe that anyone would have wanted to wreck the house in any conscious,
normal way and their inability to believe Mrs. Wilson would
have falsified her statements to cover up any such action
that forced them to consider the possibility of a paranormal explanation.

In my interview with Mrs. Wilson, she freely answered all questions without any tendency to elaborate or
sensationalize the facts.   She said that she was never really
frightened during the events, and she stated her belief that
the hand of the Lord was in these things though she did not
understand the reason.   She said that she never saw anything move, which is surprising when so much was happening in the two rooms.   This case therefore provides a striking example of the elusiveness of RSPK phenomena, the tendency for events to occur so as to avoid being observed.

The boy is a quiet chap who answered questions as
briefly as possible but who did not volunteer information.
He also said that he was not frightened.   Unlike Mrs. Wilson, he said he saw some of the objects moving, but he did
not see all of them.

Mr. Cardwell, the only witness to the events outside
the family, is a retired power company linesman.   He was
a willing witness, quite happy to talk about an experience
that changed some of his fundamental beliefs.   He said that
if he had been told about the events by someone else who
had seen and heard what he had, he would have thought the
person was lying.   But he said that his brief period in the
house during the disturbances made a believer out of him.
He was sure that there was no one other than Mrs. Wilson
and the boy in the house when he arrived, and the two events
that occurred while he was there were quite enough for him.
There can be no doubt that he was genuinely frightened by
his experience, which he freely admitted.   When his wife
went to her job on the night shift of a nearby factory, Mr.
Cardwell got in his truck and drove several miles to spend
the night in his son's home, and he did the same thing
again the following night.

The psychological situation involved a foster-child,
foster-parent relationship, and thus it adds to the evidence

from recent cases that the circumstance of a broken family
is one that may be especially prone to RSPK phenomena
(e.g., the Newark case, the Powhatan case, the "Unpubli-
cized" case). In the Pearisburg case the indications were
that the boy was happy to be in the care of Mrs. Wilson and
that he was well-liked by her and other members of the family. There were perhaps a dozen wrapped presents under
the Christmas tree, and the boy was looking forward excited-
ly to what was to be his first experience of a real Christmas. This case suggests, therefore, that the focal person
in an RSPK episode may carry the tensions and anxieties
from the environment in which they developed into another,
more favorable situation where the physical disturbances erupt
as a kind of delayed reaction.

The Pearisburg case raises with particular force the
question of the difference between the interests of those directly involved in the disturbances and the investigator. In
this instance it was evident that the members of the family
wanted to have the disturbances over and done with. Would
an investigator have been justified, under the circumstances,
to manipulate the situation in a way that seemed most likely
to cause a continuation of the unexplained events? Such a
course of action, I suggest, would have been unethical and
immoral. In addition to the wishes of the immediate members of the Wilson family, the welfare of the boy was involved, and this was the paramount consideration for the
social workers. The Wilson family showed that they could
and would protect themselves by precipitously ending their
responsibility for the child. They were reported in the
media as saying that they were genuinely devoted to the boy
and were very sorry that they had to give him up, but they
felt they had no other choice under the circumstances. I
spoke with the social worker by telephone, and she said that
she would let me know if any further trouble developed in
the new family with which the boy was placed. There has
been no further word. While I do not rule out the possibility of future contact with the boy, through the social worker,
in a followup on the case, I will say that this would have to
be managed carefully to insure that the personal welfare of
the boy would not be sacrificed where it did not coincide with
the scientific interests of the investigator.

UNDERSTANDING THE POLTERGEIST

William G. Roll (Psychical Research Foundation)

In recent poltergeist or RSPK studies several patterns have emerged. In order to determine how prevalent these are I have made a survey of RSPK cases. I have restricted this to published reports by persons held to be serious and truthful by their contemporaries. Secondly, the authors, or persons they have interviewed, must have witnessed at least one physical incident which apparently could not be explained in conventional terms. There were 116 such cases. Of these, 97 appeared in professional parapsychological books or journals. All 97 occurred after 1849 though the published accounts often came later (I have used the beginning date to designate the year for a case). I have divided the cases into four periods. The poltergeist cases receiving scientific attention fall in the period 1850-1899 where there were 25 cases, 1900-1949 where there were 38, and 1950-1974 where there were 34. Prior to 1850 there were 19 cases which fulfilled my criteria.

The survey gives a picture of the poltergeist over four centuries and an opportunity to learn which of its features change over time and therefore may be determined by extraneous factors and which are stable and may therefore express the underlying process.

THE CENTRAL PERSON

Age and Sex

Among the 116 cases, 92 (79%) seemed to be associated with a person or occasionally two persons. For the 19 RSPK cases prior to 1849, in 14 (74%) there seemed to have been focal persons; the 25 cases, 1850-99, showed central persons in 19 (76%); in the 1900-49 collection of 38 cases, there was such a connection in 30 (79%); and in the recent 34 cases, 1950-74, 29 (85%) showed this relation. The increase over the four periods of cases with focal persons is not statistically significant.

In some cases, the events followed the person out-of-doors, during visits to relatives, and so on. This was true for 39 (42%) of the 92 cases. The distribution over the

four periods is six (32%), seven (37%), 13 (43%), and 13
(45%). In two other cases no focal person was identified
but the phenomena followed the family when they moved. A
common factor runs through these cases which further points
to the link with a person: there were generally no disturbances when the focal person was asleep.

In the 92 cases with focal persons, 56 were females
and 36 males, 61 versus 39 per cent. (When more than one
person was involved, I counted the person who seemed to be
most closely associated with the phenomena; I did the same
in calculating ages.) The difference may be of borderline
significance (at the p = .05 level, chi-square test) depending
on the proportions of males and females in the general population in the times and places involved. This favoring of
women, however, was entirely due to the two early periods.
During 1612-1849 there were ten females versus four males
(71% and 29%); and during 1850-99, 16 versus three (84% and
16%). The proportions then evened out for 1900-1949 to 16
versus 14 (53% and 47%); and 1950-1974 to 14 versus 15 (48%
and 52%). If we assume that there were about as many
males as females in the population in the periods and places
in question, the difference for the second period is quite significant (X^2 = 8.9, 1 df, p < .005). I do not know the reason for this difference. Most poltergeist agents are young,
and perhaps girls then led more stressful lives than boys or
perhaps cases with girls were for some reason more likely
to be reported. In any case the two recent periods suggest
that sex is no longer associated with RSPK agency.

For 74 of the 92 persons who seemed to be associated
with the incidents, their ages were given. This ranged from
eight to 78 (the latter actually a man said to be in his late
70's; similarly a woman in her 70's is entered as 75 years
old). The average for the 43 females was 15 years and for
the 31 males 17 years, but the medians were only 13 in both
cases. This difference was the result of two people in their
70's in the fourth period. For the four time periods, the
average ages for females were 12, 15, 12, and 19; and for
males 15, 13, 14, and 21. The medians for females were
12, 13.5, 15, and 13; and for males 14, 12, 15, and 14.
The mean age for both sexes was 13. If we take account of
18 others who were only known to be adults, the mean would
probably increase to 14 years in both cases.

Health

Several of the focal persons show behavior which seem

symptomatic of a mental or psychological disorder. It is
not always clear whether the problem preceded the RSPK
incidents or was brought on by them but even in the latter
case there may have been a predisposition. In 49 (53%) of
the 92 cases with focal persons, these suffered from more or
less debilitating ailments. In 22 (24%) of the accounts, the
people were described as having seizures or dissociative
states or as being prone to such states. Sixteen of the 22
were observed one or more times as having muscular contractions, comas, convulsions, fainting fits, trances, seizures or other dissociative episodes. Four others had been
diagnosed as epileptics. Of these, three were treated for the
disease at the time of the RSPK outbreak and one had previously shown epileptic spikes in the EEG. A fifth, whose
EEG was taken some months after the incidents, produced a
short burst of such spikes. This RSPK agent and another
were prone to dissociative episodes according to their psychological tests.

     If we examine the distribution over the four periods,
1612-1849, 1850-1899, 1900-1949, and 1950-1974, the 22
RSPK agents are distributed as follows: three (21%), five
(26%), five (17%), and nine (31%). The slightly higher figure
in the last period was probably due to increased interest in
the behavior of the RSPK agent and improved methods of
observation, such as the EEG. It seems likely that the other figures would have been larger if similar diagnostic tools
had been available then. In this context it is relevant that
there were no diagnosed epileptics in the two first periods;
the first appeared in the third period, with three in the fourth
period, not counting the borderline case who was also in the
fourth. Estimates of the prevalence of epilepsy in the general population is usually quoted as .5 per cent, but in a
study which included patients who had only one known attack,
it is .74 per cent. Assuming the more conservative figure
of 1 per cent for the incidence of epilepsy in the population,
the probability of finding four or more epileptics amongst
our 92 agents is $p < .02$ (using the Poisson approximation
to the binomial). Three out of the 29 in the fourth period
is significant at $p < .001$.

     Scott Rogo warns that the association with epilepsy
"may be an artifact of reporting. ... [I]t seems to me that
if the agent has epilepsy, the family is more likely to report
RSPK since they will probably see the psi as a medical problem. Also, a trained doctor handling the patient may be
more likely to realize that the case needs to be looked into.

In other words, if you have an agent under medical supervision I think this sizably increases the likelihood of the case
getting reported at all. This could easily account for your
figure." This objection may be valid for the Midlands case
reported by James McHarg, the girl's psychiatrist. The
three other accounts were apparently not due to the medical
problems but to the publicity from the RSPK disturbances or
because the family or the police sought the aid of parapsychologists in dealing with the phenomena. If the McHarg case is
omitted, the significance for the overall relationship increases
to $p < .07$ but remains significant for the 1950-74 period at
$p = .05$.

Twenty-seven (29%) of the 92 central persons had other problems, some of which are associated with epilepsy,
such as alcoholism and hyperactivity.

In the fourth period, as a result of parapsychological
investigations or because the family had sought professional
help on their own, several of the RSPK agents received psychological or psychiatric examinations. The 13 RSPK agents
who participated in such studies were found to have repressed
agression or low tolerance of frustration. Four of them
were also among the people with dissociative episodes and
four were in the group with miscellaneous problems (two
hyperactive children, a schizophrenic, and a violent alco-
holic). Repressed agression was probably also part of the
problem for many of the RSPK agents in the previous periods,
particularly the hysterics and neurotics. Aggression and irritability are also common among epileptics. Five of the
agents in the fourth period seemed normal except for the aggression shown on the psychological tests. There is an increase in the last period in the number of people suffering
from miscellaneous problems: one (7%), seven (37%), five
(17%), and 14 (48%). This increase (significant at $p < .05$,
chi-square test) is probably the result of improved methods
of observation and increased interest in the RSPK agent in
recent times. Of the total of 49 persons with more or less
severe medical or psychological problems, 23 were in the
fourth period, representing 79 per cent of the RSPK agents
in this period. The best estimate of the proportion of RSPK
agents with organic or functional problems may come from
this period. If anything, 79 per cent may be an underestimation. It should be kept in mind that the attention of observers
usually centers on the RSPK incidents rather than on the
agent and furthermore that the period of observation is generally confined to the duration of the RSPK occurrences.

With more attention to the agent and more thorough medical
and psychological studies, more psychological or medical
problems may emerge.

John Palmer has observed in two RSPK cases he
studied, that the children were not living with their natural
parents at the time of the RSPK outbreaks. He raises the
possibility that this may have created a stressful situation
which led to the RSPK incidents.

If we set 18 as the age when a person can normally
be expected to leave home, there are 61 girls and boys at
this age or lower for whom we know where they lived (I
have included seven whose exact ages are not given but who
are referred to as boys, girls, or teenagers). Of these, 38
(62%) were living away from home and 23 (38%) were at
home when the events began. Thirty-five were girls, of
whom 21 (60%) were away and 14 (40%) at home. Of the
26 boys, 17 (65%) were away from home and nine (35%) at
home. Among the 23 boys and girls who were living at
home, in four cases there was only one parent in the home
and in three, the child was a latecomer to elderly parents.

Of the 38 children who were living away from home,
18 (47%) were 13 years or less. Since we do not know how
many children, in the populations and periods under consideration, did not live with their natural parents, a statistical
assessment is not possible. It would appear, however, that
the figures were considerably less than the 62 per cent for
poltergeist children below 19 years or the 29.5 per cent for
children below 14. It seems that many of the RSPK children
may have had a more stressful childhood than others at their
age.

Precipitating Events

In 38 (41%) of the 92 cases with focal persons, the
RSPK events began at a time when there were changes or
problems in the family's home which may have affected the
agent. In eight cases (21%) the incidents errupted after a
move to a reportedly haunted house or followed mediumistic
or spiritistic communications, or RSPK occurrences reportedly had taken place in the previous home of the focal person
or had centered around a relative. In one a sudden, startling occurrence seemed to release an RSPK outbreak. In 15
(39%) the RSPK incidents started up after the agent or the
family had moved, when a parent was away or the agent,

usually a child, had to share its bed with somebody else; in 12 cases (32%) the focal person was ill or subject to unusual psychological stress; and in two cases (5%) the incidents followed shortly after the death of relatives or friends.

The cases where precipitating events were identified are distributed as follows over the four periods, four (29%), seven (37%), 13 (43%), and 14 (48%). Again the slight increase over the four periods is probably the result of increased awareness by observers of the agent and the possibility that he or she and therefore the events, may be affected by external circumstances. Some of the precipitating events were clearly stressful. With respect to the moves or other changes in the family situation, we do not know how these affected the focal person, but changes of this type require adaptations to a new social and physical environment and may be stressful, especially for children.

Exorcism

Many of the people afflicted by poltergeists have tried to make them go away by means of exorcism and related procedures. Among the 116 cases such activities were tried in 30 (25%). These attempts were distributed as follows over the four periods: four (21%), four (16%), 13 (34%) and nine (23.5%). It is interesting that such attempts were about as common in the 20th century as in earlier ages.

Of the 30 attempts, the RSPK phenomena ceased after four (14%), there was a temporary relief after four (14%), the exorcism had no effect in 21 cases (72%)--except in five cases where the occurrences seemed to intensify during the rites. In one case it could not be determined whether the religious rites temporarily enhanced the phenomena or caused them to quiet down.

It is uncertain if the four cases which ceased after the rites did so as a result of these. For two of the four cases the duration of the RSPK eruption was not known. In two others they were two and three months. The median duration of the RSPK outbreaks was two months so these two cases had perhaps run their course when the rites were tried. In general exorcism seemed ineffective as a means to deal with RSPK.

Moves and Reduction of Stress

Once it had been noticed that the phenomena followed

a servant or other employee, this person was sometimes
dismissed, or if a member of the family, he or she was
sent to another relative. Occasionally the family as a whole
or some member would move. The phenomena at times followed the family or the focal person to the new location, but
sometimes they ceased. (In two of the cases the house was
burnt or severely damaged by fires supposedly set by the
poltergeist.)

To determine whether such moves actually tended to
shorten the course of the events we need to examine the
durations of the cases. In 31 where duration is recorded
the median is 1.13 months versus 2 months for all the cases.
To evaluate the difference statistically, the averages have to
be used: 52.4 versus 155.6 days. This difference is significant (p < .05, one tailed, chi-square test) and suggests that
the moves tended to shorten the duration of the incidents.

In 11 cases the occurrences seemed to terminate for
other reasons, but usually this happened so late in the course
of the events that the causal connection seems doubtful. For
instance, one case ceased after a year with the inception of
the girl's menses, in another after two years of psychoanaly-
sis. Only three such cases ceased before two months. In
one it was after payment of a debt incurred by a deceased
person believed to haunt the area, in another by hypnotic
suggestion, and in the third when the 10-year-old agent returned to school after having to stay home with a back in-
jury.

THE OCCURRENCES

Attenuation Effect

The proximity effect or, put differently, the attenuation of the number of incidents with increased distance from
the focal person, can only be clearly demonstrated if the
distances have been measured and if the attenuation of incidents is statistically significant. Such attenuations, first reported at the 1968 PA Convention, have now been found in
nine (26%) of the 34 cases in the 1950-1974 period.

I know of only one case where an analysis was made
for attenuation but none was found. In the Scherfede water
case, Hans Bender detected no decrease in the number of
times water appeared in relation to the position of the 13-

year-old girl who seemed to be the agent. However, the distances measured were those between the girl and the place
where the water appeared, its origin being unknown, while in
the other studies the distances were those between the person
and the starting place of the moving object.

The Focussing Effect

In RSPK the term focussing refers to repeated incidents with the same or similar objects or taking place in the
same area. In the first place there is "focussing" on the
house or area where the events are concentrated. Secondly,
there may be focussing on a special location in that area.
For instance a room or a shelf in that room may have a concentration of incidents. This is called area focussing.
Sometimes it seems that a special object, such as a kitchen
cabinet, or a special class of objects, such as stones, are
singled out. This is object focussing.

I have tried to determine whether focussing might
arise as an artifact or whether one kind of focussing may be
reduced to another. In the three cases for which we had
sufficient data for analyses, there was evidence for focussing
on types of objects, individual objects and areas which could
not be easily dismissed in other terms.

It is rarely possible to isolate the focussing effect
from the other effects in the present collection of RSPK
cases. But in 107 (92%) of the total of 116 cases there is
prima facie focussing of one or more kinds. In 89 (77%)
there is focussing on objects, either individual or types of
objects (in 12 of these there is also area focussing) and in
18 (15.5%) on areas. The evidence for focussing runs about
equally strongly through the four collections.

Unusual Trajectories and Teleportation

In the 105 cases with moving objects, "floating,"
"wavering," "zigzag," "sinuous," "hovering," or "fluttering"
movements are often reported. There are also changing
speeds in flight, levitations of objects and objects coming
around corners or rotating in the same spot. Forty-three
of the 105 cases (41%) show one or more of these features.
The proportions do not differ greatly in the four groups:
five (31%), 14 (58%), 11 (30.5%), and 13 (45%).

Cases with apparent instances of teleportation are scat-

tered throughout the collection.   Altogether there are 18 such
cases, or 17 per cent of the total of 105.   Eleven of these
also show unusual trajectories.   The teleportation cases are
distributed over the four groups as follows: one (6%), two
(8%), ten (27%) and five (17%).

Until the present survey, I have not taken teleportation seriously as a possibly genuine RSPK characteristic.
While the evidence is weak compared to more conventional
poltergeist effects, there are too many reports by serious
witnesses for easy dismissal.   I now tend to agree with Hans
Bender that this phenomenon may be real and should be taken
account of in attempts to explain the poltergeist.

Hallucinatory Experiences

In 27 (23%) of the 116 cases there were reports of
apparitions representing human figures, animals, demons,
hands, fingers, or amorphous shapes.   In 13 (11%) intelligible voices were heard, including whispering and singing;
seven of these also had apparitions.   There are other effects,
such as woundings and fires, but the apparitions and voices
are more abundant.   In the hope that they may throw light
on the RSPK process, let us take a look at them.

The 27 cases with apparitions are distributed as follows over the four periods: seven (37%), seven (28%), six
(16%), and seven (21%); and the 13 cases with intelligible
voices six (32%), two (8%), two (5%), and three (9%).   There
is a decrease in both over the four periods.   The figures
are not independent since hearing voices and seeing visions
may be related and since both were reported in seven of
the accounts.   In any case only the decrease in voices from
the first period to the last three is significant (p = .05, chi-
square test).

The decrease may be associated with a reduced tendency in more recent times to personify RSPK phenomena.
In the early cases, the observers may have been more likely
to suppose that they were dealing with a personal entity
which, if it could make knocks and throw things should also
be able to speak and make itself visible.   This is not to say
that the experiences were always hallucinatory.   Eight cases
(24%) where people outside the immediate group reportedly
witnessed the phenomena raise the possibility that there may
be an objective or physical basis to some of the experiences.

DISCUSSION

The Swedish psychiatrist, Paul Bjerre explained the underlying similarity among poltergeist cases by drawing the following analogy: "Both hysterical and especially epileptic attacks appear with similar symptomology in different individuals. One may draw an analogy between the rumblings and throwings of objects near a (poltergeist) medium with the violent energy eruptions in the other attacks. When the nerve energy moves outside the skin ... it nevertheless remains connected not only with the conscious and unconscious complex but also with certain pre-existing channels of energy. In the same way as the outpour of energy from an epileptic short circuit follows certain pathways in the nerve system, so does the transformation of the externalized energy to new energy forms and their expression follow certain schemata provided by the organism."

So far brain wave studies in parapsychology have focussed on the reception of information (ESP) or energy rather than on its transmission. In PK we seem to deal with transmission and in RSPK with sudden and recurrent transmission. If these are the results of central nervous system eruptions, poltergeist incidents may be regarded as a special class of epileptic-like symptoms of CNS malfunction.

In addition to the fact that RSPK incidents have been reported around epileptics and people with symptoms suggestive of epilepsy, several other factors make the CNS theory deserve the attention of RSPK researchers. In his 1974 study of "Epilepsy and Personality Disorders," Desmond Pond says that many epileptics show "irritability ... with sudden and unpredictable variations of mood: they are suspicious, quarrelsome, egocentric, circumstantial, religious, and [show] a slowness and stickiness of thought that borders onto mental subnormality."

The theme of aggression recurs in both the personalities of RSPK agents and in the nature of the events themselves. The "stickiness" or perseveration of people with brain dysfunctions refers to the tendency for the patient to have the same thought or carry out the same activity repeatedly. This trait does not come out strongly in the personality tests of RSPK agents but it does seem to be expressed in the incidents themselves. The focusing effects, the repetitive incidents involving an object or area, are characteristic of RSPK.

Epilepsy can be brought on by a variety of developmental and congenital defects.   Some of the 27 RSPK agents with miscellaneous complaints had problems which are sometimes associated with epilepsy.

Epilepsy is concentrated in the lower age brackets: According to a survey in 1970 by R. M. Goldenson "over half of known cases appear before age 15." Petit mal usually ceases before adulthood.   The median age for RSPK outbreaks is 14--that is, about half of the cases in the survey erupted before the age of 15.

In patients with epilepsy, seizures may be brought on by a loud voice or other startling stimulus.   Emotional and psychological disturbances may also bring on an epileptic attack.   Similarly, RSPK occurrences may be triggered by startling or stressful events in the life of the agent.   Epileptic attacks can sometimes be controlled by adjustments in the social situation of the patient.   The same seems to be true for RSPK.

Epileptics sometimes have auditory or visual hallucinations, and hallucinations are apparently caused by CNS disturbances.   Several of the RSPK cases were associated with the seeing of apparitions and hearing of voices.   Of the 33 such cases, 12 (36%) involved the agents who reportedly had epilepsy, muscular contractions and so on.   In other words more than half of the 22 agents with such complaints saw apparitions or heard voices (or relatives or visitors had such experiences).   This relationship is significant ($p < .05$, chi-square test) and seems to support the relation between RSPK and CNS eruptions.

The CNS theory for RSPK seems to fit the rotating-beam theory.   This first emerged from an examination of the Miami occurrences and was later supported by analysis of the Olive Hill disturbances.   The characteristics of movements recorded in these cases could result if energy waves were radiated from two positions on the agent's body and if they were non-synchronous.

The theory that recurrent paroxysmal events in the central nervous system are related to RSPK helps to complete the picture.   In epilepsy the neural discharge begins in a particular location (the epileptic focus) and then rapidly spreads to other parts of the brain.   The EEG transmissions resulting from different parts of the brain are out of phase, and might provide several loci of CNS discharges in addition to the place of origin. The theory that recurrent CNS disturbances are related to RSPK seems to complement the rotating-beam theory.

The most direct way of testing the CNS theory for RSPK is to take EEG recordings of the agent during the RSPK incidents using telemetry units. This has been attempted in two studies reported at the 1975 Convention by Pratt and Palmer [RIP 1975, pp. 109-15] and by Solfvin and Roll [pp. 115-20]. In neither cases were there any incidents when the central persons were wearing the EEG electrodes and carrying the telemetry units.

It is unlikely that all poltergeist agents suffer from epilepsy, even the petit mal attacks which often pass with childhood. It seems possible, however, that RSPK may be associated with CNS eruptions, whether or not these also result in epileptic symptoms. In any case, epilepsy provides some interesting parallels to poltergeist attacks and may offer insights into the nature of "seizures" outside the physical organism. The etiology of this form of CNS dysfunction and the conditions which tend to enhance or inhibit seizures have parallels in many poltergeist agents and in the development of RSPK disturbances.

RSPK occurrences are psychophysical. They simultaneously express patterns which we generally call physical and patterns which we call mental. A simple RSPK occurrence, for instance a glass in the Miami warehouse which lifted itself over the objects in front of it, suggests intelligent guidance. At the same time, the events conformed to the attenuation pattern and in other ways suggested an energetic process. Similarly, the focusing effects appear to be examples of perseveration and can also be understood in terms of wave theory. Fast-slow movements, the "floating," curved, and rotating trajectories make sense in terms of the rotating-beam theory--assuming a built-in guidance system.

Teleportations, if real, suggest in a particularly striking manner a psychological side to RSPK. Our thoughts are not limited by walls and closed space; we can easily and immediately call up ideas or images relating to distant objects. Mentation has another framework: it is a function, at least in part, of the associative cortex. Perhaps a neural discharge of sufficient strength which combines two images, such as mirror and bedroom, is reflected in the sudden appearance of an actual mirror in the room.

RSPK outbreaks are rare, but usually highly traumatic to the family or group they descend upon. The possibility that they are related to brain dysfunctions makes it possible to envisage a poltergeist therapy similar to treatments for epilepsy. The main interest of RSPK phenomena, however, may be what they suggest about ordinary people and the everyday world.

Part 3:   Presidential Address

SPACE, TIME AND MIND*

Charles T. Tart

In recent years I have discovered something which has
undoubtedly been discovered by many others before me, but
its full significance only becomes clear when you personally
make this discovery for yourself. This discovery is that the
most exciting ideas often occur when you start taking closer
look at things that are apparently obvious to everyone, things
that are so accepted that they become largely implicit habits
of thought. I have called my talk this evening, "Space,
Time and Mind" because these are three things that we all
take for granted almost all of the time. If you want to know
what space is, you look around; if you want to be more precise about it, you take out a ruler and measure it. If you
want to know what time is, you can simply feel time passing
by, or you can use a clock and measure it more precisely.
In almost all cases we don't wonder what space and time
are, we simply use our rulers and clocks without thinking.
It is a similar case with the mind. We very seldom ask
ourselves questions about what the mind is, but we use our
minds (hopefully!) in almost every action of our life.

Our field of parapsychology is an excellent one for
providing the opportunity to think more deeply about space,
time and mind. Every time that we deal with real-time psi,
such as telepathy or clairvoyance, we are confronted with instances of something that seems paradoxical in terms of our
ordinary, physical concepts of space. We arrange conditions
so there is too much space or too many barriers in space
for information to get from one point to another, yet sometimes it gets there. Whenever we set up a precognition experiment and obtain significant results, both our "common
sense" and most physicists' notions about the nature of time
are paradoxically violated. These apparent "violations" of

_____

*This is the Presidential Address, given August 10, 1977.

our accepted conceptual framework about space and time
should serve as a constant reminder that the most generally
accepted scientific concept of the mind, that it is totally
equivalent to brain and nervous sytem processes, is too
limited. Whatever the mind is, it does not seem to be fully
understandable within the ordinary conceptual framework of
space and time.

What I want to share with you this evening are the
results of almost two years of analyses and struggle with the
implications of some data of mine about time, and some of
their implications about mind. This has been the most exciting work of my parapsychological career! The data also
have implications about space, but I will not stress these
implications because, in many ways, they are familiar to
this very select group. Regardless of how profound the implications of psi phenomena seeming to violate our general
concepts about physical space are, we are quite familiar with
the violations and seldom get excited. I stress the time implications because personally they have been exciting, puzzling
and frustrating to me. Perhaps the most important personal
discovery that I made from the work I shall be describing to
you is that while I believed, as a result of the parapsychological data on it, in precognition, I did not believe in precognition at all! I discovered that while I had studied the
experimental and spontaneous case evidence for precognition
for many years, and had lectured extensively on the reality of
precognition, that belief existed in isolation on a purely intellectual level. On a deeper level, I found that I did not believe in precognition at all. The idea of a future that somehow existed and affected the present was just so ridiculous
that it had no reality at all for the rest of my psyche. When
I found that extremely significant precognitive effects had, as
it were, sneaked into my own laboratory while I wasn't looking, considerable intellectual conflict resulted, but I think the
long-term results have been very profitable. Let me begin
getting more specific now.

I believe most of us here accept the existence of several basic psi phenomena: we have studied reams of experimental evidence, collected under very good conditions, and
we know something is happening that requires explanation.
We also know that the implications of the existence of psi are
very important for our understanding of space, time and
mind. Unfortunately, our efforts to understand the nature of
psi, even though they are still in the beginning state, are
progressing very slowly. Some of the major problems that

inhibit the efficient study of the nature of psi are its unreliability, its overall level of manifestation, and the prevalence of decline effects.

A decade ago, a survey that Burke Smith and I carried out (Tart & Smith, 1967; Tart, 1973) suggested that about one in three experiments carried out by members of this Association showed statistically significant evidence for psi. While that is far more than one would expect if there were no such thing as psi, it is not a terribly good track record.

Second, even when we do get psi, that usually means we have results significant at, say, the .05 or .01 level. The vast majority of the time, the percipients are simply guessing, with a little flash of psi once in a great while. In engineering terms, we have a very poor signal-to-noise ratio, which makes study of the characteristics of psi, the signal, very difficult.

Further, even when we find a good percipient, he seldom can keep his ability. As J. B. Rhine put it so pointedly in 1947,

> As a rule a subject spoils as he continues long at the same test.... [N]othing could be more calculated to make the experimenter wring his hands in despair than to watch a good performer go bad, as so many have done with time. ... [A]ll of the high scoring subjects who have kept on very long have declined, whether or not any incident occurred. ... [I]t is a baffling field of research. We destroy the phenomena in the very act of trying to demonstrate them. Evidently the tests themselves get in the way of the abilities they are designed to measure. ... [O]bviously it cannot be brought under reliable control, either for experimental study or for practical utility as long as this is the case ..." [Rhine, 1947, pp. 189-90].

Sometimes I think it is rather heroic of us to continue working on trying to understand the nature of psi under these difficult conditions. Heroic as it is, though, I don't expect very rapid progress in understanding to be made under these circumstances. Thus I have thought for a long time that one of our major concerns should be finding some way of greatly increasing the reliability and level of psi in our experiments. Toward this end, I theorized some ten

years ago (Tart, 1966) that some important aspects of the
problems I've just noted resulted from a lack of immediate
feedback to percipients, so they could not learn to distinguish
the subtle characteristics of mental events that indicated they
were actually using psi from mere guessing processes. I
have elaborated the theory of how to teach people more reliable psi performance via immediate feedback at considerable
length, and I shall present a paper on it tomorrow morning
(Tart, 1977a; 1978 [pp. 90-122, supra]). The data I want to
report tonight come from my and my colleagues' (John Palmer and Dana Redington) two studies attempting to teach
more reliable psi performance with immediate feedback training, and so I shall review briefly the experimental procedures
used there, but not the results of the effects of feedback on
learning. Rather I shall present results dealing with unexpected precognition effects. The data on learning per
se, as well as more details of the experimental procedures, can be found elsewhere (Palmer, Tart & Redington, 1976; Tart, 1975a, 1976a; Tart, Palmer & Redington, 1977).

General Experimental Procedures

Figure 1 gives an overview of the general procedure
of my first and second studies of feedback training.* Since
my learning theory (Tart, 1966) predicted that experimental
percipients needed to have some demonstrable ESP to begin
with if the feedback training was to have much effect, we
needed relatively talented percipients, rather than unselected
ones. As percipients who can demonstrate individually significant ESP in a short period of testing are generally considered to be relatively rare, a two-stage selection procedure
preceded the formal Training Study in each case. In the first
stage, teams of student experimenters, trained by me in my
experimental psychology class at UC Davis, gave quick ESP
card-guessing tests to large classes of UC Davis students.

Students who showed individually significant ESP hitting
in this initial Selection Study stage were invited to the second
stage, the Confirmation Study.

*I would like to thank the est Foundation, the Institute for
the Study of Human Knowledge, and the Parapsychology Foundation for financial and administrative support on these studies,
as well as my many colleagues and assistants.

As we know, screening hundreds of percipients is bound to produce some who score high by chance alone, so this second, Confirmation Study where each student was individually tested was necessary to weed out most of the false positive scores. Students who scored well in both the Selection and Confirmation studies were invited to enter the Training Study. This procedure might have let a few non-talented percipients through into the Training Study, but the bulk of those who reached the final stage should have had some ESP talent. I stress this point, as it raises an interesting question later for some percipients who stopped showing individually significant ESP in the Training Study: Were they false positives who slipped through, or was their psi ability suppressed or displaced under the psychological conditions of the Training Study?

A few students, who were known to individual experimenters, who thought they might have some psychic ability, went directly into the Confirmation Study without going through the Selection Study.

In the Confirmation Study, each student percipient was tested individually on both the four-choice Aquarius Model 1000 ESP Trainer, and a ten-choice trainer, the TCT (Ten-Choice Trainer) in the first Training Study or ADEPT (Advanced Decimal Extrasensory Perception Trainer) in the second Training Study. Since individual trial target and response data, from which precognition could be scored later, was recorded only for the ten-choice machines* I shall not further describe the Aquarius machine here. As you can see from Figure 1, ten percipients completed the first Training Study, and seven percipients completed the second Training Study. "Completed" means doing 20 runs of 25 trials on either of the ten-choice machines, usually at the rate of one to three runs per hour session.

The Ten-Choice Trainer

The TCT consists of a percipient's and experimenter's

---

*In the second Training Study we did record individual trial target and response data, but as only three percipients worked with the Aquarius in the second Training Study, too little data were acquired to look for the sort of relationships described later.

SELECTION
STUDY

Screen large groups of students and some   Informal judgement by experi-
individuals with 2 quick card guessing   menters that individuals pos-
tests, score for each individual.   sess ESP ability

Invite to Confirmation Study if subject
hits at .05 level or better or, by experimenter's judgement, subject shows
special promise in spite of low score

CONFIRMATION
STUDY

Give each subject 2 runs on Aquarius,
2 runs on TCT, 2 more runs on trainer
of subject's choice, to verify ESP
ability.

Invite to Training Study if subject
continues to hit at .05 level or
better or, in experimenter's judgment, shows special promise

TRAINING
STUDY

Each subject does 20 runs of 25
trials each with immediate feedback, using the one training
machine of his choice

Evaluate Results

Figure 1

console. The experimenter also acts as agent. The two
consoles were located in separate rooms; the laboratory arrangement is shown in the lower part of Figure 2. The percipient was alone in his laboratory room (shown in the lower-
left corner of the figure) sitting in front of his console. A
closed-circuit television camera was focused on this console.
The experimenter/sender was inside a Faraday cage, con-

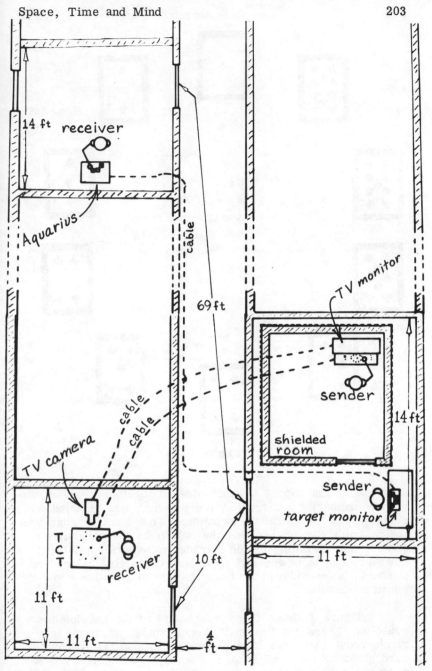

Figure 2

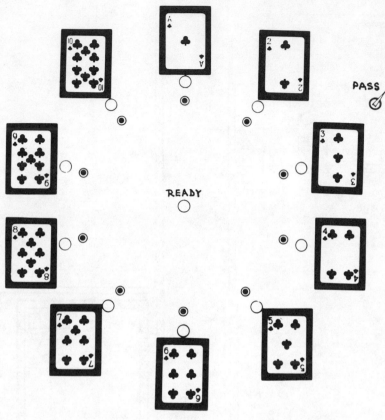

Figure 3

structed of thin copper sheets soldered together over an otherwise ordinarily constructed room, which was mounted on
rubber tires for vibration isolation. This Faraday cage was
inside another room, across the hall from the percipient's
room. The shielding of the Faraday cage was not intact,
however, due to power and apparatus connecting cables, so
it should be considered as being functional only for some
sound attenuation.

Figure 3 shows the arrangement of the percipient's
console. There are ten unlit target lamps, arranged in a
circle about 15 inches in diameter, with a miniature playing
card glued beside each lamp to identify it numerically. A
response push button is located beside each lamp. When the

ready lamp in the center of the console came on, this sig-
nalled the percipient that the experimenter/sender had selected one of the ten lamps to be the target in accordance
with the output of an electronic random number generator
(RNG), and was trying telepathically to send the target identity to him.

The percipient could respond quickly or take as much
time as he wished to make his decision.   This time ranged
from a few seconds to several minutes.   When the percipient
decided on which target he thought was the correct choice,
he pushed the response button beside it; electrical circuitry
immediately scored his response as hit or miss, recorded
hit or miss data on an electrical counter, and lighted the
correct target lamp on the percipient's console to give him
immediate feedback on whether he was right or wrong.   When
he was right a chime rang inside his console, as well as the
correct target lamp's coming on.

If a percipient thought he had no idea what the target
was on a given trial, he could push the Pass switch, signal-
ing to the experimenter/sender that he did not wish to respond and wanted a new target.   A pass was not counted as
a trial, and no feedback on correct target identity was given.
Percipients did not use the pass option very frequently.

Figure 4 shows the experimenter/sender's console with
the television monitor mounted above it.   Except for additional operating controls, this console is laid out identically to
the percipient's console.   The television monitor is very important.   In pilot work with the TCT, my students and I found
that many percipients would slowly move their hand around
the circle of unlit target lamps, trying to get some kind of
"feel" as to when they were over the correct lamp.   The
TCT was designed so that no electrical or physical differences
of any sort existed on the front of the percipient's console,
so this was totally irrelevant behavior in terms of a null hypothesis of no ESP, but psychologically it was very relevant
behavior because of the television feedback to the experiment-
er/sender.   The experimenter/sender could not only send the
abstract identity of the correct target, but also such things as
"warmer?", "colder!", or "stop, push it, this is it!".   Although I have not attempted separately to evaluate this factor,
at a minimum it keeps the experimenter/sender highly involved psychologically in the experiment.   It is my and my
experimenters' impression that it is also quite effective at
times, and we are going to try to evaluate this factor objec-

Figure 4

tively in later research. In terms of feedback training then, we were attempting to train the team of percipient and experimenter/sender, as both were receiving feedback on how effective their performances were.

Electrical counters on the TCT automatically recorded the number of trials and the number of hits. Runs were standardized at 25 trials each. If, as rarely happened, the pass option was used, the experimenter generally added additional trials to bring the total up to 25. Occasionally he forgot to do this, so a run might consist of 24 or 23 trials. On a few occasions an experimenter/sender ran a few more trials than 25, but, according to an a priori decision, no more than the first 25 trials were ever counted in the analyses.

Random Number Generator

Target selection in the first Training Study was controlled by an electronic RNG. This generator was of the "electronic roulette wheel" type. An oscillator or clock was producing more than a million output pulses per second. When the experimenter/sender depressed a push button, this drove a 1 to 10 counter over and over again. The length of time, and so the number the generator ultimately selected, was controlled by how long the experimenter/sender held down the push button. Since controllable human reaction time is, at its very best, measured in hundredths of and usually tenths of a second, this was so much slower than the clock speed that the particular output selected was totally beyond the experimenter's control, and so random.

As part of a predetermined plan, in the first Training Study we sampled 1000 numbers from the RNG before the experiment and 1000 numbers after it, and tested them for randomicity, using a chi-square analysis for equal incidence of individual targets and equal incidence of all 100 possible target doublets. The results were satisfactorily random. We did not test for possible higher level sequential effects, such as triplets, as there is no theoretical reason to expect these kinds of sequential effects of this style of random number generator. The small size of the sample used for testing randomicity has been severely criticized by Rex Stanford (1977), on the grounds that there might be subtle departures from randomicity that could aid percipients in scoring by some kind of mathematical inference. I have argued elsewhere (Tart, 1977b) that this was not likely, but since it is an important question with respect to the precognition effects I shall be reporting, I shall return to the question of departures from randomicity in more detail a little later.

In our second Training Study, done two years after the first Training Study, with an entirely new student percipient population, we used a more sophisticated model of the TCT, ADEPT, designed and constructed by Dana Redington. This was basically similar to the TCT except for the fact that the individual trial target and response data were generally recorded automatically by teletypewriter, and the random number generator was internal to the machine, rather

than external. Randomicity was satisfactory in the planned
pre- and post-experimental samples. With the TCT the individual trial data were recorded by hand, although total hits
and trials were recorded automatically. The teletypewriter
occasionally developed a malfunction in the second Training
Study. It was always clear that the teletypewriter was malfunctioning and individual trial target response data were
then recorded by hand, but the bulk were automatically recorded.

Psychological Focus on Real-Time Targets

        In the first Training Study, neither I, my experiment-
ers, nor (to my knowledge) the percipients had any formal
interest in precognition. Our conception of the experiment
was that we were trying to train real-time ESP, whether it
was clairvoyance or telepathy. The same focus on real-time
hits existed for the second Training Study; although I discovered significant precognitive effects in a retrospective
analysis of the first Training Study data while we were mid-
way through the second Training Study, I deliberately re-
frained from saying anything about it to the experimenters
and percipients until the study was over, in order not to
shift this psychological focus.

        Figure 5, showing the temporal sequence of target
generations, further defines this focus. Given that a target
has already been generated and the TCT or ADEPT activated
(ready light comes on on the percipient's console) for trial
N, the percipient would take a variable period of time, from
a few seconds to several minutes, to decide on what he
thought the target was. Then he would push a response button, giving himself immediate feedback as well as giving the
experimenter/sender immediate feedback on what the percipient's response had been. The experimenter/sender recorded the response on his record sheet in the first Training
Study (the target had already been noted), turned off the TCT,
and then pushed a button on the RNG to select the next target. When a selection had been made, in a second or so,
he switched on the selected target lamp for trial N+1. The
time sequence of responses was basically the same for
ADEPT in the second Training Study.

        During the time the percipient was trying to use ESP
to determine what the current, real-time target was, the target for the next trial had not yet come into existence, nor

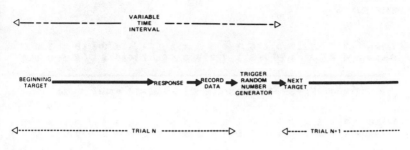

Figure 5

could it be inferred from any knowledge of current events,
given the nature of the RNG.   All of the experimenter/send-
er's attention was focused on the real-time target.   Any significant effects relating responses to future targets, then,
would be attributable to precognition.

Scoring Responses

For evaluating the presence of ESP and its relation
to the learning hypothesis, I was interested in real-time hits,
and all initial scoring was done for such hits.   The top third
of Figure 6 shows a sample of actual data from a run by one
of the percipients in the first Training Study, E1S5.   The
top row shows the 25 targets that were sequentially generated,
the second row the percipient's responses to each one.   Real-
time hits are circled; there were six of them for this particular run.   This happened to be an individually significant run,
as the one-tailed binomial probability of six or more hits in
25 trials is three in 100.

I mentioned earlier that while intellectually I accepted
the reality of precognition, on a deeper level I did not believe in it at all.   Although I knew that it was common to
look for immediate precognitive effects in parapsychological
studies, and while I had said that I was going to do it, I had
not done it at the time the initial publication of results, The
Application of Learning Theory to ESP Performance (Tart,
1975a), was on the verge of appearing.   I do not honestly
know whether I would have even gotten around to looking for
precognition, or simply kept myself busy with other work.
About that time, however, a colleague from the Genetics Department at UC Davis, Lila Gatlin, asked for copies of my

E1S5, Run #3

Targets   3 7 ⑤② 7 ⑨ 6 0 7 8 3 7 4 8 ⑤ 1 ④ 9 0 ⑦ 9 4 3 8 5
Responses   4 8 ⑤② 4 ⑨ 7 5 1 7 2 8 3 9 ⑤ 7 ④ 5 6 ⑦ 2 5 0 6 4

_____

REGISTER SHIFT FOR +1 TEMPORAL DISPLACEMENT   #TRIALS = 24

Targets   3 7 5 2 7 9 6 0 7 8 3 7 4 8 5 1 4 9 0 7 9 4 3 8 5
Responses   4 8 5 2 4 9 7 5 1 7 2 8 3 9 5 7 4 5 6 7 2 5 0 6 4

_____

REGISTER SHIFT FOR −1 TEMPORAL DISPLACEMENT   #TRIALS = 24

Targets   3 7 5 2 7 9 6 0 ⑦ 8 3 7 4 8 5 1 4 9 0 7 9 4 3 8 5
Responses   4 8 5 2 4 9 7 5 1 ⑦ 2 8 3 9 5 7 4 5 6 7 2 5 0 6 4

Figure 6

raw data so she could try out various information theoretic
approaches on them.   The analyses she carried out did not
take into account real-time factors in the data, such as intervals between runs, but they did suggest that in addition
to highly positive hitting on the real-time target, there was
highly significant missing on the +1 precognitive target, so
I was inspired to analyze my data systematically for temporal displacement effects.   This register displacement technique for scoring such effects is illustrated in the middle
and lower thirds of Figure 6.

ESP Missing in the First Training Study

        The ten percipients who completed the first Training
Study showed exceptionally significant results in terms of
real-time hitting.   For their total of 5000* trials, we would

_____

*In the original publications of these ESP learning results
(Tart, 1975a; 1976a), I worked with total run scores and did
not realize that the total number of trials was slightly less
than 5000, namely 4994.   The current total analysis here
retains the convention of 5000 trials to be consistent with
the original publication, as it is a conservative error: the
data are slightly more significant than the results here calculated.

expect 500 hits by chance, but 722 were observed. The two-tailed probability of such an occurrence, using the normal approximation to the binomial, is $2x10^{-25}$. For the group as a whole, this corresponded to an average of about 3.61 hits per run of 25, rather than the chance expected average of 2.50.

There is considerable individual variation in scoring, of course, with five of these ten percipients apparently having their overt manifestation of ESP suppressed under the change of psychological conditions of the Training Study, at least in terms of real-time hitting: their scores did not reach significance. The other five percipients all showed exceptionally significant individual scoring. The least significant of these five averaged 3.90 hits per run, with an associated probability of $4x10^{-5}$, two-tailed, and the most significant percipient averaged 6.20 hits per run, with a probability of $4x10^{-28}$, two-tailed.

In scoring for hits on the +1 future trial (after subtracting a few trials that were lost when an experimenter inadvertently only gave 24 trials in a run, as well as the routine loss of one trial per run on the displacement analysis), there were 4790 trials where hits could have occurred. By chance we would expect approximately 479 hits. Only 318 occurred; this has an associated, two-tailed probability of $8x10^{-15}$. Thus some part of the percipients' minds were occasionally using precognition to know what the +1 future target was and then affecting the conscious calling of the real-time target to be sure it was not what the +1 target would be. All other possible future displacements over the run (+2, +3, ... +24) were checked, but were not of obvious significance, and so they will not be reported on further in this paper.

Past temporal displacements were also checked, and a rather regular pattern was found for the -1 (immediately past) and -2 (two trials back) displacements. Figure 7 is a bar graph of this for one percipient, E1S1, whose pattern is representative of that of many other percipients. This particular percipient made 78 real-time hits, when 50 would be expected by chance, with an associated probability of $4x10^{-5}$, two-tailed. On the +1 future scoring, he made only 25 hits when 47 would be expected, another highly significant score, with a probability of $6x10^{-4}$, two-tailed. His avoidance of the immediate past trial was even greater: he made only 13 hits when 47.8 would be expected, which has a probability of

10^{-7}, two-tailed. For the -2 displacement he made only 29 hits when 46 would be expected, significant avoidance of the -2 target. On the -3 displacement he made 42 hits when 44 would be expected, a negligible departure from chance. As I said, this is a typical pattern for the past displacements: significant avoidance of the immediately past target, significant, but not as great avoidance of the second past target, falling off to generally chance variations by about the third target and further back. The mean CRs (Critical Ratios, Z-scores) for the -1, -2, and -3 displacements for the ten percipients in the first Training Study are -4.93, -2.67, and +.13.

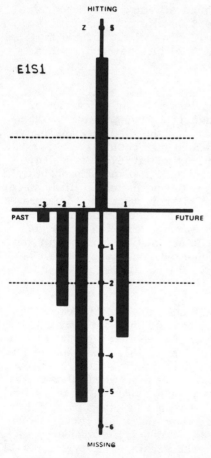

Figure 7

At first glance this pattern seems to be in accordance with what we know about most people's psychological guessing habits, namely that they underestimate the probability of a target XX doublet, and so rarely call what the immediately past target has been. This avoidance apparently carries over to a lesser extent for two trials past the target and then is pretty much inoperative.

Real-Time Hitting and Precognitive Missing

Although discovering such extremely strong precognitive missing was important to me personally in making me struggle with the concept of precognition, precognitive missing per se is probably not an exciting finding to most of you. What became more exciting as I examined the data was the discovery that the precognitive avoidance of the +1 future target was not an isolated event, haphazardly scattered throughout the data, but was quite strongly and negatively related to the degree of real-time hitting shown by various percipients. Figure 8 plots the magnitude of real-time hitting and +1 missing (hitting in one case) for each individual percipient. The vertical axis is the CR of the hitting or missing. I deliberately ordered the real-time hitting scores from the highest on the left (a CR of 11.03) down to the greatest degree of missing on the real-time target to the right. The consequent good ordering of +1 missing scores that then results is an indication of the strength of the relationship between these two measures. If hitting in real time and missing on the +1 future target had nothing to do with each other, these scores should be independent of each other. But the correlation here is -.84, which has a two-tailed probability of less than .005. A rank order correlation coefficient, which makes fewer assumptions about the characteristics of the numerical scaling, gives a correlation of -.89, a negligible change.

As a further check on the solidity of this relationship, I added the data from three more percipients who had, in accordance with a pre-data analysis decision, been excluded from formal data analyses because they did not complete the first Training Study. These three percipients had 11, ten and six runs respectively. One of them was scoring quite significantly when he decided he could not take the time to continue the experiment (CR = 2.11); the others were near chance expectation for real-time hits. When their data were included, the correlation change from -.84 to -.82 was negligible.

The small squares beside each individual percipient's data in Figure 8 indicate significant results from a t-test, applied post hoc to each individual's data, comparing the hitting on the real-time targets with the missing on the +1 future targets applied over each percipient's 20 runs. Six of the ten percipients show such significant differences, including one percipient whose real-time hitting was not individually significant. As I will comment later, I think this latter finding suggests an interesting answer to the question of why did some of these carefully selected percipients apparently stop showing ESP in the Training Study.

Replication of Effects in the Second Training Study

In terms of the magnitude of real-time ESP shown,

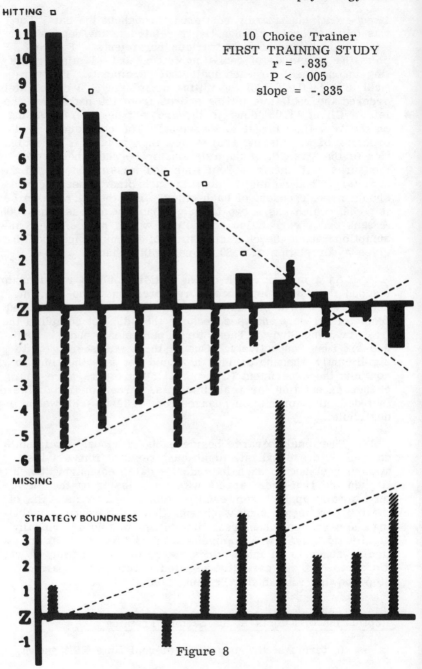

Figure 8

the second Training Study, which will be reported on in a future publication (Tart, Palmer & Redington, 1977), was much less successful for the ten-choice machine data than the first Training Study was. Our second Selection Study and Confirmation Study procedure (described fully in Palmer, Tart & Redington, 1976) simply did not give us individual percipients with ESP scores as high as we had in the first Training Study. The group of percipients who completed the first Training Study had Confirmation Study scores ranging from 2.50 to 6.00 hits per run of 25 (chance is 2.50), with a mean group score of 4.78, while the corresponding range was 2.75 to 4.50, with a group mean of 3.61 hits per run, for the percipients who completed the second Training Study. Using a t-test, the difference in ESP talent levels of the percipients going into the two studies was significantly different (p < .05, two-tailed).

Ideally, we should have run more students through our Selection and Confirmation study procedures until we picked up enough highly talented percipients to make the ESP talent level comparable to that of the first Training Study, but a lack of time, money and manpower prohibited this. Thus we used the percipients we had, but predicted, before the second Training Study, that our overall yield of ESP would be smaller than it had been in the first Training Study. Regretfully, this prediction was confirmed! It is not, of course, the most powerful prediction one could make, as it is a fairly general finding that second studies of a problem do not give as strong results as the first studies.

Seven percipients completed the second Training Study. The overall group mean (2.61) did not differ significantly from chance expectation, although two of the seven percipients showed individually significant results. One of them showed individually significant real-time hitting (average of 3.20 hits per run, p < .05, two-tailed), but the other showed individually significant real-time missing (average of 1.85 hits per run, p < .05, two-tailed), so they effectively canceled each other out in the total.

Figure 9 shows the individual percipient results for real-time hitting and +1 precognitive scoring, plotted in the same manner as Figure 8. The prediction I made on the basis of the first Training Study's finding, that there would be a strong relationship between real-time hitting and +1 missing, was confirmed. The correlation coefficient between hitting in the two time registers was -.73, p < .05, one-

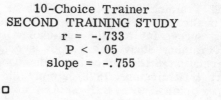

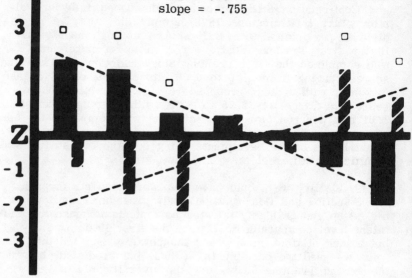

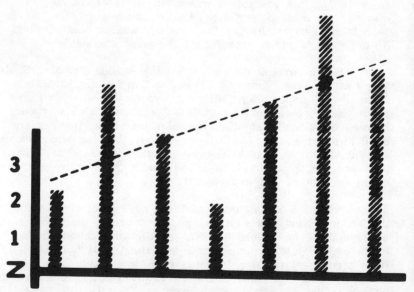

Figure 9

tailed.   The more conservative rank order correlation coefficient was -.79, a slight increase.   As predicted, five of the seven percipients showed individually significant t-test differences between their real-time scores and their +1 precognitive scores.   Figure 9 suggests that there might be some curvilinearity in the relationship, but I tend to doubt that this is so although it should be kept in mind for future studies.   The significant replication of the negative relationship between real-time and +1 future scoring, even when the overall yield of psi in the second Training Study was so much less than in the first Training Study, convinced me that the relationship is both real and strong, strong enough to be of practical significance as well as statistical significance.

In terms of real-time hits, the percipients from the second Training Study amounted to a sampling of the lower end of the distribution sampled in the first Training Study, so I combined the results of these two Training Studies, as shown in Figure 10.   Here the strong negative relationship between real-time hitting and +1 hitting stands out very clearly.   The correlation is -.85, p < .001, two-tailed.   The more conservative rank order correlation is also -.85.   The highly successful ESP percipients strongly suppressed hitting on the immediately future target while the ones who, perhaps because of the increased psychological pressure of the Training Study, tended to switch toward ESP missing on real-time targets--an incorrect focusing of their ESP--showed a suggestive tendency to switch to hitting on the immediate future target.   This switching toward hitting on the immediate future target is quite interesting, and I shall comment on it later.

A significant negative relationship between real-time hitting and +1 precognitive hitting has not, to my knowledge, previously been reported in the literature.   This may be due, at least partially, to the fact that it has not been looked for. Insofar as this is true, I hope that those of you with relevant data will examine it for this sort of relationship.   I suspect that it may also be unreported because of a procedural difference in my two Training Studies from most parapsychological studies, namely that in my studies there was a sequential generation of targets "on line."   That is, no future target came into existence until a call had been made on the present target.   In most parapsychological studies of precognition, especially those using shuffled decks of cards for targets, the entire sequence of future targets is generated simultaneously during the shuffling procedure, rather than being generated one by one.

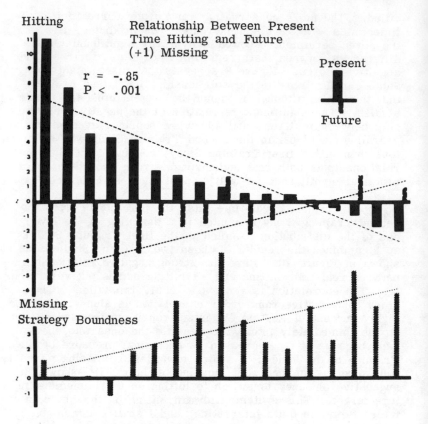

Figure 10

Control Procedures

When I first discovered this relationship, and in the
almost two years I have worked with it, I have been nagged
by the question of whether the relationship might have been
artifactually generated by some sort of peculiar non-randomicity in the target sequences, or some other sort of statistical
artifact.   Given the novelty of this relationship and its potential importance, I think it appropriate to be concerned
with any possible artifacts here, so I shall take a few minutes to describe the kinds of control analyses I have carried
out that have satisfied me that the relationship is not arti-
factual.

I mentioned earlier that I made an a priori decision to test the randomicity of the electronic RNGs used with the TCT and with ADEPT before and after each Training Study, but not during it. This was because numerous studies (André, 1972; Braud et al., 1976; Honorton & Barksdale, 1972; Matas & Pantas, 1971; Miller & Broughton, 1976; Schmidt, 1970; 1973; 1975; 1976; Schmidt & Pantas, 1972; Stanford & Fox, 1975; Stanford et al., 1975) have shown that human agents can influence the output of electronic RNGs simply by wishing for some output to come up more frequently. While I conceived of these Training Studies as training ESP, and wanted the percipients to use ESP, their task, both as defined to them and in terms of what they were rewarded for, was to push a button that corresponded to the current time target. While utilizing some kind of ESP is the obvious way to do this, unconsciously utilizing some kind of PK to influence the electronic RNG to match the percipient's response preferences would also produce hits. Thus I anticipated that there might be unusual numerical patterns appearing in the target data collected, and so made the decision to check the RNG for satisfactory operation before and after each study, but not during the studies. I do believe there was some PK influence on the RNG in the first Training Study, although I have not yet devised a satisfactory way of separating this from ESP effects, which I believe were predominant.

As I began to carry out analyses of various internal effects in the data, it became important to conduct classical randomicity tests on the target sequences actually used in order to allow for any effects resulting from possible lack of randomicity. In examining the data of the first Training Study, I found that two of the high scoring percipients had statistically significant departures from randomicity at the singlet and doublet levels in their target sequences, using chi-square at the singlet and the generalized serial test (Davis & Akers, 1974) at the doublet levels.* The magnitude of these departures from randomicity seemed to be rather small in comparison with the magnitude of the ESP effects, but, to be on the safe side, I recalculated the relationship between real-time hitting and +1 future hitting after deleting the data of these two percipients. This changes the correlation coefficient from -.84 to -.81. The change is negligible, and the latter figure is still significant at the .02 level, two-tailed.

---

*I wish to thank Lila Gatlin for carrying out these tests.

In testing the target sequences of the seven percipients of the second Training Study by chi-square tests, one percipient's target showed significant departure from randomicity although he was a percipient whose real-time hitting score was at chance. Conservatively deleting his data from those of the other seven percipients in the second Training Study, the correlation changes from -.73 to -.74, a negligible change, and the latter correlation is still independently significant (p < .05, one-tailed). If the data of all three of the percipients are deleted from the combined correlation across the two studies, the correlation negligibly changes from -.84 to -.82.

The next control analysis resulted from detecting a systematic kind of non-randomicity in almost all of the target sequences of the first Training Study, namely a great lack of XX doublets. That is, there were not enough 1,1's or 2,2's etc. in the target sequences--only 193, when there should have been 500.

This is a striking discrepancy, and one which is of practical significance, for these particular XX doublets are not simply any target doublet but, given common human qualities, ones which are psychologically significant to people. My first question was how could this have happened? There was no such problem in the formal randomicity testing sequences before and after the study.

Through using the electronic RNG from the first Training Study and questioning one of the experimenters, I think I now understand the lack of XX doublets. In order to select a new target on the RNG, a push button on its panel was depressed, held down for a second or two, and let up. This push button was not of the type that made a tactically discernable click when it was depressed, but simply one that got harder to push as you pushed it further in. Thus it was not sensorily obvious if you had indeed pushed the button in far enough to activate the generator. What apparently happened is that an experimenter would sometimes push and release the button to get the next target, look at the RNG and see that the same number was still in the readout, and so assume that he had not pushed the button in sufficiently to activate the generator. So he would push it again to get a new target. This would lead to a systematic depletion of XX doublets. (Part of the lack of XX target doublets might also have been caused by unconscious PK by the percipients and/or by the experimenters. Given the common human underestimation of the frequency of target **XX** doublets, unknowingly PKing the RNG to reduce the frequence of such doublets would make it appear that the RNG was working "correctly." I see no way of objectively testing this hypothesis, however, and mention it only to provoke thought.)

How serious is this effect? Since it is generally known that people tend to avoid calling the previous target, whose identity they know through feedback (due to their fallacious belief that **XX** doublets are rare in a true random number generator) we now have an interesting case where **XX** doublets were actually rare from this particular generator, so their habit of not calling **XX** doublets should increase their scores. Indeed, it will, but a simple approximation shows that the effect is quite small. Assume the worse case, where we have no **XX** doublets at all. This means that there are only nine alternative targets on each trial (barring the very first trial of each run) and so the probability of a hit on any trial is one-ninth rather than one-tenth. For the experiment as a whole, then, with 5000 trials we would expect 556 real-time hits by chance rather than 500 hits.

There were 722 hits and, with the one-ninth hit probability figure put in, this yields a CR of 7.49. The probability of such a result by chance is less than 10^{-13}, two-tailed. Applying the same correction in a somewhat more sophisticated fashion (allowing for passes and occasional missing data due to ambiguous handwriting, as well as a systematic depletion of end trials) to +1 hits, we expect 454 +1 hits by chance alone, but there were only 301, yielding a CR of 7.62, with an associated probability of less than 10^{-13}, two-tailed. Even generously allowing for lack of **XX** doublets then, we still have exceptionally significant real-time hitting and exceptionally significant +1 precognitive missing.

I have not been able to figure out any way in which the lack of **XX** doublets per se would create a correlation between real-time hitting and +1 missing. As an empirical control, there was no lack of **XX** doublets in the second Training Study target sequences, yet the relationship is there just about as strongly as in the first Training Study, so I do not believe the lack of **XX** doublets in the first Training Study is of any real relevance to the relationship reported here.

Third, the possibility has been suggested that there are higher order biases or sequential dependencies between the targets in my first Training Study data (Gatlin, 1978; Stanford, 1977). This has led Gatlin to hypothesize, if I understand her correctly, that percipients, by keeping track of previous targets through the immediate feedback, may have gradually estimated what these biases were and then used them as a basis for a (non-conscious) strategy of math- ematical inference that would increase their scores above chance expectation, in addition to, or perhaps without even any need to invoke ESP. I am not convinced there are any significant sequential dependencies of the third order and higher that are of any consequence, but I felt that this kind of hypothesis needed to be tested, not only in terms of its importance to the data of the first Training Study that was already in, but because many studies are now employing im- mediate feedback, so this is a question of general interest.

The hypothesis of scoring high by mathematical infer- ence as a result of figuring out target biases needs to be cast in a specific and testable form to be viable, and mathe- matical inference is the sort of thing that allows precise ex- pression. A colleague in the Computer Sciences Department of the University of California at Berkeley, Eugene Dronek, and I have now completed what we believe is a very powerful test of this hypothesis, and we shall be preparing the results for publication in the near future. We set ourselves the task of devising a computer-assisted inferential calling strategy that would have enormously more power than what we could reasonably attribute to human percipients. We gave our pro- gram powers such as an absolutely perfect memory for all previous targets to date, all previous target doublets, etc., up to all previous target sextuplets, as well as perfectly ac- curate and well-nigh instantaneous (in human terms) comput- ing capacity to assess possible biases. To get an overview of what the program does, assume that the 101st trial is coming up. To make its call, our inference program looks at all 100 previous targets which have come up on previous trials. It has already sorted them into a singlet file, a doublet file, and so on through a sextuplet file. It looks at the singlet file, asks what has been the most frequent singlet to date, and, given 100 trials, what is the exact binomial probability that a singlet should have come up with such an observed frequency compared to the null hypothesis that all singlets have an equal probability of one-tenth? This binom- ial probability is computed and stored. The program then asks if there is relevant information in its doublet file. That is, say the 100th target was a 7; does the doublet file have any information on what 7s have been followed by in the previous 100 trials? If not, it will guess on the basis of the most improbable (compared to the null hypothesis) target to date in the singlet file, but if the doublet file does have relevant information, it will again compute the exact binomial probability of that many or more doublets having occurred in the 100 trials to date, compared to the null hypothesis of equal probability for all possible doublets. This binomial probability will then be compared to the binomial probability of the highest singlet to date. If the highest doublet to date is less probable, i.e., represents more of a departure from the model of sequential independence than the highest singlet to date, the program will use that doublet information as the basis of its guessing strategy. Similarly if there is a relevant triplet, quadruplet, quintuplet, or sextuplet, the most radical departure from the model of equal probability and sequential independence will be used as a basis for the guessing strategy. On the 102nd trial, all computations will be re-done because there is now a data base of 101 trials instead of 100, etc., so the program constantly updates itself in order to get the maximum information from all the material to date. Because of this updating, it is quite sensitive to locally shifting biases, as well as general biases.

Figure 11 is a comparison of what our inferential strategy program, with all of its advantages, can do on the target sequences, compared to the scores of the actual percipients of the first Training Study. As you can see, the inferential strategy program manages to reach statistical significance on only two of the ten target sequences, and it is generally scoring well below the actual percipients' scores. In two cases of percipients who did not show individually significant ESP scores, the inferential strategy program did better, although it did not reach statistical significance. In general, the inferential strategy program can only get about 30 per cent as many hits above mean chance expectation as the actual percipients achieved. Further, the strategy program shows patterns in its calling output that do not look anything like those used by the actual percipients. I doubt very much that the percipients were doing much of the kind of estimation that the calling program was. Thus, given this very powerful test of how much biases can be capitalized on, the bulk of the data is still attributable to ESP.

However, our main concern in this kind of control, given our focus this evening, is, might some kind of deliberate estimation strategy create the relationship found between real-time hitting and +1 precognitive missing? The

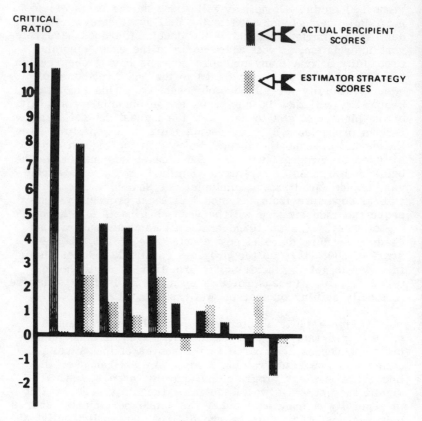

Figure 11

answer is no. I had the inferential strategy program's calls,
working with a memory span up to the triplet level, * punched
on IBM cards in the same format as the percipients' calls
were, and compared them to the actual percipients' calls.
The resulting correlations do not look at all like those obtained with the actual percipients. The relationship between

---

*I used the triplet level (no memory categorizations at high-
er levels) because the inferential strategy program scores as
high as it ever will by the triplet level (and often the doublet
or singlet level) on this target data, which empirically argues
that there are no relevant higher order biases that percipients might have used in an inferential strategy.

real-time hitting and +1 hitting for the inferential strategy
program, for example, is highly positive, rather than negative.   Indeed, there are extremely significant positive correlations across almost all temporal displacement register
scorings because the estimator program is constantly adjust-
ing itself to fit the characteristics of the target distribution
to date.

To give you an example of the flavor of this, Figure
12 shows a computer printed graph of the temporal displacement scoring over all possible registers (-24 to +24) for one
of the significantly scoring percipients (E1S1) of the first
Training Study.   Notice the crowding of effects around the
origin (real time), the strong negative scores on +1, -1,
and -2 registers, and the approximately equal number of
positive and negative CRs computed.   Figure 13 shows the
same kind of analysis done on the inferential strategy output
for the target sequence of the same percipient.   Notice the
massive block of positive displacements in the past direction,
and the tremendous preponderance of positive correlations in
the future direction.   Clearly, whatever percipients are doing
does not look at all like a powerful estimation strategy.

Let me make it clear that Dronek and I are not claiming that we have devised the most powerful inferential strategy
for taking advantage of possible biases that might exist in
target sequences.   We are claiming that we have devised a
very powerful one.   We would like our inferential strategy to
stand as a challenge to other investigators to see if they can
devise a more powerful strategy, actually model it, and
demonstrate empirically that it is more powerful.   Given our
results to date, however, I am convinced that the strong relationship between real-time hitting and +1 missing found in
my Training Studies is not due to any kind of statistical artifact.

We have a novel finding--what might it mean?   I
shall now present a theory I have devised to explain this
phenomenon, which will bring us back to concepts of space,
time and the mind.   I should note that I am deeply indebted
to Enoch Callaway, a colleague at the Langley Porter Neuro-
psychiatric Institute, who, after seeing a preliminary analysis
of these data, suggested that the effects resembled a neural
inhibitory surround, and started the train of thought in me
that led to the following theory.

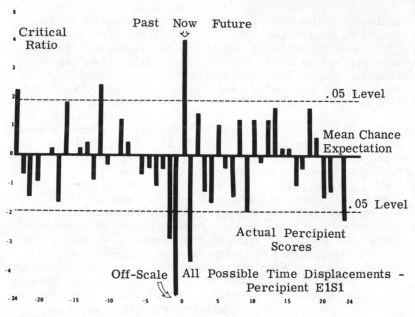

Figure 12

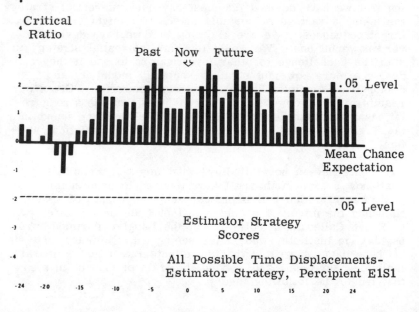

Figure 13

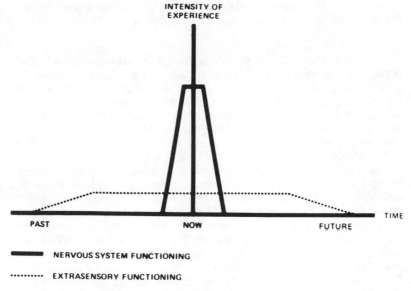

Figure 14

The Duration of the Present

There are two general senses in which the concept of the "now" or the "present" is used. One refers to our immediate psychological experience; there is a certain small duration of time that I think of and experience as the present. There is also the mathematical concept of the present, namely a temporal point of zero width, zero duration, sandwiched between past and future. The mathematical concept is a useful abstraction for a large variety of applications, but is a poor representation of the psychological present. We simply don't experience our present as having no duration!

In Figure 14 I have sketched a model of the experienced present. The vertical axis represents the intensity of experience, the horizontal axis is time in a conventional sense, with the now at the center of it. The heavy lines show a band width for the experienced present, probably on the order of one- or two-tenths of a second. That is where all of our ordinary experience is concentrated, and it is obviously intense: we perceive it. The band width of this experienced present is slightly variable; meditative tech-

niques or other psychological changes can sometimes make
the present seem shorter or more fleeting, or bigger and
wider.

For those of you who are familiar with electrical fil-
ters, the experienced present is like a high-gain, narrow
band-width filter. The experienced present is its pass band.
Everything within that narrow pass band comes through very
strongly, but as soon as signals fall outside that pass band
they come through very weakly or not at all. The one- or
two-tenths of a second band width of the experienced present
is probably a function of the neural circuitry that underlies
immediate memory. Sensory input and other kinds of psychological processes are, in a sense, literally held or stretched
out for one- or two-tenths of a second. Dynamically, we
could picture this pass band of the experienced present as
ordinarily moving along horizontally from past to future on
our physical concept of time. Whether experience within
this pass band of the experienced present is actually continuous, or consists of discrete frames, with awareness of the
frame intervals suppressed, is an interesting question we
shall leave for the future.

There is an older psychological term for the experienced present, the "specious present," a term which I shall
not use, as it implies a theoretical commitment to the mathematical abstraction of the present as having no duration, as
being more real than what we experience! Keep in mind
that the mathematical concept of time is an abstraction,
even if extremely useful, and we should not casually deny
our own experience in favor of abstractions.

Precognition and the Experienced Present

The model of the theory shown in Figure 14 postulates
that there is some other temporal dimension of mental functioning, an extended temporal dimension different from our
ordinary one. We may talk about time "flowing at a different rate" compared to ordinary time, or some such analogy,
but the important property of some aspect of the mind existing in an extended dimension of time is that the experienced
present of that part of the mind has, compared to ordinary
time, a greater duration for its now, a wider pass band than
our ordinarily experienced present. This wider pass band
is shown in Figure 14 by the light, dotted line. I have no
idea what the exact shape or duration of the pass band of

this second temporal dimension of the mind is, so I have
simply shown it tapering off at some temporal distance in
the past and future, without attempting to represent anything
exactly.

I am proposing that this extended aspect of the mind,
which is activated on those occasions when psi abilities are
used, has two properties different from our ordinary consciousness. Our ordinary consciousness seems both spatially
and temporally localized with respect to ordinary spatial and
temporal constraints on physical brain and nervous system
processes. It operates in what we call "real time." The
first property of this extended dimension of the mind is that
it is not so spatially localized as the ordinary one, and so
somehow can pick up information at spatial locations outside
the sensory range of the body/brain/nervous system. The
second property of this extended dimension of the mind is
that the center point of its experienced present can be located at a different temporal location than the center point of
the experienced present of ordinary consciousness. That is,
it may be centered around a time that, by ordinary standards,
is past or future, although it is probably usually centered on
the same temporal location as ordinary consciousness. Further, the size of this extended dimension of the mind's experienced present, its pass band, is wider than the pass
band of our ordinarily experienced present. Even if the experienced present of this extended dimension of the mind is
centered on the ordinary present, what is now in this extended dimension of the mind may include portions of time
that, from our ordinary point of view, are past and future,
as well as present. Similarly in a spatial way, what is
here to this extended dimension of the mind may include aspects of physical reality that are there or elsewhere to our
ordinary consciousness.

Since our ordinary consciousness is ordinarily fully
identified with and preoccupied with body/brain/nervous system functioning, very little basic awareness, if any, is left
over to be aware of activity in this extended dimension of
the mind. Thus its experienced intensity is ordinarily quite
low, usually below conscious threshold, and so it is accord-
ingly drawn as quite low in Figure 14. To put this more
precisely, in my systems approach to consciousness (Tart,
1974; 1975b; 1975c; 1976b; 1977c; 1977d), I postulate basic
awareness as something different from consciousness: consciousness is a combination of the more basic awareness we
have with the properties of the physical brain/body/nervous

system. It is a Gestalt, an interactive creation. Because awareness is ordinarily fully identified with, influenced by and influencing body/brain/nervous system processes, we commonly, but mistakenly, equate the two. In the theory I am presenting here tonight, basic awareness can sometimes be withdrawn from its total identification with ordinary body/brain/nervous system processes and then takes in the activity of this extended dimension of the mind.

When a percipient is asked to use ESP, his first task is to disregard incoming sensory input. After all, we set up conditions so that no sensory input that reaches the percipient contains any relevant information about the ESP target. Second, he must disregard or inhibit his ongoing fantasies and any guessing strategies he has that attempt to figure out the RNG, since we design random number generators to be equiprobable and sequentially independent. (Note the slight lack of randomicity of some of the target sequences in the first Training Study is not really relevant to the points made here.) Third, he must try to contact or tune in to that aspect of his mind which exists in or is capable of existing in and using this extended spatial and temporal dimension of the mind.

Considering the temporal aspects of ESP, we have a problem. If the percipient's desire is to obtain real-time, concurrent information by ESP (the state of the apparatus or the mental processes of the experimenter/sender in another laboratory room), then simply tapping into the wider experiential present of this extended dimension of the mind is not sufficient. This wider experiential present includes information about past and future events, as well as present events. Since the percipient desires to get present-time information, this past and future information is noise, which may interfere with the detection of the desired target.

Recall now that the primary psychological set of the experimenters and percipients in my Training Studies was on getting the real-time target information via ESP. Occasionally experimenters or percipients might have had a temporary interest in precognitive events, but while I cannot assess this precisely, the constant focus on real-time targets in our strategy sessions and the like definitely made the real-time target the focus of most attention. By focusing on the real-time target, this implicitly defined the temporal boundaries of that real-time information as the immediately past (-1) target and the immediately future (+1) target. What the

percipient wanted was now, not past or future. Spatially, the
experimenters' and percipients' attention was fixed on a particular location for the desired target information, namely
the experimental apparatus and/or the experimenter/sender's
mind. The target information was not sensorially here to
the percipient, but at a specific there, out of many possible
elsewheres.

Figure 15 models the psychological processes a percipient must carry out, consciously or unconsciously, in
order to use ESP successfully for getting real-time information. His basic awareness or consciousness is receiving a
variety of irrelevant sensory information and irrelevant internal process information that must be ignored or inhibited.
A particularly important source of irrelevant information here
is his memory of what recent past targets have been, combined with that common human tendency to try to outguess
the random number generator, leading to a guessing strategy.
Note that I want to carefully distinguish here call strategies,
which produce the final response, and guessing strategies,
which are only a subset of call strategies. A guessing
strategy is, by definition, irrelevant with a random target
source, but the call strategies may include psychological
processes which are relevant. Some of those kinds of calling strategies will be discussed in my paper on the expanded
learning theory model of tomorrow (Tart, 1978 [pp. 90-122,
supra]).

In addition to disregarding irrelevant information then,
he must, at least occasionally tap into that extended dimension of the mind that can use ESP, but since that aspect of
the mind is getting, as an integral part of its experienced
present, information about past and future (and possible targets that are spatially elsewhere, as well as the desired
ones) as well as real time, present information, he must
further carry out some kind of discrimination process. This
discrimination process must clearly identify the past, present and future aspects of the ESP information being gathered,
and then actively suppress the past and future aspects of the
ESP information in order to enhance the detectability of the
desired real time ESP information. That is, a kind of contrast sharpening must be employed.

The output of the discrimination process then, consists of a mixture of information, some of it designed to
positively influence the percipient to call the identity of the
present-time target, and some of it consisting of negative,

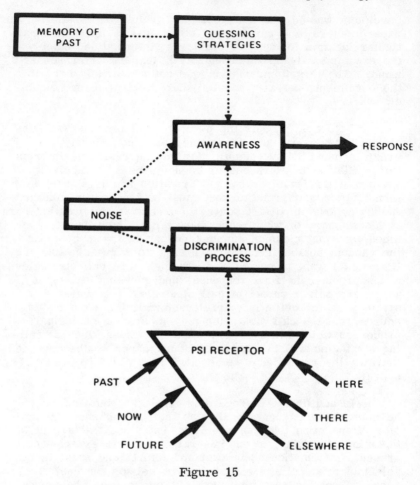

Figure 15

inhibitory tendencies <u>not</u> to call the target numbers belong-
ing to the immediately future and immediately past targets.
This combination of tendencies probabilistically increases the
chances of a correct call.   These non-conscious psi-receptor
and discrimination processes obviously work intermittently
and imperfectly, although they might be capable of much better functioning, are influenced by factors we cannot yet specify, and are probably affected by both systematic and random
noise.   Perhaps the positive and inhibiting components of
this process work semi-independently.   Systematic and random noise may occur at all stages of this discrimination and
calling process.

In spatial terms, the discrimination process must further identify targets that are at the correct location there, and discriminate them from target identity information that is here to ordinary consciousness, i. e. , there is target identity information available via psi about targets spatially adjacent to the currently desired target: this psi-acquirable but incorrect information must be discriminated and rejected.

Trans-Temporal Inhibition

What I am postulating, then, is an active inhibition of precognitively and postcognitively acquired information about the immediately future and the immediately past targets, which serves to enhance the detectability of ESP information with respect to the desired real-time target. As the inhibition extends over time, I have named this phenomenon trans-temporal inhibition.

Except for the unusual (in terms of our ordinary concepts) feature of extending over time rather than space, trans-temporal inhibition is like a widely used information processing strategy in our nervous systems called lateral inhibition (Von Békésy, 1967). This is a general phenomenon, found in all sensory systems, whereby a highly stimulated neuron sends out inhibitory impulses to neurons and receptor endings which are laterally/spatially adjacent to it, thus suppressing their initially weaker output unless they are also strongly stimulated. Lateral inhibition is illustrated for touch receptors in the skin in Figure 16.

If you press on your skin with a sharply pointed object, say under the middle receptor shown in Figure 16, not only is the touch receptor immediately under that point strongly stimulated but, because of the mechanical deformation of the skin also shown in the figure, receptors laterally adjacent to the stimulation point are also stimulated, although not as intensely. The neural impulses from the receptors at this first stage of detection, then, would show rapid firing (the neural code for high intensity) immediately under the stimulated point, but also fairly rapid firing on each side of it, gradually tapering off with distance, so that you have a neural signal pattern suggesting that you were stimulated by a blunt, rounded object, rather than by a point. The stimulated receptor under the point, however, sends out lateral inhibitory impulses which suppress the weaker, less frequent impulse trains from the laterally adjacent receptors, so by

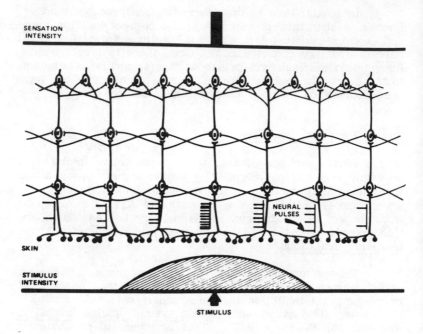

Figure 16

the time you are several steps up in the neural chain, you have recovered a pattern indicating point stimulation. In engineering, this kind of contrast enhancement effect is referred to as edge detection; it was used on the signals transmitted from the Viking landers on Mars, for example, to produce crisp, clear pictures, even though the actual signal received was rather noisy. The phenomenon of trans-temporal inhibition, then, suggests that a generally useful information processing procedure also operates for ESP.

Although I have not yet fully worked out the implications, I suspect that we will find a similar phenomenon for the spatial dimensions of targets. That is, when ESP works well detecting a spatially distant target that is surrounded by other targets, there will be an increased missing or inhibition on the immediately surrounding targets. Such a phenomenon could be called trans-spatial inhibition. As will be discussed later, possible widening of the band width of the extended dimension of mind needs also to be taken into account in empirically looking for this.

All right. We started with an unexpected finding of
extremely significant precognitive missing, missing which
was highly correlated with real-time ESP hitting. The relationship was solidly confirmed in a second study. This relationship, plus the inspiration of Enoch Callaway's remark
about neural inhibitory surrounds, plus my personal struggle
to think about precognition in spite of my prejudices, led to
a theory about an extended dimension of the mind and the
consequent necessity of trans-temporal inhibition in order for
ESP to work effectively. A good theory should make more
and more sense out of the data. Let's look at some applications of the theory to the data from my two Training Studies.

Strategy Boundness

In showing the +1 displacements, real-time hits, and
-1 past displacements score patterns of percipient E1S1 in
Figure 7, I indicated that the highly significant degrees of
missing on the immediately past target seemed to be caused,
at first glance, by maladaptive guessing habits on the percipient's part--namely, a mechanical avoidance of calling
whatever the previous target had been. Ideally, the RNG is
so constructed that there are no sequential dependencies between targets, so this strategy, while common among people,
is maladaptive. Even considering the experimenter error
which led to a deficiency of target doublets in the First
Training Study, mindless and automatic avoidance of the immediately past target is a poor strategy for using ESP.
There are some XX doublets, and ESP could allow hits on
them.

In postulating the existence of trans-temporal inhibition,
I also postulate that the effect is roughly symmetrical in time,
as symmetry seems to be a basic principle in the world. In
principle, then, there is probably an extrasensory postcognitive inhibition against calling the immediately past target,
mixed in with not calling it through mechanical avoidance of
the target, given knowledge of it because of the feedback.
Although I have no independent measure of the degree of such
postcognitive avoidance, I decided to assume that the magnitude of the extrasensory postcognitive -1 avoidance for each
percipient would be equal in magnitude to that of his +1 precognitive avoidance. I could then subtract the magnitude of
the +1 precognitive avoidance from the magnitude of the -1
avoidance, and the remainder left over would be a component
I have named maladaptive strategy boundness. Strategy bound-

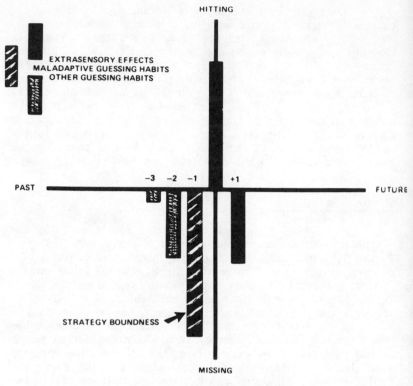

Figure 17

ness is thus a measure of mechanical avoidance of the previous target via ordinary psychological processes.

Figure 17 shows this kind of partialing-out applied to the data of percipient E1S1. On the assumption that extrasensory postcognitive avoidance is equal to extrasensory precognitive avoidance, you can see how I have split the magnitude of the -1 score, and gotten a strategy boundness measure for this particular percipient. A similar procedure was carried out individually for all other percipients in both Training Studies.

My understanding of the optimal way to try to use ESP is that any sort of calculation processes are irrelevant. This includes any kind of guessing strategy which involves keeping track of what the past targets have been and then trying to outguess the random number generator. This is not only a waste of time, given sequential independence of the random number generator, but, as I mentioned earlier, since there is only a limited amount of awareness available, this kind of maladaptive guessing strategy uses up some awareness which might otherwise be used to activate relevant mental processes for actually using ESP.

On theoretical grounds, then, we would expect that the more maladaptive strategy boundness a percipient showed, the less real-time ESP he would show. Since trans-temporal inhibition of the future (and, by assumption, of the past) is also adaptive for enhancing real-time ESP, we would also expect that with more strategy boundness there would be less missing on the +1 target; that is, the contrast between real-time hitting and +1 missing would be less with increased strategy boundness. The data seem to bear this out quite strongly.

Because the signs for the arithmetical computations of missing, strategy boundness, etc., require a good deal of attention to follow in terms of their relationships, I have taken the value of strategy boundness resulting from the above computations and made it positive to make the following discussion clearer.

In originally computing the correlations between real-time hitting, +1 future hitting, and -1 past hitting for percipients in the combined two Training Studies, I found that +1 future hitting correlated significantly negatively with real-time hitting ($r = -.85$, $p < .001$, two-tailed), but the magnitude of -1 past hitting did not correlate significantly with either the magnitude of real-time hitting ($r = -.24$) or with the magnitude of +1 future missing ($r = +.14$). When strategy boundness is factored out as described above, however, it is significantly correlated with the other two measures. Strategy boundness correlates $r = -.64$, $p < .01$, two-tailed with present time hitting, and $r = +.83$, $p < .001$, two-tailed with +1 future missing. Referring back to Figures 8, 9 and 10, the magnitude of each individual percipient's strategy boundness score is plotted in the lower part of the graph, and the strength of the relationship is quite clear.

Applying the symmetry assumption to trans-temporal inhibition then, takes some meaningless data, the absolute magnitude of the -1 past deviations, and partials it into highly meaningful data. There is only one problem: although I

checked with three mathematicians about the validity of this
partial correlation procedure, and they all thought it would
not artifactually lead to a high correlation if none actually
existed, this has turned out to be wrong! Recently Eugene
Dronek set up a computer program to check this procedure
empirically. It took the actual CR values for real-time hitting and +1 missing for each of the 17 percipients in the
combined Training Studies, and then drew a sample of 17
digits from the computer's random number generator program. If that particular sample of 17 digits showed a very
low correlation (less than ± .2) with both the real-time hitting and the +1 missing scores, thus duplicating the original
data pattern, a strategy boundness score was then computed
on these random numbers as if they were the -1 deviation
score, and the correlation of this strategy boundness figure
computed with both real-time hitting and +1 missing. One
thousand correlations were generated in this way. Unfortunately, it turns out that the procedure artifactually gener-
ates quite high correlations! Thus I am not at all sure that
the maladaptive strategy boundness measure I have just described to you is really valid. Obviously we need independent measures of postcognitive avoidance and strategy boundness. Nevertheless, I intuitively feel this strategy boundness
measure is reflecting something quite important, and I've presented it to you for its stimulus value.

Persistence of Inhibition

        Recall now that the theory of trans-temporal inhibi-
tion says that if the psi-receptor and appropriate discrimination processes are working on trial N, not only does this
positively influence you to call a digit that corresponds to
the actual identity of the target at that time, but it inhibits
or prejudices you against calling the digit which is the identity of the target on trial N+1 in the immediate future. Now,
human psychological processes generally have some degree
of "inertia," i.e., our immediate past is constantly having
some influence on the present. It follows then that after
making a call on trial N, on trial N+1 a problem exists.
The percipient is likely still to be carrying some inhibitory
bias against calling the digit which corresponds to the identity
of the target on trial N+1. Thus the operation of trans-temporal inhibition is likely to produce a kind of "stuttering" of
ESP, a break in its continuity. If you hit by using ESP, you
are more likely to miss on the next trial than if you hadn't
hit, an affect we might call psi stuttering. In terms of the

data available for analysis, we should expect to see fewer
hit doublets, two hits in a row, than would be expected if
every trial were independent of the previous one.

The appropriate test for this is to use the actually obtained proportion of real-time hits to recalculate the probability of a hit. Then the probability that a real-time hit will
be followed by another real-time hit is simply the square of
this empirically obtained proportion, given the assumption
that real-time hits are temporally independent of one another.
Calculating this, I found that in the first Training Study there
was a deficiency of real-time hits following real-time hits:
only 86 when about 106 would be expected. This has a CR
of -2.07, p = .02, one-tailed. More importantly, the degree of lack of real time hit doublets is strongly and negatively correlated with the degree of real time hitting: r =
-.71, p < .025, one-tailed. That is, the more a percipient
showed real-time hitting, the more this hitting tended to be
broken up and not occur sequentially, as we would expect
from the trans-temporal inhibition theory.

This same relationship was found in the data of the
second Training Study (r = -.40), but while it is in the right
direction, the correlation does not reach significance with
the smaller number of percipients and a much more restricted range of ESP. Such a lowering of the range of ESP
would automatically lower the estimate of the true population
correlation coefficient. If the data from the two Training
Studies are combined, r = -.60 between real-time hits and
real-time hit doublets, with an associated p < .01, one-
tailed.

We would also expect that the degree of lack of real-
time hit doublets would correlate with our direct measure of
trans-temporal inhibition, the degree of missing on the +1
precognitive target. It does, although not quite so outstand-
ingly. In the first Training Study, r = +.48, which does
not quite reach the .05 level of significance; in the second
Training Study, r = +.47, also below the level of statistical
significance. When the two Training Studies are combined to
produce a larger sample size, r = +.47, with an associated
probability of p < .05, one-tailed.

Thus this persistence of inhibition aspect of the theory
of trans-temporal inhibition has received good support.

Shifting the Focus: A Case Study with Ingo Swann

    As I mentioned earlier, percipients and experimenters in both my Training Studies were usually focused on getting real-time hits and trying to learn to do better on real-time hits. This implicitly defined the immediate boundaries of the now as the +1 and -1, future and past, target events. The trans-temporal inhibition theory, however, is not restricted to this particular focus.

    We have many studies of precognition which have shown successful calling of events which are much further ahead in the future than the minute or two of one trial. The trans-temporal inhibition theory would predict in general that inhibition missing of targets would immediately surround the future target focused on, in terms of its immediate past and immediate future, regardless of how far ahead that target event is in the future. If percipients were trying to guess the targets 20 trials ahead, for example, we would expect to see missing on the 19th and 21st trials ahead.

    In actual situations the predictions might be somewhat more complicated if the percipient's focus included more than one trial. Say that he was trying to get the target on the 20th trial, but was also thinking about the 21st trial ahead. Then we might expect the inhibition to be on the 19th and 22nd trials. I have not yet worked out whether there should be a definite relationship between the width of the focus of interest of the percipient's attention (the pass band of the experienced present of the extended dimension of the mind) and the size of the inhibition, but there are some interesting future possibilities there. To use our filter analogy, we should be able to shift the center point and/or the band width of the filter that is used in psi.

    An interesting opportunity to test this prediction occurred spontaneously when the noted artist and psychic, Ingo Swann, attended a small meeting of parapsychological researchers at my home in October, 1976. I spent the evening presenting much of the above data (minus the material on the lack of pairs of hits) and the basic theory about trans-temporal inhibition, although I did not say much about the possibility of shifting the center point of the experienced now of this extended dimension of the mind. Swann was quite intrigued by my data, especially in terms of learning to use ESP and precognition better, and made a number of useful comments on the studies. This included his own observation that what I was calling maladaptive strategy boundness was conceptually similar to a concept that he and the Stanford Research Institute researchers, Russell Targ and Harold Puthoff, had worked out, "analytical overlay." Swann wanted to try my ADEPT training device, and a few days later was able briefly to visit my laboratory.

I looked forward to his visit with great interest, for he would be the first percipient who, because he had heard about trans-temporal inhibition, would knowingly (to me) be psychologically set to have some concern with the immediate, +1 future target, as well as the real-time target. I predicted that he would probably show hitting on the +1 future target rather than missing as well as real-time hitting, but missing on the +2 future target because of trans-temporal inhibition. I did not, of course, inform Swann of this prediction, as that might have altered his psychological focus.

Swann did five runs on ADEPT in the course of a little over an hour, all of the time available for him to work with the training machine on this visit. In one run he inadvertently did 29 trials instead of the usual 25, so we had a total of 129 trials. His performance is shown in Figure 18. He made 21 real-time hits in the five runs, where only 12.9 would be expected by chance, so $p = 9 \times 10^{-3}$, one-tailed. He showed a lack of pairs of real-time hits in a row, as would be predicted from the persistence of inhibition aspect of the theory, although with such a small number of trials the effect did not reach statistical significance (CR = -.77).

On the +1 future target, he made 19 hits when only 12.4 were expected by chance, $p = .03$, one-tailed, as predicted. On his +2 precognition hits, he scored only seven hits when 11.9 would be expected by chance, $p = .07$, one-tailed. This is not quite independently significant (CR = -1.50, $p = .07$, one-tailed), but using a t-test comparison between +1 hitting and +2 hitting, as it was used to compare real time and +1 hitting for percipients in the Training Studies, the difference is statistically significant (t = 2.59, 4 df, $p < .05$, one-tailed).* This is pushing the assumptions

---

*In comparing run scores between real time, +1, and +2 hits, we deal with a shortened run length in each case (25, 24, 23), so the chance expected number of hits is slightly lower (2.5, 2.4, 2.3) with each further displacement. This was compensated for in doing t-tests by testing the null hypotheses "[real time hits] = [(+1 hits) +(.1)]" and "[(+1 hits)+(.1)] =[(+2 hits)+(.2)]."

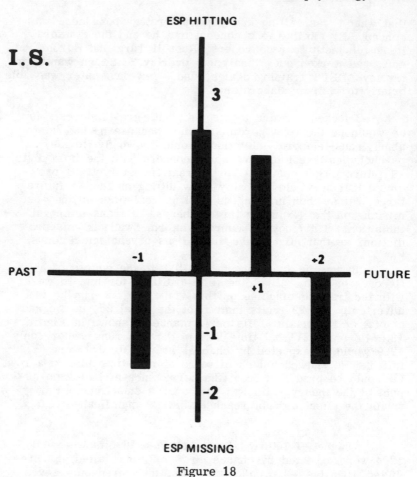

Figure 18

of the t-test somewhat, but the main point is that the scores are quite strongly in the theoretically expected direction.

It is also interesting to note, from Figure 18, Swann's performance on the -1 past displacement. It is only slightly larger than the +2 missing displacement, indicating a very low degree of maladaptive strategy boundness. This is precisely what we would expect for someone with high ESP abilities.

The Generalized Trans-Temporal Inhibition Test

Given the existence of a trans-temporal inhibition, I now believe that a more sensitive test for the presence of ESP, in the data of percipients run under conditions comparable to those of the present studies (where targets are generated one by one) is to look at the contrast, the difference between hitting on the target on which ESP is focused and missing on the immediately adjacent (in our case, +1 precognition) targets. If we could always assume that our instructions to a percipient to focus on the real-time target were completely effective, the particular measures to test the difference between would always be real-time hits versus +1 precognitive hits (and/or -1 post-cognitive hits in non-feedback studies). As Ingo Swann's data demonstrated, however, the focus of ESP hitting and the consequent inhibition may be shifted to other than the real time and +1 targets. Indeed, I had suspected such shifts had occurred for at least one of the percipients of the first Training Study and at least one of those of the second Training Study, but for a long while I had not seen how to test this objectively rather than do a purely post-hoc analysis. I have now devised a more general test for trans-temporal inhibition which allows for the fact that a percipient might focus somewhat off from the real-time target and/or have a somewhat wider pass band than just the designated target. I suspect this may be partially post hoc because of the influence of looking at my data at great length, but it does follow from the theory. The ultimate test will be others' application of it. The test works as follows.

If psi is operating and trans-temporal inhibition is present to some degree, but the focus of a percipient's ESP is not necessarily on the real-time target, it is nevertheless more likely to be focused close to the real-time target than distantly from it. Thus I took as a contrast measure the first four data registers, the real-time, +1, +2, and +3 precognitive registers. Within these four registers, I created a contrast score for each percipient by taking the absolute magnitude of the difference between the highest (usually a hitting) score and the lowest (usually a missing) score. For most percipients this meant the difference between real-time hits and +1 misses, but for a few this was the +1 precognitive hits minus the -2 precognitive misses, etc. As a control for each percipient, I randomly selected (using my Texas Instrument SR-52 calculator's random number program) four other precognitive registers from the remaining +4 to

+24 precognitive registers of that percipient, and computed
a contrast score between the highest and lowest of these
four registers. If ESP and trans-temporal inhibition effects
are concentrated on or near real time, the designated focus
of attention, then the control contrast scores we compute
from the registers further away from real time should, in
general, be less. The results support this prediction.

In the first Training Study the mean contrast score,
in CR units (unit normal deviation) was 6.90 around the real-
time focus, while the control contrast score had a mean of
only 1.96. This difference is highly significant: t = 3.13,
p < .01, one-tailed. The significance comes from both the
high scores per se (t = 2.80, p < .025, one-tailed), and the
low scores per se (t = 3.09, p < .01, one-tailed). In the
second Training Study, the contrast scores are again significant, with a mean contrast score of 2.76 in real time and
adjacent registers, compared to a mean contrast score of
1.76 in the control registers: t = 3.37, p < .01, one-tailed.
The significance here is contributed primarily by the high
scores in the experimental versus control registers.

We have an interesting result then. The data of the
second Training Study were not independently significant for
real-time hitting (CR = +.85) because the data of a strong
psi misser balanced out the data of a strong psi hitter.
This study was statistically significant when evaluated by
contrast scores. The real-time psi misser who wiped out
the significance on overall real-time hits was a percipient
who may very well have been inadvertently focused on the
+1 future target; the difference between +1 hits and +2
misses is independently significant by a post-hoc t-test for
him. I hope then that this contrast measure may serve to
find evidence of ESP in many experiments that were initially
considered failures in terms of overall hitting. Insofar as
trans-spatial inhibition is real, similar relationships between
hitting and missing contrasts should be looked for in existing data. Studies using playing cards in the DT mode, e.g.,
call for the strong sort of spatial discrimination that might
call for trans-spatial inhibition.

Which Leads Us to ...

It is traditional for scientific papers to end with a
call for further research, and I shall do that, not simply out
of respect for tradition, but because I am quite excited about

the implications of the findings I have reported to you, and where they might lead. A number of early obvious research possibilities have been suggested as we went along, but let me just mention some here.

First and foremost, I would be most happy to see this strong relationship between hitting on real-time target and missing on +1 future target replicated by others. First attempts should use carefully screened percipients who have some psi ability and use on-line target generation, as in my Training Studies, but if the effect can be found with other experimental procedures, so much the better. I particularly would like to see further tests on using the contrast effect as a more sensitive measure for the presence of ESP than the conventional number of real-time hits, as well as its application in the generalized trans-temporal inhibition test. Along that line, I strongly hope that others who have data where spatial discrimination was required, which means most ESP experiments, will look for the sorts of relationships that might provide empirical evidence for the concept of trans-spatial inhibition. I have no time tonight to even begin talking about the extension of this theory into PK.

There are a number of important questions that need to be asked about trans-temporal inhibition. For example, my measures have not been in seconds or minutes of clock time, but the psychological units of one trial to the next. Although I have some response-time data from the percipients in the second Training Study, I have not had a chance to look at it yet. Is trans-temporal inhibition necessary only in terms of psychologically adjacent targets, as from one trial to the next, or is it more closely related to clock time? If trials were a long distance apart in clock time, say many minutes, would trans-temporal inhibition be unnecessary because the "strength of the signal" from the future event would be diminished sufficiently by temporal distance so that it wouldn't need to be inhibited? Does this mean that trans-temporal inhibition is even more necessary with rapid calling? Might a reason for the poor success rate that often accompanies rapid-fire massed trials be that the signals from future or spatially adjacent events are so strong that the trans-temporal inhibition discrimination strategy cannot deal with them very well?

Along a similar line, our most striking ESP results often come with free-response targets, where we usually have trials separated by very long periods of time. This might cut the need for trans-temporal inhibition because interference from the future may be greatly reduced. Further, in a free-response situation, subsequent targets usually have very little resemblance to each other, so there may be even less need to discriminate among similar targets, further reducing interference so ESP can manifest more strongly. Perhaps the much higher psi quotients I have gotten from percipients on my ten-choice training machines are due to the fact that they represent an approach toward the free-response situation, more so than the four-choice Aquarius machine, although this finding may be mixed up with the fact that percipients usually responded much faster on the Aquarius machine, thus putting subsequent targets much closer to one another and possibly adding more confusion this way.

The concept of maladaptive strategy boundness needs further investigation with measures that are independent of the ESP data per se. I should imagine that various existing psychological tests of cognitive functions which measure rigidity of function, as well as special purpose tests we might devise, could enable us to categorize percipients as to how much they could be, as it were, in the "here and now" on each trial, which I believe is optimal for making ESP function, versus how much their awareness is being taken up by strategies that maladaptively bind them to the past.

For a long time I have thought that the statistical measures we commonly use in parapsychological research are valid, but really not very sensitive. Already we have learned that variance tests sometimes show significant evidence of psi operating in data that look otherwise insignificant. I wonder how many other ESP experiments that we think were insignificant have more subtle indications of ESP in them, such as might be revealed by the generalized trans-spatial inhibition test?

I began my talk this evening by mentioning how exciting it can be to question our generally accepted concepts of space, time and mind. I have used up quite a bit of ordinary time by now! The work I have talked about this evening has been the most exciting research in my entire professional career: I hope I have conveyed some of that excitement and promise to you, and that we will all help each other to learn more about space, time and mind.

Thank you.

REFERENCES

André, E.   Confirmation of PK action on electronic equipment.   Journal of Parapsychology, 1972, 36, 283-293.

Braud, W.; Smith, G.; Andrew, K.; & Willis, S.   Psychokinetic influences on random number generators during evocation of "analytic" vs. "nonanalytic" modes of information processing.   In J. D. Morris et al. (eds.), Research in Parapsychology 1975 (Metuchen, N. J.: Scarecrow Press, 1976), pp. 85-8.

Davis, J., & Akers, C.   Randomization and tests for randomness.   Journal of Parapsychology, 1974, 38, 393-407.

Gatlin, L.   Comments on the critical exchange between Drs. Stanford and Tart.   Journal A. S. P. R., 1978, 72, 77-81.

Honorton, C., & Barksdale, W.   PK performance with waking suggestions for muscle tension versus relaxation.   Journal A. S. P. R., 1972, 66, 208-214.

Matas, F., & Pantas, L.   A PK experiment comparing meditating versus non-meditating subjects.   Proceedings of the Parapsychological Association, 1971, no. 8, 12-13.

Millar, B., & Broughton, R.   A preliminary PK experiment with a novel computer-linked high speed random number generator.   In J. D. Morris et al. (eds.), Research in Parapsychology 1975 (Metuchen, N. J.: Scarecrow Press, 1976), pp. 83-4.

Palmer, J.; Tart, C.; & Redington, D.   A large sample classroom ESP card-guessing experiment.   European Journal of Parapsychology, 1976, 1, no. 3, 40-56.

Rhine, J. B.   The Reach of the Mind.   New York: Wm. Sloane, 1947; pp. 189-90.

Schmidt, H.   A PK test with electronic equipment.   Journal of Parapsychology, 1970, 34, 175-81.

Schmidt, H.   PK tests with a high speed random generator.   Journal of Parapsychology, 1973, 37, 105-18.

Schmidt, H.   Observation of subconscious PK effects with
    and without time displacement.   In J. D. Morris et
    al. (eds.), Research in Parapsychology 1974 (Metuch-
    en, N. J.: Scarecrow Press, 1975), pp. 116-21.

Schmidt, H.   PK experiment with repeated time displaced
    feedback.   In J. D. Morris et al. (eds.), Research
    in Parapsychology 1975 (Metuchen, N. J.: Scarecrow
    Press, 1976), pp. 107-9.

Schmidt, H., & Pantas, L.   Psi tests with internally dif-
    ferent machines.   Journal of Parapsychology, 1972,
    36, 222-32.

Stanford, R.   The application of learning theory to ESP per-
    formance: A review of Dr. C. T. Tart's monograph.
    Journal A. S. P. R., 1977, 71, 55-80.

Stanford, R., & Fox, C.   An effect of release of effort in
    a psychokinetic task.   In J. D. Morris et al. (eds.),
    Research in Parapsychology 1974 (Metuchen, N. J.:
    Scarecrow Press, 1975), pp. 61-3.

Stanford, R.; Zenhausern, R.; Taylor, A.; & Dwyer, M.
    Psychokinesis as psi-mediated instrumental response.
    Journal A. S. P. R., 1975, 69, 127-34.

Tart, C.   Card guessing tests: learning paradigm or ex-
    tinction paradigm?   Journal A. S. P. R., 1966, 60,
    46-55.

Tart, C.   Parapsychology.   Science, 1973, 182, 222.

Tart, C.   On the nature of altered states of consciousness,
    with special reference to parapsychological phenom-
    ena.   In W. G. Roll et al. (eds.), Research in Para-
    psychology 1973 (Metuchen, N. J.: Scarecrow Press,
    1974), pp. 163-218.

Tart, C.   The Application of Learning Theory to ESP Per-
    formance.   New York: Parapsychology Foundation,
    1975. (a)

Tart, C.   States of Consciousness.   New York: Dutton,
    1975. (b)

Tart, C.   Discrete states of consciousness.   In P. Lee et

al., Symposium on Consciousness (New York: Viking, 1975), pp. 89-175. (c)

Tart, C. Learning to Use Extrasensory Perception. Chicago: University of Chicago Press, 1976. (a)

Tart, C. The basic nature of altered states of consciousness: a systems approach. Journal of Transpersonal Psychology, 1976, 8, no. 1, 45-64. (b)

Tart, C. Toward conscious control of psi through immediate feedback training: some considerations of internal processes. Journal A. S. P. R., 1977, 71, 375-407. (a)

Tart, C. Towards humanistic experimentation in parapsychology: A reply to Dr. Stanford's review. Journal A. S. P. R., 1977, 71, 81-102. (b)

Tart, C. Drug-induced states of consciousness. In B. Wolman et al. (eds.), Handbook of Parapsychology (New York: Van Nostrand/Rheinhold, 1977). (c)

Tart, C. Putting the pieces together: A conceptual framework for understanding discrete states of consciousness. In N. Zinberg (ed.), Alternate States of Consciousness (New York: Free Press, 1977), pp. 158-219. (d)

Tart, C. Consideration of internal processes in using immediate feedback to teach ESP ability. In W. G. Roll (ed.), Research in Parapsychology 1977 (Metuchen, N. J.: Scarecrow Press, 1978), pp. 90-122.

Tart, C.; Palmer, J.; & Redington, D. Effects of immediate feedback on ESP performance: A second study. Unpublished manuscript, 1977.

Tart, C., & Smith, B. Research activity by members of the Parapsychological Association over the past decade. Paper, 1967 annual meeting of the Parapsychological Association, New York.

Von Békésy, G. Sensory Inhibition (Princeton, N. J.: Princeton University Press, 1967).

BRIEF GLOSSARY

AGENT   In telepathy, the person whose mental states are to be apprehended by the percipient.   In GESP tests, the person who looks at the target.

ASTRAL PROJECTION   see   OUT-OF-BODY EXPERIENCE

CALL   An individual guess to a specific target.

CLAIRVOYANCE   ESP of a physical event.

DECLINE EFFECT   A decline in scoring during a series of trials.

DIFFERENTIAL EFFECT   A differential scoring rate between two procedural conditions within the same experiment.

DISPLACEMENT   An ESP response to a target other than the intended one.

DT [Down Through] PROCEDURE   The clairvoyance method in which the cards are called down through the pack before they are checked.

ESP [Extrasensory Perception]   Information obtained by a person about an event without the use of known means of information.

ESP CARDS   Cards bearing one of five standard symbols: circle, cross, square, star, and wavy lines.

FREE VERBAL RESPONSE METHOD (FVR)   Any procedure in which the range of targets is not known to the subject, such that he is free to make any response he wants.

GESP [General Extrasensory Perception]   Any method designed to test the occurrence of ESP which permits either telepathy or clairvoyance or both to operate.

MATCHING PROCEDURE   Any procedure in which the subject matches one set of cards (or objects) against another.

OUT-OF-BODY EXPERIENCE (OBE)   A state in which one's "self" is experienced to be located at a specific place outside the physical body.   Also called astral projection.

PERCIPIENT   The person who is receiving information through ESP, especially information coming from an agent or sender.

PK   see   PSYCHOKINESIS

POLTERGEIST   see   RSPK

PRECOGNITION   ESP of a future event.

PSI   Psychic ability in general, including ESP and PK.

PSI-HITTING   Exercise of psi ability in a way that hits the target at which the subject is aiming.

PSI-MISSING   Exercise of psi ability in a way that avoids the target the subject is attempting to hit.

PSYCHIC   Pertaining to psi; also, someone who is a sensitive.

PSYCHOKINESIS (PK)   A physical effect produced by a person without known intermediaries.

PSYCHOMETRY   The ESP method in which an object (known as a token object) is used to obtain information about events associated with it.

RETROCOGNITION   ESP of a past event.

RSPK   Recurrent spontaneous psychokinesis.

RUN   A group of consecutive trials.

SENSITIVE   An individual who purportedly has strong psi ability.

SPONTANEOUS CASE   An unplanned natural occurrence apparently involving psi.

SUBJECT   The person whose psi ability is being tested.

TARGET   The aspect of the subject's environment toward which he is asked to direct his psi ability, such as an ESP card or a rolling die.

TELEPATHY   ESP of a mental event.

THETA   Pertaining to aspects of the self which appear to survive death.

TOKEN OBJECT   see   PSYCHOMETRY

TRIAL   A single attempt by the subject to use his psi ability.

NAME INDEX

Akers, Chuck 140
Anderson, Margaret 3, 4
André, Eve 160
Atkinson, Richard 5

Backster, Cleve 169
*Bailey, Kathleen 143-6
*Barker, David Read 26-7,
 179
Barker, Patricia 156
Bartlett, F. C. 66
*Beloff, John 41-8
Bender, Hans 189, 191
Bergson, H. 66
*Bisaha, John P. 146-51
Bjerre, Paul 192
*Braud, Lendell 135-43
*Braud, William 1, 15,
 16-7, 103, 123-134, 135-
 43
Brier, Bob 123
Brookes-Smith, Colin 141
*Broughton, Richard 41-8

Cadoret, Remi 4
Callaway, Enoch 225, 235
Cardwell, Marvin 177, 181
Cayce, Charles Thomas
 156
*Child, Irvin 1, 48, 174
Cox, William E. 141
Cruci, K. 69-70

*Davis, James W. 65-84,
 84-90, 140, 163-8
Dean, E. Douglas 123
Delmore, Bill 112
Dronek, Eugene 222, 225,
 238
*Dunne, Brenda J. 146-51

Ebbinghaus, Hermann 65,
 66
*Edge, Hoyt L. 169-74
Emmerich, David 70

Feather, Sara 67, 70
*Freeman, John A. 84-90

Gamble, J. 69-70
Gatlin, Lila 209, 219, 222
Glaze, J. A. 74, 75
Goldenson, R. M. 193
*Greyson, Bruce 27-8

Haight, JoMarie 81
Harary, S. B. 69
Hart, Hornell 12
Hilgard, Ernest 5
*Honorton, Charles 15-6,
 40, 53, 128, 142
Houtkooper, J. 163

James, William 66
Jenkins, J. J. 54
*Jungerman, John A. 157-62

---

*Convention participants are identified by asterisks

255

SUBJECT INDEX

AAAS see American Association for the Advancement of
      Science
ADEPT [Advanced Decimal Extrasensory Perception Trainer]
      201, 207, 208, 219, 241
Agents see also Percipients; Subjects
    telepathic 54, 58
Aggression 186, 192; see also Personality traits
Algorithms, pseudo-random 158
Allobiofeedback 123-34; see also Biofeedback
Altered states of consciousness see also Consciousness;
        Out-of-body experiences; Psi-conducive states
    and internal states 18, 95
    and out-of-body experiences 14
American Association for the Advancement of Science (AAAS)
      5, 6
American Society for Psychical Research (A. S. P. R.) vii, 8,
      12, 28
American University 1, 8, 23
Amsterdam 163
Anpsi 169
    cockroaches 170
    rats 112
ANS see Autonomic nervous system
Anthropology 27
Anxiety 182; see also Personality traits
Apparitions 191; see also Hallucinations
Application of Learning Theory to ESP Performance 209
Aquarius ESP Trainer 201, 246
Artifacts see Controls
A. S. P. R. see American Society for Psychical Research
Association for the Understanding of Man 54
Association ranking sheet 74, 75, 76, 77, 78, 86
Associative-mediation hypothesis 53, 60-1, 63
Attenuation effect 189-90, 194
Autonomic nervous system (ANS) 131; see also Nervous
      system
Awareness 229

258